D1068733

MERGERS AND ACQUISITIONS FROM A TO Z

• FOURTH EDITION •

MERGERS

AND

ACQUISITIONS

FROM A TO Z

· FOURTH EDITION ·

Andrew J. Sherman

AMACOM

AMERICAN MANAGEMENT ASSOCIATION

New York • Atlanta • Brussels • Chicago • Mexico City • San Francisco
Shanghai • Tokyo • Toronto • Washington, D.C.

Bulk discounts available. For details visit:
www.amacombooks.org/go/specialsales
Or contact special sales:
Phone: 800-250-5308
Email: specialsls@amanet.org
View all the AMACOM titles at: www.amacombooks.org
American Management Association: www.amanet.org

This publication is designed to provide accurate and authoritative information in regard to the subject matter covered. It is sold with the understanding that the publisher is not engaged in rendering legal, accounting, or other professional service. If legal advice or other expert assistance is required, the services of a competent professional person should be sought.

Library of Congress Cataloging-in-Publication Data

Names: Sherman, Andrew J., author.
Title: Mergers and acquisitions from a to z / Andrew J. Sherman.
Other titles: Mergers & acquisitions from A to Z
Description: Fourth Edition. | New York : AMACOM, [2018] | Revised edition of
    the author's Mergers & acquisitions from A to Z, c2011. | Includes index.
Identifiers: LCCN 2017045559 (print) | LCCN 2017048455 (ebook) | ISBN
    9780814439036 (ebook) | ISBN 9780814439029 (hardcover)
Subjects: LCSH: Consolidation and merger of corporations. | Small
    business—Mergers.
Classification: LCC HD58.8 (ebook) | LCC HD58.8 .S484 2018 (print) | DDC
    658.1/62—dc23
LC record available at https://lccn.loc.gov/2017045559

About AMA
American Management Association (www.amanet.org) is a world leader in talent development, advancing the skills of individuals to drive business success. Our mission is to support the goals of individuals and organizations through a complete range of products and services, including classroom and virtual seminars, webcasts, webinars, podcasts, conferences, corporate and government solutions, business books, and research. AMA's approach to improving performance combines experiential learning—learning through doing—with opportunities for ongoing professional growth at every step of one's career journey.

22 23 24 PC/LSCH 10 9 8

Contents

4.

5.

6.

7.

Acknowledgments

The author would like to thank Timothy Burgard and his team at AMACOM Books, for all of their hard work on the editing and organization of the manuscript.

I would like to thank my partners at Seyfarth Shaw for their unconditional support including Chairman Pete Miller, Corporate Department Chair Paul Mattingly, M&A Practice Group Chair Susie Saxman and my colleagues Steve Meier, Andrew Lucano, Lisa Damon, Laura Maechtlen, John Shine, and Bob Bodansky as well as the entire corporate M&A team in the D.C. office.

For general research support, I am very grateful for the efforts of Nick Rosenberg and Anjali Vohra, M&A associates at Seyfarth Shaw, and Eric Czubiak, my nephew and rising 3L at USC Law. As always, my assistant, Evelyn Capps was a key player in pulling everything together and helping to produce an organized and informative manuscript.

And in perpetuity, I gratefully acknowledge my wife, Judy, my son, Matthew, and my daughter, Jennifer, for tolerating my commitment to writing over the years, when clearly we could have been doing something together a bit more fun.

Introduction to the Fourth Edition

"It was the best of times; it was the worst of times."

When Dickens first shared this quote with the world, he was not refer-ring to the current state of the merger and acquisition (M&A) markets but he might as well have been. In the time between the publication of the third edition of this book in 2010 and today, the overall financial markets and the levels of M&A activity have experienced both polar opposites and everything in between. From the seemingly insatiable appetite for middle-market companies that private equity firms and other buyers had in 2006 and 2007, thereby driving valuations through the roof, to the fast ending to the party and the sobering effects of a virtual halt in 2008 to 2009, sending valuations on a downward spiral, to the tepid economic recovery and GDP growth from 2012 to 2016, this was not a good time if you prefer merry-go-rounds to roller-coaster rides at the amusement park.

According to Mergermarket, there were 17,369 deals announced worldwide in 2016 and 4,951 deals in the United States, with a total value of $3.25 trillion. These figures represent a wide variety of indus-tries driven by a wide range of strategic and financial buyers with the biggest deal of the year being AT&T's proposed high-profile acquisi-tion of Time Warner for over $100 billion, which at the time of publi-cation had been challenged by the Department of Justice (late 2017). Merger and acquisition activity in the United States increased slightly in terms of the number of deals from the first quarter of 2017, the total deal value being 3,554 deals worth $678 billion, an 8.9 percent increase over Q1 of 2016.

In January of 2017, the value of M&A deals worldwide for the month totaled $280 billion, the second largest January for M&A on record, but things began to cool as the reality of the challenges to imple-menting the economic and tax aspects pieces of the Trump agenda began to set in. By midyear 2017, global M&A deals were at $1.59 trillion, down well over 15 percent from 2016 deals at the half-year point.

Mergers and acquisitions are a vital part of both healthy and weak economies and are often the primary way in which companies are able to provide returns to their owners and investors. Mergers and acquisitions play a critical role in both sides of this cycle, enabling strong companies to grow faster than their competition and providing entrepreneurs with rewards for their efforts, while ensuring that weaker companies are more quickly swallowed or, worse, made irrelevant through exclusion and ongoing share erosion.

Mergers and acquisitions have played a variety of roles in corporate history, ranging from the "greed is good" corporate raiders buying companies in a hostile manner and breaking them apart in the 1980s to today's trend of using mergers and acquisitions for strategic growth and to foster industry consolidation.

During the 1980s, nearly half of all U.S. companies were restructured, more than 80,000 were acquired or merged, and over 700,000 sought bankruptcy protection in order to reorganize and continue operations. The 1980s featured swashbucklers and the use of aggressive tactics to gain control over targets. The 1990s were equally dynamic in terms of companies evolving through upsizing and growth, downsizing, rollups, divestitures, and consolidation, but focused on operational synergies, scale efficiencies, increases in customer bases, strategic alliances, market share, and access to new technologies. This period, however, came to a crashing end with the bursting of the tech bubble and the global recession that followed.

The wave of M&A activity seen from 2004 to 2007 was driven by the more general macroeconomic recovery and several key trends. First, many companies had exhausted cost cutting and operational efficiencies as a means of increasing profitability and were looking to top-line growth as a primary enabler of shareholder return. The increased pressure to grow turned the spotlight on the opportunity to achieve growth through acquisition. Second, the M&A market had been supported by the return of corporate profits and, with them, improved stock price valuation. The improved valuations enabled corporations to leverage their internal currencies to acquire target companies that were willing to swap their illiquid private stock for valuable public-company shares. Third, interest rates were hovering at historical lows, enabling firms to cost-effectively utilize debt to finance acquisition-based growth.

From 2008 to late 2009, the wave of M&A activity was driven by weak economic conditions around the globe. The strong, cash-rich companies and firms began bargain shopping, picking off distressed and downtrodden competitors at a fraction of their market value compared to expectations just a short twelve to eighteen months earlier. Today, many large and midsize companies have begun to refocus on their core business lines, triggering divestitures and spin-offs of underperforming divisions or subsidiaries. Private equity firms and even hedge funds, under pressure to provide returns to their limited partners, have turned stepchild investments into small buckets of cash in order to hold off a tyranny or management overthrow.

Yet, although so many dollars have been changing hands, the number of readily available resources for business executives and professional advisors to turn to for strategic and legal guidance on mergers and acquisitions remains very limited. This book is intended to be such a resource.

There is no more complicated transaction than a merger or acquisition. The various issues raised are broad and complex, from valuation and deal structure to tax and securities laws. The industries affected by this rapid activity are also diverse, from banking and computer software companies to retailers and health-care organizations. It seems that virtually every executive in every major industry faces a buy or sell decision at some point during her tenure as leader of the company. In fact, it is estimated that some executives spend as much as one-third of their time considering merger and acquisition opportunities and other structural business decisions. As we will see in the chapters to follow, the strategic reasons for considering such transactions are also numerous, from achieving economies of scale, to mitigating cash flow risk via diversification, to satisfying shareholders' hunger for steady growth and dividends.

The degree to which the federal government intervenes in these transactions varies from administration to administration, depending on the issues and concerns of the day. During the Reagan-Bush years, the government took a passive role, generally allowing market forces to determine whether a given transaction would have an anticompetitive effect. During the Clinton years, regulatory bodies took a more proactive approach, with more intervention by the U.S. Department of Justice and the Federal Trade Commission, such as a refusal to provide the necessary approval for the proposed merger of Staples and Office Depot in mid-1997. The second Bush administration took a more laissez-faire approach, only to have the European Union take a more aggressive role in preventing potentially anticompetitive mergers. The European Competition Commission's landmark rejection of GE's proposed acquisition of Honeywell in 2001 signified a shift in the role that the EU played in the global M&A marketplace. Under the Obama administration, we saw an increase in antitrust and regulatory oversight, but also experienced an anxiousness to facilitate transactions that will be beneficial from an economic recovery perspective. Transactions such as AT&T/Time Warner were approved, yet the Draft Kings/Fan Duel and Walgreens/Rite Aid transactions failed to secure antitrust approval. Under the Trump administration, we are likely to see a Bush-like approach to M&A approvals and some regulatory and tax reform that will directly and indirectly impact M&A activity.

Recent years since the publication of the Third Edition have seen upticks in cross-border transactions, aggressive acquisitions by private equity, strategic tech and social media consolidations, and participation in a wide variety of industries.

What can we learn and what can we predict about the future when we observe transactions as diverse as:

- Microsoft buys LinkedIn for $26.2 billion in 2016.

- Facebook buys WhatsApp for $19.5 billion in 2014 and buys Instagram in 2012 for $1 billion.

- Google buys Motorola's patent portfolio for $13 billion in 2012.

- Apple buys Dr. Dre's BEATS Music for $3 billion in 2016.

- Priceline buys OpenTable for $2.6 billion in 2014.

- Sycamore Partners (private equity) acquired control of retailer Staples for $6.9 billion in June of 2017.

- Amazon buys Whole Foods in June of 2017 for $13.4 billion (sending ripples of fear and concern throughout the retail and grocery industries as to what's next for Amazon and its already well-established online retail dominance).

- Dupont and Dow announce a merger in December 2015 (that was expected to finally close in late 2017) to create a $150 billion chemical and industrial behemoth, and soon thereafter Huntsman (the political family) Corporation and Clariant merge to create a $14 billion chemical giant (and drive over $300 million in cost savings).

- Defense contractors were active in 2017 in anticipation of Trump administration upticks in budget, with Northrop buying Orbital ATK for $7.5 billion and United Technologies merging with Rockwell at a deal valued at over $20 billion.

- Yahoo sells the bulk of its assets to Verizon for $4.48 billion in 2017 and spins off other strategic assets to newly created Altaba (whose shares climbed in the summer of 2017).

- *High Times* magazine is sold to a group of private investors led by Adam Levin and Damion Marley (Bob's son) for $70 million as the legalization of marijuana in many states has led to a surge of interest in its content and readership.

- Medical supply manufacturer Becton, Dickinson, and Co. announced plans in May 2017 to buy rival C.R. Board for $24 billion and in a similar transaction, Actelcon was sold to Johnson & Johnson for $31.4 billion. Both deals fetched much higher than usual valuations for transactions in this industry.

- Longtime rivals QVC and Home Shopping Network agreed to merge in July of 2017 to drive efficiencies and synergies in an all-stock transaction valued at $2.1 billion—both companies cited a need to stay competitive with Amazon among their reasons for doing the deal.

- Cabela's agrees to sell to rival Bass Pro Shops in 2016 for $4.2 billion, creating an outdoorsman and outfitters that will have a significant market share and brands in specialty retailing.

- 7-11 acquires the Sunoco chain of gas stations in 2016 for $3.3 billion in a classic vertical integration transaction that will strengthen both brands as co-branded locations roll out aggressively in 2018–2020.

- Reckitt Benckiser Group (UK) acquires Mead Johnson Nutrition for $16.6 billion in 2017 as it considers the sale of its own food division that includes the French's mustard brand (which spice maker McCormick recently bid $4.2 billion to acquire).

- Technology and government contract services giant Computer Sciences Corporation (CSC) merges with a spin-off of Hewlett Packard to create a $25 billion combined entity.

- Nestle pursues upscale retail concepts in buying Blue Bottle Coffee Shops in 2017, to compete in part with the Starbucks rollout of its high-end Reserve brand of coffee bars.

- JAB Holdings (a growing chain of coffee and breakfast concepts) buys bakery/café chain Panera Bread Company for $7.5 billion.

- Burger King buys Popeye's for $1.8 billion in early 2017, and Arby's owner Roark Capital buys Buffalo Wild Wings restaurant chain for $2.9 billion in late 2017.

- Honeywell is buying Evoqua to expand its water technologies offering for $3.6 billion at the same time it's spinning off its aerospace division as it shifts pieces around the strategic chess board.

- Standard Life and Aberdeen Asset Management join forces in Europe to create a $4.7 billion money management and financial services firm.

- Leidos acquires the IT services division of Lockheed Martin in 2016 for $4.6 billion.

- MBE Worldwide buys its rival franchisor Post Net in May 2017 to create a combined specialty retailer with more than 3,200 locations in more than thirty countries.

- Coach reaches out to a younger, hipper target demographic customer as it acquires rival Kate Spade for $2.4 billion in May of 2017.

- Janitorium and building services conglomerate ABM Industries buys rival GCA Services for $1.25 billion in July of 2017 to further strengthen its market share and range of commercial services.

- Payment processing and financial services conglomerate Vantiv acquires rival Worldpay Group PLC (UK) for $10 billion in July of 2017.

- Single-family home Landlords Invitation Homes and Starwood Waypoint Homes announced a $4.3 billion merger in August of 2017, which combined would create an entity with over 82,000 homes for rent in over a dozen major cities—the primary impact of the deal was to create efficiencies as foreclosure sales and bargain-home prices become scarcer.

- VF Corp, the owner of clothing brands North Face and Timberland, announced plans to buy Williamson Dickie Manufacturing for $820 million in August of 2017 to expand its clothing and underwear brands—Dickies is an established "career apparel" branch, which competes with Carhartt and Duluth-Trading Co.

- Kellogg is diversifying its breakfast snack offerings by buying protein-bar maker RX Bar for $600 million in October of 2017.

- Facebook buys virtual reality equipment maker Oculus in 2014 for $2 billion, with an eye on the rapidly growing VR market. By 2017, its bet had more than paid off as VR hardware was among the hottest products in consumer electronics with Microsoft, HTC, and Samsung all playing catch-up to Oculus.

- Discovery Communications acquires Scripps Networks (including the Food Network and HGTV) for over $11 billion in August 2017 to drive a consolidation in content and channel programming.

But not *all* deals planned came to fruition, either due to antitrust or regulatory concerns, loss of transactional momentum, or shifts in the marketplace. Kraft-Heinz's attempted takeover of Unilever for $143 billion in 2016 ran out of gas. The Walgreens–Rite Aid merger derailed due to antitrust concerns in mid-2017, though Rite Aid did ultimately agree to sell 2,186 out of its total 4,600 shares to Walgreens for $5.18 billion, ending over two years of negotiations. Health-care giant Anthem terminated its plan to acquire rival Cigna for $54 billion in May of 2017, citing legal, regulatory, and shareholder approval challenges. The fantasy sports company merger between Draft Kings and Fan Duel was called off in early 2017 as neither company was confident that it could overcome antitrust challenges to the deal filed by the Federal Trade Commission in late 2016. And Abercrombie and Fitch shelved its talks with potential suitors in July of 2017 when retailer valuation concerns failed to produce viable offers from Express, American Eagle, and others. It was especially challenging for Abercrombie to fetch a reasonable valuation when many of their rivals, including Wet Seal, American Apparel, and Aeropostale, had filed for bankruptcy in the previous twelve months. And many deals failed to meet strategic expectations and "cratered" on a post-closing basis, such as Starbucks's decision to close all 379 Teavana stores in July of 2017 after paying $620 million for the tea specialty stores in 2012.

A wide variety of M&A trends are emerging that will probably predict the next five to seven years of activity through 2025, or at least through the publication of the fifth edition. These include:

- The Trump effect of the 2016 election has caused massive uncertainty in the markets, leading many executives to sit on the sidelines as they await clarity and actions on tax reform, trade barriers, health-care reform, infrastructure spending, immigration reform, and foreign policy.

- China is not going away anytime soon as an acquirer and cross-border dealmaker as its economy slowly creeps toward capitalism: Several estimates are that up to $1.5 trillion will be allocated to cross-border M&A over the next ten years (2018–2028).

- The aging of the baby boomers and rise of the millennials will trigger the greatest intergenerational wealth transfer in the history of mankind—in many cases via M&A—estimated at over $40 trillion over the next twenty years according to the latest report by Mass Mutual.

- Cash stockpiles swelled to $10+ trillion worldwide by the fall of 2017, as cash sitting in thousands of corporate treasuries sat on the sidelines in search of reasonable yield in returns.

Recent years have also seen a significant increase in merger and acquisition activity within industries that are growing rapidly and evolving overall, such as health care, information technology, education, infrastructure, and software development, as well as in traditional industries such as manufacturing, consumer products, and food services. Many of these developments reflect an increase in the number of strategic buyers and a decrease in the amount of leverage used, implying that these deals were being done because they made sense for both parties, which is very different from the highly leveraged, financially driven deals of the late 1980s.

The small- to middle-market transactions have clearly been the focus of this book in each of its editions since the 1990s. Fortunately for this audience, middle-market transactions continue to attract compelling valuations.

Companies in the small- to middle-market segment need to understand the key drivers of valuation, since they are often able to focus their operating goals in order to maximize the potential valuation range. Therefore, it is important to know that the multiple a company achieves for its business is directly correlated with the following seven characteristics:

1. Strong revenue growth
2. Significant market share or a strong niche position
3. A market with barriers to entry by competitors
4. A strong management team
5. Strong, stable cash flow
6. No significant concentration in customers, products, suppliers, or geographic markets
7. Low risk of technological obsolescence or product substitution

Successful mergers and acquisitions are neither an art nor a science, but a *process*. In fact, regression analysis demonstrates that the number one determinant of deal multiples is the growth rate of the business. The higher the growth rate, the higher the multiple of cash flow that the business is worth.

A study of deals that close with both buyer and seller satisfied shows that those deals largely followed a sequence, a pattern, a series of steps that have been tried and tested. This book focuses on conveying this process to the reader, as we seek to understand the objectives of both buyer and seller in Chapters 2 and 3, move through the process of negotiations and closing in Chapters 4 through 11, and focus on closing and beyond in Chapters 12 through 15.

For example, when a deal is improperly valued, one side wins big while the other loses big. By definition, a transaction is a failure if it does not create value for shareholders, and the easiest way to fail, therefore, is to pay too high a price. To be successful, a transaction must be fair and balanced, reflecting the economic needs of both buyer and seller, and conveying real and durable value to the shareholders of both companies. Achieving this involves a review and analysis of financial statements; a genuine understanding of how the proposed transaction meets the economic objectives of each party; and a recognition of the tax, accounting, and legal implications of the deal.

A transaction as complex as a merger or acquisition is fraught with potential problems and pitfalls. Many of these problems arise either in the preliminary stages, such as forcing a deal that shouldn't really be done (i.e., some couples were just never meant to be married); as a result of mistakes, errors, or omissions owing to inadequate, rushed, or misleading due diligence; through not properly allocating risks during the negotiation of the definitive documents; or because integrating the companies after closing became a nightmare. These pitfalls can lead to expensive and protracted litigation unless an alternative method of dispute resolution is negotiated and included in the definitive documents. This book is designed to share the pitfalls of such transactions, with the hope that buyers and sellers and their advisors can avoid these problems in their future transactions.

Finally, with merger and acquisition activity continuing to grow at rapid rates, and entrepreneurs and venture capitalists continuing to form new entities and pursue new market opportunities, it is critical to have a firm grasp of the key drivers and inhibitors of any potential deal. With so much money on the line, it is essential to understand how to maximize price and valuation goals while ensuring that the transaction is successfully consummated.

Andrew J. Sherman
Washington, D.C.
Fall 2017

1.

The Basics of
Mergers and Acquisitions

Over the past few decades, we have seen countless examples of companies, such as Amazon, Facebook, General Electric, Google, and Cisco, that have grown dramatically and built revenues through aggressive acquisition programs. Seasoned executives and entrepreneurs have always searched for efficient and profitable ways to increase revenues and gain market share. The typical strategic growth options are as follows: organic, inorganic, or by external means. Examples of organic growth are hiring additional salespeople, developing new products, and expanding geographically. The best example of inorganic growth is an acquisition of another firm, something that is often done to gain access to a new product line, customer segment, or geography. Finally, *external* revenue growth opportunities include franchising, licensing, joint ventures, strategic alliances, and the appointment of overseas distributors, which are available to growing companies as an alternative to mergers and acquisitions as a growth engine. Figure 1-1 discusses the benefits of organic versus other forms of growth.

This book focuses primarily on mergers and acquisitions (M&A) as a means of growing, although toward the end of the book certain external means are explored as well.

Figure 1-1. M&A Basics: Buy Versus Build

At the heart of all decisions regarding mergers and acquisitions, regardless of the global financial crisis, is a fundamental question: Are we better off *buying* a new capability, market entry, customer base, earnings opportunity, and so on, or attempting to *build* it ourselves? The dedication of financial and human resources to organize growth must be based on long-term, sustainable value creation for the company's stakeholders, but achieving this objective through growth may require a high level of patience and may result in some lost opportunities. The allocation of resources to M&A will tend to expedite the achievement of growth objectives, but it also increases the *level of risk* if deals are not structured and negotiated properly. What variables should a growing company consider in striking the right balance between organic growth (*build*) and mergers and acquisitions (*buy*)? These include:

➡ The competitiveness, fragmentation, and pace of your marketplace and your industry
➡ Your access to and cost of capital
➡ The specific capabilities of your management and advisory teams
➡ The strength and growth potential of your current core competencies
➡ The volatility and loyalty of your distribution channels and customer base
➡ The degree to which speed to market and scale are critical in your business (including typical customer acquisition costs and time frames)
➡ The degree to which your company operates in a regulated industry

UNDERSTANDING KEY TERMS

The terms *merger* and *acquisition* are often confused or used interchangeably. It is important to understand the difference between the two. A technical definition of the words from David L. Scott in *Wall Street Words: An A to Z Guide to Investment Terms for Today's Investor* is as follows:

MERGER

A combination of two or more companies in which the assets and liabilities of the selling firm(s) are absorbed by the buying firm. Although the buying firm may be a considerably different organization after the merger, it retains its original identity. The merger of equals between XM and Sirius to form Sirius XM is an example.

ACQUISITION

The purchase of an asset such as a plant, a division, or even an entire company. For example, Oracle's acquisition of Sun Micro-systems was a significant technology transaction in 2009.

On the surface, this distinction may not really matter, since the net result is often the same: Two companies (or more) that had separate ownership are now operating under the same roof, usually to obtain some strategic or financial objective. Yet the strategic, financial, tax, and even cultural impact of a deal may be very different, depending on the type of transaction. A *merger* typically refers to two companies joining together (usually through the exchange of shares) as peers to become one. An *acquisition* typically has one company, the *buyer*, that purchases the assets or shares of another, the *seller*, with the form of payment being cash, the securities of the buyer, or other assets that are of value to the seller. In a *stock purchase* transaction, the seller's shares are not necessarily combined with the buyer's existing company, but are often kept separate as a new subsidiary or operating division. In an *asset purchase* transaction, the assets conveyed by the seller to the buyer become additional assets of the buyer's company, with the hope and expectation that, over time, the value of the assets purchased will exceed the price paid, thereby enhancing shareholder value as a result of the strategic or financial benefits of the transaction. See Figure 1-2 for a better understanding of the M&A cycle.

Large corporations are acquiring strategic targets with the aim of attaining goals that they could not have achieved prior to the credit crisis and the resulting lower valuations; it was an opportune moment for Bank of America to acquire Countrywide for a significantly low value and increase its market share in the mortgage industry. A few of the Wall Street banks were acquired in 2008 on fears of impending liquidation or bankruptcy and, by 2016, were rewarded for their risks—

Figure 1-2. The Cyclical Nature of Mergers and Acquisitions

Mergers and acquisitions activity is often driven by cycles—both at a macro level in the overall marketplace, reflecting such factors as the availability of capital and the state of the economy, and at a micro level based upon where this *particular* buyer or seller stands in its growth plans or life cycle. Some acquiring companies are at an early stage of the cycle and may be looking for their first major deal as a platform for additional acquisitions, while others may be nearing the end of their cycle and are looking only for smaller "tuck-in" transactions. Other buyers may now appear to be more like sellers, since they are now in the phase of the cycle where they have digested what they have purchased and are ready to divest themselves of assets that are not a strong fit or that have failed to meet their strategic objectives. The M&A strategic cycle in some ways mimics the human digestive cycle:

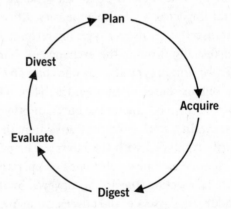

look how nicely the public bank stocks had recovered by the end of 2017. However, the essential characteristic of these deals, which have attracted extensive media coverage, is that the target entities would ideally have preferred not to be acquired. Protection-driven and risk allocation–driven deal terms are more hotly contested.

A notable trend has emerged in recent times where the participants in the "voluntary," if you will, deals are mainly midsize businesses. These so-called middle-market transactions utilize bank debt, which is available, although at a higher cost and in tougher circumstances than previously. Thomson Financial reports that there were more than $10 billion in U.S. midcap private equity deals in the early part of 2016. Efficient companies that have not been exposed to the subprime hullabaloo are preferred targets for financiers, perhaps also because they have simpler balance sheets and a realistic revenue stream. Indeed, the circumstances under which banks are willing to provide debt financing are tougher than have been seen in a long time—most banks were exposed not only to subprime mortgage loans, but also to different layers of securities and derivatives backed by these subprime mortgages that are now standing still in an illiquid market, and the banks holding them are unsure of what their value actually is today.

The major criteria that banks are looking at today are:

- Banks are more likely than not to lend to buyers who are not highly leveraged and whose balance sheets reflect a sound financial position.

- The potential for earnings, reflected in earnings ratios, is the make-or-break factor for a deal. Banks are assuring themselves of the earnings capability of buyers in the event of an economic slowdown following six solid years of economic growth from 2011–2017.

- Banks are likely to take a less active role in the syndication process; therefore, other participants in the deal may have to step up their involvement in this process.

- Banks are likely to demand, on average, a greater equity contribution by the buyer than was previously required to be assured of the sponsoring capacity of equity participants.

What factors have led to this sizable halt in the frenzied M&A market seen until the first half of 2008?

- ▶ A housing-led U.S. recession (that spilled over into global markets)
- ▶ Overleveraged financial institutions
- ▶ Falling asset prices (equities, real estate, commodities, and resources)
- ▶ Frozen credit markets (interbank, consumer, and business)
- ▶ Weak consumer household balance sheets
- ▶ Forces of inflation versus forces of deflation
- ▶ Global synchronization and interconnectivity exacerbating all of these factors

The forecast for the next few years can be broadly positioned as follows:

- It is (and will be for some time) a buyer's market in global M&A after years of sellers calling the shots.

- Cash is king, and genuine post-closing synergy is queen. As Mark G. Shafir, Citigroup's global head of M&A, said in late 2008 when forecasting the M&A marketplace in 2009, "Companies that have access to cash will clearly have the opportunity to buy things for what look like once-in-a-generation prices." This same mantra held true in 2014–2016, when many cash-rich buyers stepped up to the plate to do deals, although as of early 2017, well over $3 trillion in case reserves were still firmly on the sidelines.

- The conventional wisdom is that, in such an environment, buyers are likely to turn to stock-for-stock deals, as this minimizes their cash outlays. But these deals are difficult to pull off because a corporate sale often triggers covenants in the seller's credit agreements, forcing debt repayment. Under normal circumstances, the buyer would refinance the debt. That has become a tough task, with the high-yield debt and investment-grade markets largely shut to new issues.

- The "buy and flip" model is dead (or at least hibernating) for a while (as it should be)—in 2017 the focus is on deal flow with medium- and long-term value creation (the window for exit strategies is narrow).

- Look for pockets of opportunity in growing/needed sectors, regions, and technologies.

In view of this unexpected crisis situation that businesses find themselves in, the ten key reasons for deals that are likely to take place in the coming months are as follows:

1. Mergers are the most effective and efficient way to enter a new market, add a new product line, or increase distribution reach, such as Disney's late 2009 acquisition of Marvel, which gave it access to new content, channels, and product development. Some classic examples includes Walgreens' proposed acquisition of Rite Aid for $9.4 billion in October 2015, which was later adjusted to $7 billion when some divestitures would be required to obtain antitrust approval and then reduced to select assets when the federal government digs in its heels. Bank of America acquiring Countrywide Financial, a company that

was severely hit by the subprime mortgage crisis, and Merrill Lynch as a way to offer a much broader spectrum of financial services is another example. But as of 2012, the strategic effects of these acquisitions had not yet been fully realized. Apple's 2015 acquisition of Beats Electronics from hip-hop star Dr. Dre for $3 billion was a good example of product line expansion.

2. In many cases, mergers and acquisitions are being driven by a key trend within a given industry, such as:
   - Rapidly changing technology, which is driving many of the deals in high technology
   - Fierce competition, which is driving many of the deals in the telecommunications and banking industries
   - Changing consumer preferences, which is driving many of the deals in the food and beverage industry
   - The pressure to control costs, which is driving many of the deals in the health-care industry
   - A reduction in demand, such as the shrinking federal defense budget, which is driving the consolidation in the aerospace and defense contractor industries

3. Some transactions are motivated by the need to transform a firm's corporate identity or even to be transformative for the buyer overall, where the target company may lead the buyer in a new direction or add significant new capability. In 2003, the video game company Infogrames, for example, gained instant worldwide recognition by acquiring and adopting the old but famous Atari brand. Similarly, First Union adopted the brand of acquisition target Wachovia in hopes of benefiting from Wachovia's reputation for high quality and customer service; the firm was subsequently acquired by Wells Fargo but *not* rebranded. Another example of this is Google's $1.65 billion acquisition of YouTube in 2006; YouTube continues to retain its own brand. Microsoft's acquisition of LinkedIn in 2016 for $26.2 billion and Facebook's 2015 acquisition of WhatsApp for $19.5 billion and of Instagram in 2014 for $1 billion were social media industry examples of consolidation of assets but driven by the desire to own globally recognized brands.

4. Many deals are fueled by the need to spread the risk and cost of:
   - Developing new technologies, such as in the communications and aerospace industries

- Research into new medical discoveries, such as in the medical device and pharmaceutical industries
- Gaining access to new sources of energy, such as in the oil and gas exploration and drilling industries

5. The global village has forced many companies to explore mergers and acquisitions as a means of developing an international presence and expanding their market share. This market penetration strategy is often more cost-effective than trying to build an overseas operation from scratch.

6. Many recent mergers and acquisitions have come about from the recognition that a complete product or service line may be necessary if a firm is to remain competitive or to balance seasonal or cyclical market trends. Transactions in the retail, hospitality, food and beverage, entertainment, and financial services industries have been in response to consumer demand for "one-stop shopping," despite the slowdown in consumer demand overall.

7. Many deals are driven by the premise that it is less expensive to buy brand loyalty and customer relationships than it is to build them. Buyers are paying a premium for this intangible asset on the balance sheet, which is often referred to as *goodwill*. In today's economy, goodwill represents an asset that is very important but that is not adequately reflected on the seller's balance sheet. Veteran buyers know that long-standing customer and other strategic relationships that will be conveyed with the deal have far greater value than machinery and inventory.

8. Some acquisitions happen as a result of competitive necessity. If the owner of a business decides to sell that business, every potential buyer realizes that its competitors may buy the target, and therefore must evaluate whether it would prefer to be the owner of the business that is for sale than to have a competitor acquire it.

9. In 2009, during the peak of the weak economy, some M&A deals were driven more by survival than by growth. In these types of transactions, companies need to merge in order to survive and cut costs efficiently; an example was the merger in July of 2009 between Towers Perrin and Watson Wyatt or the need to refocus on the core, such as eBay's sale of Skype or its acquisition and then subsequent spin-off of PayPal.

10. Some transactions are taking a new twist to an old page in the M&A playbook. Years ago, IBM transformed itself into a consulting-driven, value-added services business. In 2009, three similarly situated companies followed the same path, with Xerox merging with ACS, Hewlett-Packard buying EDS, and Dell Computer purchasing Perot Systems, all in an attempt to diversify and refocus on higher-margin and value-added consulting and services-oriented revenue streams. In 2016, Lockheed's acquisition of Leidos for $4.6 billion was another example of this type of strategic revenue-mix diversification strategy.

WHY BAD DEALS
HAPPEN TO GOOD PEOPLE

Nobody ever plans to enter into a bad deal. But many well-intentioned entrepreneurs and business executives enter into mergers and acquisitions that they later regret. Classic mistakes include a lack of adequate planning, an overly aggressive timetable to closing, a failure to really look at possible post-closing integration problems, and, worst of all, projecting synergies to be achieved that turn out to be illusory. As is evident in the ten key drivers just discussed above for today's deals, the underlying theme is the goal of post-closing synergy. What is synergy, and how can you be sure to get some?

The key premise of synergy is that "the whole will be greater than the sum of its parts." But the quest for synergy can be deceptive, especially if there is inadequate communication between buyer and seller, a situation that usually leads to a misunderstanding regarding what the buyer is really buying and what the seller is really selling. Every company says that it wants synergy when doing a deal, but few take the time to develop a transactional team, draw up a joint mission statement of the objectives of the deal, or solve post-closing operating or financial problems on a timely basis. We must work hard to improve M&A failures to create post-closing value rates estimated as high as 80 percent.

WHY DO BUYERS BUY,
AND WHY DO SELLERS SELL?

In Chapters 2 and 3, we'll look at the basic reasons why a buyer buys and a seller sells in the context of a merger or acquisition. The basic reasons are the same even in crunch times such as these, although the benefits that buyers and sellers get out of deals have changed to a notable extent. The goal here is twofold: (1) to educate you as a prospective buyer or seller on how to define your own goals and objectives, and (2) to provide some insight into the motivations of the other party to the transaction, which will usually facilitate a more successful and mutually rewarding transaction. These motivations are summarized in Figure 1-3.

Figure 1-3. Common Seller Motivations

The desire to retire

Lack of successors

Business adversities

Inability to compete

Lack of capital to grow

Inadequate distribution system

To eliminate personal guarantees or other personal obligations

No ability to diversify

Age and health concerns

A particular amount of money is needed for estate planning

Irreconcilable conflict among owners

Losing key people or key customers

Common Buyer Motivations

The desire to grow

Opportunity to increase profits

Desire to diversify

Value-driven acquisition strategy

Buying up competitors

Using excess capital

Achieving new distribution channels or efficiencies

Diversifying into new products or geographic markets

Particular people, existing businesses, or assets are needed

Access to new or emerging technologies

Need to deploy key people or resources efficiently

Strategic fit between buyer and seller's current operations

Motivations in an Acquisition

For the seller, the key motivators in an acquisition (discussed in more detail in Chapter 2) usually include one or more of the following:

- ► An owner who is nearing retirement or is ready for an exit
- ► Inability to compete as an independent concern
- ► The need or desire to obtain cost savings through economies of scale
- ► Access to the greater resources of the acquiring company

For the buyer, the key motivators in an acquisition (which will be discussed in more detail in Chapter 3) usually include one or more of the following:

- ► Revenue enhancement
- ► Cost reduction
- ► Vertical and/or horizontal operational synergies or economies of scale
- ► Growth pressures from investors
- ► Underutilized resources
- ► A desire to reduce the number of competitors (increase market share and reduce price competition)
- ► A need to gain a foothold in a new geographic market (especially if the current market is saturated)
- ► A desire to diversify into new products and services

Motivations in a Merger

It is important to note that a merger is a different animal from an acquisition, and thus a different set of objectives typically emerges for both parties.

► To restructure the industry value chain
► To respond to competitive cost pressures through economies of scale and scope (e.g., the merger of Hewlett-Packard and Compaq, or the $5.5 billion purchase of BJ Services by Baker Hughes)
► To improve process engineering and technology
► To increase the scale of production in existing product lines
► To find additional uses for existing management talent
► To redeploy excess capital in more profitable or complementary uses
► To obtain tax benefits

In a classic merger, there is no buyer or seller, although one party may be quarterbacking the transaction or have initiated the discussion. Therefore, the culture and spirit of the negotiations are different from those for an acquisition. In a merger, data gathering and due diligence are two-way and mutual, with each party positioning its contribution to the post-merger entity to justify its respective equity share, management, and control of the new company.

Before turning to the details of structuring and negotiating these complex transactions, let's take a look at the individual perspective of both buyer and seller in Chapters 2 and 3. An understanding of each party's goals and objectives is critical to understanding the overall dynamics of the transaction.

2.

Preparing for the Dance:
The Seller's Perspective

Some time ago, two houses in my neighborhood went up for sale. The sellers took very different approaches to preparing for the transactions. One couple, who were nearing retirement, began the process almost two years prior. Every weekend they would work on a different part of the house or the garden, taking steps to increase the value and hence raise the ultimate selling price. The proceeds would represent the bulk of their retirement nest egg, and every dollar of value was critical. Naturally, there were certain items that could not be specifically addressed, such as new wallpaper and paint, because they did not know the needs and wants of the possible buyer. In such cases, they took steps to make the rooms more generic, so as to appeal to the varying tastes of prospective buyers. The other couple, in their midthirties with three young children, seemed to have started preparing about one week before the first prospective buyer arrived. They were on their way to their next home, and although the selling price mattered, it really affected only the size of their next mortgage. In fact, with three wild and destructive kids, it seemed that they were taking steps to decrease the value of the house on a weekly basis! Clearly, their approach to the buyer was "take it as is and perhaps it will meet your needs."

Prospective buyers came into the transaction knowing that a lot of time, care, and attention would need to go into the house after the closing.

In many ways, these two approaches mirror the attitudes of sellers of businesses. Some companies become available for sale only after years of planning and preparation, with the sellers laying the groundwork for maximizing value. These sellers take the time to anticipate the needs and wants of different types of buyers, yet they realize that some items must be kept "plain vanilla" because each buyer will have different objectives and motivations. Other companies become available for sale because of boredom on the part of the founding entrepreneur or competitive or financial issues that may have appeared only recently. Although each circumstance will be different, these sellers simply may not want to make the significant capital investments necessary to continue operations. Or the industry may have become less profitable, or there may be irreconcilable shareholder or management disputes driving the transaction. In these cases, the buyer is likely to be purchasing a "fixer-upper," and the price and valuation will be negotiated accordingly. In rare cases, a hasty decision to sell may be made for positive reasons, such as an industry being perceived as hot by the financial markets, thereby creating an ability to sell at an increased price for a limited time. Or a competing business opportunity may have been presented and the company needs to diversify its assets in order to pursue that opportunity.

There are many reasons why the owners of a business may consider selling it, the most obvious of which is that businesses, like any asset, are valuable. As with many things of value, there is a market for the trade of companies—a market where people with different expectations for the future will value the same company differently, thus enabling a buyer and seller to come to a mutually agreeable "trade." Some of the common reasons why companies are sold include:

Retirement. The owner plans to retire.

Undercapitalization. A significant infusion of cash is required to take the business to the next level.

Partner dispute or business divorce. A partner wants or needs to be "cashed out" because of a dispute or the unwinding of the business.

Risk reduction. The owner wants to reduce risk from personal guarantees or liabilities.

Death or illness. An owner or partner has a serious health issue.

Poor management. The owner does not have the skills to manage the business.

New business idea. The owner is ready to move on to the next idea or opportunity.

Glass ceiling. The owner has taken the growth and development of the business as far as it can go without the resources and platform offered by a much larger entity.

Burnout. Running a business full-time can be very demanding, and not everyone can sustain these pressures for a long period of time.

Relocation. Some businesses are tied to specific locations and do not relocate well.

Lack of bench strength. The founder or leader is very dynamic but has failed to groom an effective management team or heir apparent (or even an effective board of directors or advisory board).

Serial entrepreneurship. Some entrepreneurs are well qualified to build businesses to a certain level, but then prefer to sell them and use the proceeds to build other businesses rather than take the existing company to the next level, which may require a skill set or degree of patience that they lack.

Inadequate distribution system. Channels are expensive to build; it is much easier to leverage a preestablished distribution system.

No ability to diversify. The wealth of the owner may be exclusively tied up in the business, creating substantial personal financial risk.

Estate planning. When there is no family member as a successor, a business often needs to be sold for estate-planning purposes.

Personnel. Key people or key customers have been lost and the business needs new management to continue operations.

Regardless of the seller's specific motivations or timetable, an exit strategy and plan of action are critical to protect the value of the business. This process is outlined in Figure 2-1. There is usually a direct correlation between the amount of time a seller spends preparing for the transaction and the price ultimately paid for the business.

Figure 2-1. The Selling Process and Seller's Decisional Path

Reaching the Decision to Sell

1. Understanding Your Motivations and Objectives
2. Building the Foundation for Value
3. Timing and Market Factors

Getting the House in Order

1. Assembling Your Advisory Team
2. Legal Audit and Housekeeping
3. Identifying and Inventorying Your Tangible and Intangible Assets
4. Establishing Preliminary Valuation Ranges
5. Preparing the Offering Memorandum
6. Estate and Exit Planning

Marketing Strategy

1. Targeting Qualified Buyers
2. Use of Third Party Intermediaries
3. Narrowing the Field of Candidates

Choosing a Dance Partner

1. Selecting the Most Qualified and Synergistic Candidate (or Financial Candidate, depending on your objectives)
2. Preliminary Negotiations
3. Execution of Confidentiality Agreement
4. Preliminary Due Diligence

Fighting It Out

1. Execution of More Detailed Letter of Intent or Memorandum of Understanding
2. Extensive Negotiations and Strategic Adjustments
3. Structuring the Deal
4. Accommodating the Buyer's Team for Legal and Strategic Due Diligence
5. Doing Due Diligence on the Buyer

Preparing for the Closing

1. Preparation and Negotiation of the Definitive Legal Documents
2. Meeting Conditions to Closing
3. Obtaining Key Third Party Consents

THE CLOSING: Post-closing Issues

1. Monitoring Post-closing Compensation/Earn-Outs
2. Facilitating the Post-closing Integration Plan
3. Post-closing Challenges—See Chapter 13.

CONDUCTING A THOROUGH EOTB ANALYSIS

In preparing for the sale of a company, the seller and its advisory team should conduct a strategic EOTB analysis, where EOTB means "eyes of the buyer." What will buyers see when the due diligence veil is removed? What value drivers will they really see? How does the acquisition of your company solve a problem or create a significant opportunity for them? The EOTB analysis should be done on a "no-holds-barred, no sacred cows" basis, with candor and integrity as the guiding principles. At no point should the EOTB session resemble the children's fable "The Emperor's New Clothes." The seller must be honest and non-defensive as well as strategic throughout this process.

Key questions will include:

- ▶ How do *we* add value to *their* business model?
- ▶ How do we strengthen their core capabilities or revenue streams?
- ▶ Where are the imported and exported cross-selling opportunities (e.g., products and services that they will be able to offer to *our* clients and, conversely, that we can offer to *their* clients and customers)?
- ▶ What holes in their management team or organization structure do our people help to fill?

A thorough EOTB process will help a seller uncover key value drivers, help in drafting a stronger offering memorandum, and get the advisory team thinking about obvious and some not-so-obvious buyers.

PREPARING FOR THE SALE OF THE COMPANY

From the seller's point of view, the key to the process is *preparation,* regardless of the motivation for selling. This means taking all the necessary steps to prepare the company for sale from a corporate housekeeping perspective. A seller must anticipate the questions and concerns of a prospective buyer and be prepared to provide the appropriate information for review. In addition, a seller should understand the pricing parameters for selling the business in preparation for discussing the financial terms and conditions.

The preparation process should always begin with a strategy meeting of all members of the seller's team. It is the job of this team to:

- ▶ Identify the financial and structural goals of the transaction.
- ▶ Develop an action plan and timetable.
- ▶ Understand the current market dynamics and potential pricing range for the business.
- ▶ Determine who are the logical buyers of the business and why the business for sale would be a compelling asset for each of the specific target buyers.
- ▶ Identify the potential legal and financial hurdles to a successful transaction (e.g., begin thinking about what problems may be "transactional turn-offs" to a prospective buyer), such as unregistered trademarks, illegal securities sales, or difficulties in obtaining a third-party consent.
- ▶ Outline and draft the offering memorandum.
- ▶ Develop a definitive "to do" list in connection with corporate housekeeping matters, such as preparation of board and shareholder minutes and maintenance of regulatory filings.
- ▶ Identify how and when prospective buyers will be contacted, proposed terms evaluated, and final candidates selected.

Step 1: Selecting the Seller's Team

One of the most important steps in the preparation process is the selection of a team of advisors to orchestrate the sale of the business. The team will help the company's internal preparation and create the offering memorandum that summarizes the key aspects of the company's operations, products and services, and personnel and financial performance. In many ways, this *offering memorandum* is akin to a traditional business plan, and it serves as both a road map for the seller and an informational tool for the buyer.

When selecting the members of the team, a seller should choose people who:

- ▶ Understand the seller's motivation, goals, and post-closing objectives.
- ▶ Are familiar with trends in the seller's industry.
- ▶ Have access to a network of potential buyers.
- ▶ Have a track record and experience in mergers and acquisitions with emerging growth and middle-market companies.
- ▶ Have expertise with the financing issues that prospective buyers will face.
- ▶ Know tax- and estate-planning issues that may affect the seller both at closing and beyond.

At a minimum, the team should include the following members:

1. **Investment banker/financial advisor.** An investment banker or financial advisor counsels the seller on issues relating to market dynamics, trends, potential targets, valuation, pricing, and deal structure. He assists the seller in understanding the market, identifying and contacting prospective buyers, and negotiating and evaluating offers. Finally, in many cases, multiple offers may have divergent structures and economic consequences for the seller, so the banker conducts an evaluation of each offer.

2. **Certified public accountant.** A certified public accountant (CPA) assists the seller in preparing the financial statements and related reports that the buyer (or buyers) inevitably request. She advises the seller on the tax implications of the proposed transaction. The CPA also assists in estate planning and in structuring a compensation package that maximizes the benefits associated with the proposed transaction.

3. **Legal counsel.** The transactional attorney is responsible for a wide variety of duties, including:
   - Assisting the seller in presale corporate "housekeeping," which involves cleaning up corporate records, developing

strategies for dealing with dissident shareholders, and
shoring up third-party contracts

- Working with the investment banker in evaluating competing offers
- Assisting in the negotiation and preparation of the letter of intent and confidentiality agreements, such as those in Figure 2–2, which should be signed by all potential buyers who are provided access to the seller's books and records
- Negotiating definitive purchase agreements with the buyer's counsel
- Working with the seller and the CPA in connection with certain post-closing and estate- and tax-planning matters

Figure 2-2. Sample Confidentiality Agreement

THIS CONFIDENTIALITY AGREEMENT ("Agreement") is made as
of this _____ day of _____ , 20___ by and among
Company1, Inc., a _____ corporation ("Company1") and
Company2, Inc., a _____ corporation ("Company2") and
each of the undersigned representatives of each of Company1 and
Company2, respectively (the "Representatives"). Company1 and
Company2 are collectively referred to hereinafter as the "Parties."

   WHEREAS, the Representatives executing this Agreement shall
include, but are not limited to, the following individuals: On behalf
of Company1, _____ , and on behalf of Company2, _____ ;
provided, however, that any additional Representatives also shall execute a copy of this Agreement;

   WHEREAS, Representatives of the Parties intend to meet on
_____ , 20___ to discuss certain transactions related to the
businesses of the Parties, including a potential purchase and sale
transaction between the Parties or other possible combinations of
Company1 and Company2 (all of which shall be referred to hereinafter
as the "Transaction");

   WHEREAS, each of the Representatives, in the course of meetings
and discussions relating to the Transaction, may disclose certain confidential and proprietary information regarding each Party's business
plans, financial and operational data, services, products, and product
development plans;

WHEREAS, each of the Parties desires to protect its proprietary rights and further desires to prevent unauthorized disclosure of any information regarding its individual business plans, financial and operational data, products, and services;

WHEREAS, the Representatives collectively desire to prevent unauthorized disclosure by any one of them of any information regarding the Transaction and the business plans, financial and operational data, products and services associated therewith;

WHEREAS, the Parties intend to have the "Confidential Information" as defined below treated as being confidential and/or proprietary.

NOW, THEREFORE, in consideration of the premises and the mutual covenants contained herein, the parties agree as follows:

1. Definition of Confidential Information. In connection with the Transaction being discussed among the Representatives, each of the Parties and their Representatives may disclose certain information intended to remain as proprietary and confidential, including information regarding business plans, financial data, operational data, product development plans, products, and services. The information furnished by either of the Parties or by any Representative is hereinafter referred to as "Confidential Information" and such Confidential Information shall belong to the Party furnishing the same (through one or more of its Representatives) and shall be treated as Confidential Information as provided herein. Confidential Information shall also include all discussions in connection with, and all information in any medium in any way related to, the Transaction.

The term "Confidential Information" shall not include information that was or becomes generally available to the public other than as a result of a disclosure by a Representative or by a Representative's affiliates, agents, or advisors including, without limitation, attorneys, accountants, consultants, bankers, and financial advisors (collectively "Affiliates").

2. Use of Confidential Information. The Representatives of a Party shall not use any Confidential Information disclosed by the Representatives of the other Party or pertaining to the Transaction for its own use or for any purpose other than to carry out the discussions between the Parties and to further the evaluation of the Transaction and the business relationship between the Parties.

3. Permitted Disclosure. A Party or its Representatives may disclose Confidential Information if required by a governmental agency or court of competent jurisdiction, or the rules thereof; provided, however, each Party agrees to give to the other prompt notice of the receipt of the subpoena or other process requiring or requesting disclosure of Confidential Information.

4. Proprietary Rights. All Confidential Information furnished by a Party or its Representatives to the other Party or its Representatives shall remain the property of the Party furnishing the same and shall be promptly returned or destroyed at the request of the Party furnishing the Confidential Information.

5. No License or Right to Reproduce. Nothing contained in this Confidentiality Agreement shall be construed as granting or conferring on any Party or its Representatives, any rights, by license or otherwise, to reproduce or use in any other matter any Confidential Information disclosed hereunder by the other Party or its Representatives or pertaining to the Transaction, except to further the Transaction and the business relationship between the Parties.

6. Noncompetition. For a period of one (1) year from the date of this Confidentiality Agreement, no Party nor any of its respective Representatives shall, directly or indirectly, on behalf of itself or any other person, use any Confidential Information disclosed by the other Party or its Representatives or pertaining to the Transaction, except in connection with the furtherance of the Transaction and the business relationship between the Parties.

7. No Further Obligation. Neither the disclosure nor receipt of Confidential Information shall obligate a Party to undertake any business relationship with the other Party in connection with the Transaction. The Parties and the Representatives understand and acknowledge that neither Party is making any representation or warranty, express or implied, as to the accuracy or completeness of the Confidential Information, and that only those representations or warranties that are made in a definitive purchase and sale or merger agreement when, as, and if executed, and subject to such limitations and restrictions as may be specified in such definitive agreement, will have any legal effect.

8. No Waiver. Failure to enforce any provision of this Agreement shall not constitute a waiver of any other term herein and any waiver of any breach shall not be construed as a waiver of any subsequent breach. If any provision of this Agreement is held to be invalid, void, or unenforceable, the remaining provisions shall continue in full force and effect without being impaired or invalidated. This Agreement shall be construed and governed in accordance with the laws of the State of _____.

9. Termination. This Agreement shall terminate on the earlier of the execution of a) definitive agreement by the Parties, b) the unanimous agreement of the undersigned parties, or c) one year from the date hereof.

10. Entire Agreement. This Confidentiality Agreement embodies the entire understanding among the Parties and their respective Representatives with regard to the Transaction, the Confidential Information, and all other subject matter described or contained herein. This Agreement may not be amended, changed, altered, or modified in any way, except by a written document signed by the Parties. This Agreement may be executed in a number of counterparts that, when taken together, shall constitute one and the same instrument.

Step 2: The Action Plan

An action plan is a natural outcome of the meeting with the deal team. It is important to be realistic about the time investment required and the expected amount of time before completion of a transaction. While some deals are completed within sixty to ninety days, it is more common for the sales process to take approximately six months. An action plan can help ensure that the process runs smoothly and should outline the list of deal milestones and expected completion dates.

Step 3: Market Dynamics and Valuation

When entering a sale process, it is critical to understand the current market dynamics affecting the potential valuation range for the business. Market trends and merger and acquisition activity provide great insight into whether a sector is hot (and will support buoyant valuations) or cool (with valuations that may be somewhat depressed). Understanding the industry structure, growth drivers, consolidation trends, and macroeconomic conditions (e.g., low interest rates or high oil prices) can set the stage for a more detailed valuation analysis. The current macroeconomic conditions, in particular, have brought about a striking change in how sellers prepare for the dance—the credit crunch and the ensuing recession have changed the bullish tendencies that were operating in the M&A market in the 2008–2010 time frame but then settled in to some degree of normalcy by 2015–2017. Tightened lending standards and difficulty in procuring funds through public or private equity markets indicate that sellers and, indeed, buyers face a different landscape today. Many banks that had to write off subprime assets have since successfully built up their capital, but spiking default rates in 2008 prompted them to further tighten their lending standards. After historically low default rates in 2006 and 2007, Standard & Poor's reports that corporate defaults for the first five months of 2008 had already exceeded full-year 2007 defaults. Sellers that have a visibly attractive price/earnings ratio are enjoying their newly found leverage in the liquidity-focused M&A market. The preference is for sellers whose earnings are likely to withstand the turbulent times of 2009 and onward until the cyclical flow changes and then, by 2015–2017, had refocused beyond multiples. Sellers must be aware of the fact that, in such troubled and volatile times, buyers are very likely to reexamine their decision to go ahead with a deal at every milestone of the process or, indeed, reexamine the terms and conditions, including the purchase price, at every such milestone.

Valuation is a paramount business issue for buyers and sellers alike. However, valuation is not a precise science—it is based upon both objective facts and subjective beliefs and assumptions about the future performance of the business in question. The value of a business, ultimately, is based upon what a buyer is willing to pay, just as houses can be valued by skilled and analytical real estate appraisers but a house is worth only what the buyer ends up paying the seller. Fortunately for sellers of businesses and real estate, competition provides a healthy and normalizing force to ensure that sellers obtain near the maximum of what a buyer is willing to pay. In fact, eBay, an online marketplace where goods are sold by auction, provides compelling insight into how competition affects the prices paid for assets. In an eBay transaction, the price that the seller receives typically is not the maximum that the "winner" was willing to pay, but rather just a little more than the maximum that the second-highest bidder was willing to pay. The phenomenon of auctions plays into the sale of businesses, even in the absence of a formal auction. So long as there is perceived competition for a deal, then buyers have an incentive to increase their offer price.

While competitive market dynamics help to ensure that sellers obtain a good price for their businesses, many companies are sold without the presence of extensive buyer competition. But, in the absence of strong and visible competition, how can prices be "fair"? Fortunately, there are analytical tools available that help both buyers and sellers estimate what the market is willing to pay. By analyzing comparable historical transactions, looking at comparable public-company trading multiples, and conducting net present value (discounted cash flow) analyses, buyers and sellers can quickly understand the price range for which a particular type of business will sell.

The topic of valuation is examined more thoroughly in Chapter 9. Here's a recap of four things that a seller should have in mind in the current economic context:

1. Examine to one's satisfaction whether the lending sources that potential bidders are counting on are likely to see the deal through in this difficult, volatile credit market.
2. Valuation should not be so unreasonable and unrealistic that it could introduce unneeded stress in the negotiation process and drive potential bidders away.
3. As will be discussed in Step 7, it is critical to make sure that the "house is in order."
4. A cardinal principle that holds true regardless of taxing economic times is that overall benefits that are likely to accrue to the seller are much more useful than an attractive monetary offer. A buyer may not offer gigantic sums of money and may be a hard negotiator, but a buyer's ability to close the deal is typically more valuable than the money that is brought to the table.

Step 4: The Target List

A key step in any merger or acquisition process is generating a list of potential targets. The first step in generating the target list is determining the set of categories of companies that would be likely to be interested in the selling entity. Once all the potential categories are identified, determining which companies belong in each of the categories is a relatively straightforward exercise.

After the initial target list has been created, the next step is applying a logical filter to reduce the list to a more focused set of buyers. As acquirers, companies that clearly cannot afford the purchase, were recently acquired themselves, or have never purchased a business before, are inferior to companies with strong balance sheets (or buoyant stock) that have a history of successfully buying and integrating companies.

Step 5: The Legal Audit

The next step in the preparation process is to get the company ready for the buyer's analysis and due diligence investigation. A pre-sale legal audit should be conducted in order to assess the state of the company; it is critical to identify and predict any problems that will be raised by the buyer and its counsel. The legal audit should include corporate housekeeping and administrative matters, the status of the seller's intellectual property and key contracts (including issues regarding their assignability), regulatory issues, and litigation. The goal is to find the bugs before the buyer's counsel discovers them for you (which would be embarrassing as well as costly from a negotiating perspective) and to eliminate as many of the bugs as possible before the first buyer is considered. For example, now may be the time to resolve any disputes with minority shareholders, complete the registration of copyrights and trademarks, deal with open issues in your stock option plan, or renew or extend your favorable commercial leases. It may also be a good time to set the stage for the prompt response of those third parties whose consent may be necessary in order to close the transaction, such as landlords, bankers, key customers, suppliers, or venture capitalists. In many cases, there are contractual provisions that can prevent an attempted change in control without the consent of these parties. If there are bugs that can't be exterminated, don't try to hide them under the carpet. Explain the status of any remaining problems to the prospective buyers and negotiate and structure the ultimate deal accordingly.

The legal audit should include an examination of certain key financial ratios, such as debt-to-equity, turnover, and profitability. The audit should also look carefully at the company's cost controls, overhead management, and profit centers to ensure the most productive performance. The audit may also uncover certain sloppy or self-interested business practices that should be changed before you sell the company. This strategic reengineering will help build value and remove unnecessary clutter from the financial statements and operations.

Even if you don't have the time, the inclination, or the resources to make such improvements, it will still be helpful to identify these areas and address how the company *could* be made more profitable to the buyer. Showing the potential for better long-term performance could earn you a higher selling price, as well as assist the buyer in raising the capital needed to implement the transaction.

Step 6: Preparing the Offering Memorandum

The next step in the preparation process is to identify a marketing strategy to attract prospective buyers. This strategy should include developing a profile of the ideal buyer, identifying how and when buyers will be identified, determining who will meet with potential buyers, and gathering a set of initial materials to be given to potential buyers and their advisors. These initial materials are often referred to as the *offering memorandum*. This offering memorandum should include the following information:

- ▶ Executive summary
- ▶ Market opportunity
- ▶ History
- ▶ Business overview
- ▶ Products, services, and pricing
- ▶ Current ownership profile
- ▶ Property, plant, and facilities
- ▶ Manufacturing and distribution
- ▶ Sales, marketing, and growth strategy
- ▶ Competitive landscape
- ▶ Management team and organizational overview
- ▶ Risks and litigation
- ▶ Historical financial information
- ▶ Normalized or recast financial data (with footnotes)
- ▶ Projected financial performance
- ▶ Future growth opportunities
- ▶ Supplemental materials

The Offering Memorandum is used as a marketing tool for the sale of the business. This is the key opportunity to communicate the company's key attributes, the size and growth of its market, and its potential profitability. However, the company must be presented accurately, with a fair portrayal of the problems and challenges that it faces.

The offering memorandum is not sufficient, however. The other tools needed in the seller's toolkit are shown in Figure 2-3.

Figure 2-3. Tools in the Seller's Toolkit

➡ Model confidentiality agreement
➡ Teaser one-pager
➡ Two- or three-page high-level executive summary
➡ Definitive confidential information memorandum
➡ Short all-approved script for contacting buyers
➡ PowerPoint presentation for management presentations
➡ Strategy and positioning on key deal points and/or hurdles to closing

Step 7: Getting the House in Order

A key step before marketing the company is ensuring that the business is truly ready for sale. Once the process has been started, all questions are fair game and the state of affairs will be available for full review. As a result, it is necessary to develop a definitive "to do" list in connection with corporate housekeeping matters, such as preparation of board and shareholder minutes and maintenance of regulatory filings. Once the transaction process has been started, things move very quickly. There is rarely time to deal with housekeeping matters during this process.

Step 8: The Game Plan

Once the preparation for the transaction is complete, the process can be managed in any number of ways. A major decision at this stage is in determining how closely the process should match a formal auction. A formal auction typically involves sending standardized company materials to a large audience and providing the targets with specific dates for management meetings and when offers are due. This formal process can lead to very positive results; however, no buyer likes an auction. An auction ensures that the winner values the deal more than other auction participants do, and as a result, some companies refuse to participate in auctions, thus closing the door to potential buyers.

A less formal approach, however, can yield similar if not better results than an auction. In this approach, the investment banker coordinates more informally with identified buyers and ensures that all of the target buyers are contacted simultaneously. In addition, each of the targets is examined more closely for strategic fit, and often the communication and marketing materials are tailored to underscore the strategic rationale of the proposed transaction. There are multiple benefits to this approach. First, each buyer is different, and a tailored message may be better received. A likely buyer may review a large number of potential deals (even if it only participates in a few of them), and helping the evaluator come to the proper conclusion can be best accomplished through more focused communication. Second, for each pairing of buyer and seller, there are different synergies to be had. If a seller truly wants to maximize the value obtained from the buyer, understanding the synergies available is critical and necessary. Finally, investment bankers typically have interacted with many of the target buyers in the past. As a result, a less structured process allows the investment banker the opportunity to solicit more candid, direct feedback about the proposed transaction—feedback that is typically not available when the process is more structured.

The last option for running a merger and acquisition process is to have the CEO of the company contact the targets directly. This is rarely the best option, largely because of the challenge of price negotiations. An intermediary can preserve the good working relationship between two CEOs, despite differences in price expectations. When two CEOs are working together directly, however, price can become an emotional and personal roadblock to productive discussions.

COMMON PREPARATION MISTAKES

Once you have assembled your team, conducted an internal pre-sale legal audit, and pulled together "the good, the bad, and the ugly" in a detailed offering memorandum, you are ready to start contacting potential buyers. To maximize the selling price, however, you must take certain strategic and reengineering steps in order to build value in the company and to avoid the common mistakes that sellers make. To properly reengineer and reposition the company for sale, hard decisions need to be made and certain key financial ratios need to be analyzed in critical areas such as cost management, inventory turnover, growth rates, profitability, and risk mitigation techniques. The next chapter gives some insights into the buyer's perspective, while Chapters

4 through 12 discuss the process itself. But before turning to Chapter 3, take a look at a few of the common preparation mistakes that sellers make in getting ready to sell their company.

- **Impatience and indecision.** Timing is everything. If you seem too anxious to sell, buyers will take advantage of your impatience. If you sit on the sidelines too long, the window of opportunity in the market cycle to obtain a top selling price may pass you by.

- **Telling others at the wrong time.** Again, timing is critical. If you tell key employees, vendors, or customers that you are considering a sale too early in the process, they may abandon your relationship in anticipation of losing their jobs, their customer, or their supplier, or from a general fear of the unknown. Key employees, fearful for their jobs, may not want to chance relying on an unknown buyer to honor their salary or benefits. Be sure to conduct a *"WHO KNOWS WHAT, WHEN, HOW, AND WHY?"* analysis to determine disclosure scopes and time frames. A related problem for companies that are closely held (or if one person owns 100 percent of the shares) is how to reward and motivate key team members who may have contributed to the company's success over time but will not be participating in the proceeds of the sale at closing. It is critical that their interests be aligned with those of the seller and that they work hard and stay focused on getting to the closing table. A bonus plan or liquidity event participation plan can be an effective way to bridge that gap and allow such people to participate in the success and share in the proceeds at closing without owning equity in the seller's company. Vendors and customers will want to protect their interests, too. Yet these key employees and strategic relationships may be items of value in the sale; the buyer may count on their being around after the deal closes. If you wait too long and disclose your news at the last minute, employees may feel resentment at having been kept out of the loop, and key customers or vendors may not have time to react and evaluate the impact of the transaction on their businesses or, where applicable, provide their approvals.

- **Retaining third-party transactions with people you're related to.** If there are relationships that will not carry over to the new owner, shed these ghost employees and family members. They should follow you out the door once the deal is secured.

■ *Leaving loose ends.* Purchase minority shareholders' interests so that the new owner won't have to contend with their demands after the sale. Very few buyers will want to own a company that still has remaining shareholders who may present legal or operational risks. It's akin to the real estate developer who needs 100 percent of the owners of the lots where a development is planned to agree to sell before he can proceed with his plans: A lone straggler or two can break the deal. The same goes for minor vendor disputes and others who are likely to come out of the woodwork at the last minute and may derail the transaction.

■ *Forgetting to look in your own backyard.* In seeking out potential buyers, look for those who may have a vested interest in acquiring control of the company, such as key customers, employees, or vendors.

■ *Deluding yourself or your potential buyers about the risks or weaknesses of your company.* Your credibility is on the line—a loss of trust by the potential buyer usually means that she will walk away from the deal.

OTHER CONSIDERATIONS FOR THE SELLER

The Importance of Recasting

Since privately owned companies often tend to keep their reported profits—and thus their tax obligations—as low as possible, *financial recasting* is a crucial element in understanding the real earnings history and future profit potential of your business. Since buyers are interested in the *real* earnings of a business, recasting shows how your business would look if its philosophy matched that of a public corporation, in which earnings and profits are maximized. As part of the offering memorandum, you should recast your financial statements for the preceding three years. For example, adjust the salaries and benefits to prevailing market levels, eliminate personal expenses (expensive car leases, country club dues, and so on), and exclude nonworking family members. Recasting presents the financial history of your business in a way that buyers can understand. It translates your company's past into a valuable, salable future, and it allows sophisticated buyers the opportunity for meaningful comparisons with other investments being considered.

Selling the Pro Forma

The price that a buyer may be willing to pay depends on the quality and reasonableness of the profit projections you are able to demonstrate and the future growth opportunities that you are able to substantiate. The profit and loss statement, balance sheet, cash flow, and working capital requirements are developed and projected for each year over a five-year planning period. Using these documents, plus the enhanced value of your business at the end of five years, you can calculate the discounted value of the company's future cash flow. This establishes the primary economic return to the buyer for her acquisition investment.

Price vs. Terms

Many sellers get caught up in an over-focus on price when the real action is in the terms. Naturally, an all cash at closing set of terms leaves very little to the imagination, but offers are rarely presented in this fashion, especially in a buyer's market. Pay careful attention to the *exact* terms being proposed, as they can make a reasonable price seem attractive and make an attractive price seem very ugly once they are fully understood.

Prequalifying Your Buyers

It is critical that you prequalify the potential buyers, especially if you contemplate a continuing business relationship after closing the deal. Thus, the buyer must demonstrate the ability to meet one or more pre-closing conditions, such as availability of financing, a viable business plan for post-closing operations (especially if the seller will be receiving part of its consideration in the form of an earn-out), or a demonstration that the post-closing efficiencies or synergies are bona fide. Take the time to understand each potential buyer's post-closing business plan, especially in a rollup or consolidation, where the seller's upside will depend on the buyer's ability to meet its business and growth plans.

GETTING DEAL TERMS
AND STRUCTURE THAT FIT THE SELLER'S
OBJECTIVES, PERSONAL NEEDS, AND
POST-CLOSING PLANS

In addition to taking the other steps discussed in this chapter, the seller should meet with his legal and financial advisors *well before* the sale to address personal and estate-planning needs. The seller's net worth, lifestyle requirements, post-closing plans, charitable goals, and estate-planning objectives are all relevant to the type of offer and deal structure that he may be willing to accept. A twenty-eight-year-old seller who is already planning her next venture may have different goals and needs from those of a forty-six-year-old seller whose triplets are seniors in high school or a seventy-six-year-old seller who is finally ready for retirement and life as a philanthropist and patriarch. It is also critical that the proper estate-planning techniques, trusts, and other tools to maximize wealth, protect assets, and minimize tax liabilities are recommended by the right advisors far enough ahead of the proposed transaction that adequate time is available to put these documents and structures in place in a manner that will prevent them from being set aside or disregarded down the road.

3.

Initiating the Deal:
The Buyer's Perspective

Business strategists often say that it is cheaper to buy a business than to organically build a business. This approach, together with today's low interest rates and sellers' somewhat more realistic expectations of their enterprise valuation, has created a very attractive set of market conditions for cash-rich buyers. Our domestic market has clearly experienced major industry consolidation through acquisitions and rollup strategies. Despite all of the excitement, however, the purchase of an existing business is a complex and challenging task. Buying a company for the right price is both an art and a science. Experienced buyers and their advisors often develop a sixth sense, an instinct, a gut feel for the potential problems *and* opportunities inside a company that is for sale. They use these instincts to mitigate risk and to uncover hidden intangible assets. Indeed, the market situation and macroeconomic conditions tend to influence these instincts even though we tend to hear the oft-repeated maxim "invest in a downturn." This chapter leads the buyer through the process, with a focus on preparation for the deal, creating an acquisition plan, and preliminary negotiation tips, as we begin to understand the buyer's perspective.

ASSEMBLING THE TEAM

Every buyer needs to develop both an internal working team and a set of experienced external advisors, such as lawyers, accountants, investment bankers, valuation experts, and in some cases insurance or employee benefits experts. The internal work team should include representatives from the finance, sales and marketing, strategic planning, and operations departments. An effective buyer's team not only will be creative and aggressive, but also will not lose focus on the core fundamentals that drive the acquisition strategy, such as product mix, distribution, integration, and expansion of the customer base. To successfully acquire companies and enhance shareholder value, there must be cohesive thinking and constant communication among team members. For middle-market companies, the chief executive officer is typically the quarterback of the acquisition team, but it can be someone appointed by the CEO. The quarterback must clearly define both the responsibilities and the authority of each team member, including who speaks on behalf of the buyer, who contacts prospective sellers, who negotiates with the selected sellers, and so forth. All parameters of the team's operations must be clearly set.

One key decision with respect to assembling the team is whether to use an investment banker to find and evaluate targets, or whether the deal flow will be generated internally through screening, networking, and industry contacts. In many cases, the sellers (or at least those that have declared their businesses eligible for sale) may have hired intermediaries. Using an investment banker can save valuable time and money and can put you at parity with the seller's representation; chasing after the wrong sellers or even trying to figure out which companies have expressed an interest in selling can be costly and time-consuming. In addition, an investment bank is likely to have resources and access to information that is unavailable to the company. Finally, an investment bank can provide invaluable counsel on valuation and negotiation. The potential of saving several million dollars (or more) through smart bargaining almost always justifies the acquisition of valuation and negotiation expertise.

DEVELOPING AN ACQUISITION PLAN

Mergers and acquisitions often play a key role in a company's growth. The achievement of certain corporate goals and objectives may involve the external acquisition of assets and resources that are needed for growth, a step that may be more efficient than internal expansion. A growing company that is considering an acquisition should always begin with an *acquisition plan* that identifies the specific objectives of a transaction and the criteria to be applied in analyzing potential target companies. Figure 3-1 provides an outline of the acquisition process.

Figure 3-1. The Buyer's Acquisition Process

The buyer's planning and implementation of an acquisition program typically involves the following steps:

1. Develop acquisition objectives. (Why? What? Where? How? Who?)
2. Analyze the projected economic and financial gains to be achieved by the acquisition.
3. Assemble an acquisition team (managers, attorneys, accountants, and investment bankers) and begin the search for acquisition candidates.
4. Perform due diligence analysis of prime candidates (test the premise of the deal).
5. Initial negotiations and valuation of the selected target. (How much can we *really* pay and how? Determine price and terms.)
6. Select the structure of the transaction.
7. Identify sources of financing for the transaction.
8. Engage in detailed bidding and negotiations.
9. Obtain all shareholder and third-party consents and approvals.
10. Perform phase II confirmatory due diligence. (Were our assumptions accurate? Do deal terms need to change? What protections do we need?)
11. Structure the legal documents.
12. Prepare for the closing.

13. Hold the closing.
14. Implement post-closing tasks and responsibilities.
15. Oversee the integration of the two entities.
16. Focus on long-term integration.

The acquisition plan also identifies the value-added efficiencies and cost savings that will result from the proposed transaction and answers the fundamental question: *How will the buyer's professional management or brand equity enhance the performance or profitability of the seller's company on a post-closing basis?* The possible answers may vary, but generally they include a desire to accelerate growth in revenues and profits, strengthen the buyer's competitive position, broaden existing product lines, or break into new geographic markets or market segments as part of a diversification strategy. The heart of the plan identifies the targeted industries and lists the criteria for evaluating candidates within these targeted industries. Why is change planning a key part of any acquisition strategy? For the same reason that synergy is a key consideration in mergers and acquisitions. If a buyer pays exactly what the business is worth on a stand-alone basis, then any benefit obtained from the planned changes (i.e., synergy) is profit to the buyer. Conversely, if a buyer adds no value to the seller's operations, then paying fair value does not make the buyer any better or worse off than it would be without the transaction. This basic economic principle provides the reason why buying companies makes sense in today's economy. Simply, if a company is worth more to a buyer than to a seller, then there is reason to do a deal where both parties win.

Step 1: Identify Your Objectives

The first step in developing an effective acquisition plan is to identify key transactional and strategic objectives (see Figure 3-2). Although the reasons for considering growth through acquisition will vary from industry to industry and from company to company, certain strategic advantages provided by an acquisition should be considered and should ultimately be adjusted over time and drive long-term shareholder value. In periods of global economic downturn and recession, the key objectives of buyers change. As revenue slows and profit margins are reduced, many prospective buyers switch their focus to cutting costs and maintaining earnings or to smaller "tuck-in" transactions to address missing puzzle pieces in their business model or to adjust their products and service offerings to meet leaner or pickier demand. There is a tendency to protect one's balance sheet—an approach that leads to the deferral of growth and postponement of low-priority investments, the shelving of large acquisitions, and the sale of assets. A recent study by McKinsey & Company reports that many companies simply freeze: 60 percent of the companies studied by McKinsey made no portfolio moves at all in downturns, compared with only 40 percent that made no moves in upturns. The "best-growth" buyers take a different approach. They view a downturn as a time to increase their market share in the face of weakness and make acquisitions that support that premise.

Figure 3-2. Strategic Acquisition Objectives of the Buyer

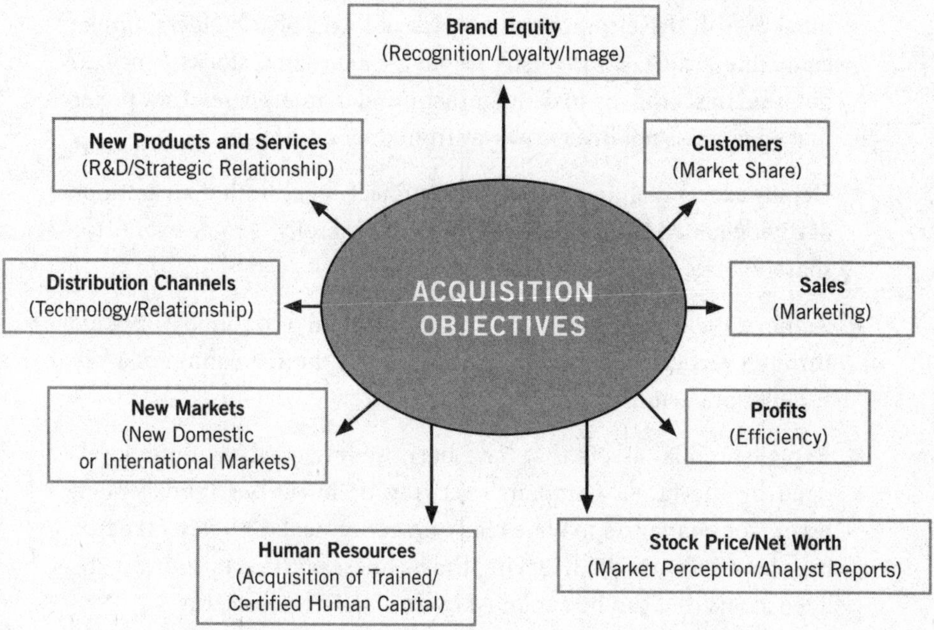

When articulating the acquisition objectives, the rationale for processing a transaction will vary and may include all or some of the following goals:

■ Achieve certain operating synergies and economies of scale with respect to production and manufacturing, research and development, management, or marketing and distribution. For example,

1-800-flowers.com announced in early 2009 that it would start making non-core (i.e., non-floral) acquisitions in order to harvest the efficiencies of its established distribution channels, brand recognition, and loyal customer base, but also to even out its revenue stream, which is still heavily weighted toward holidays such as Valentine's Day and Mother's Day and by 2016 was a much more diversified company.

- Obtain the rights to develop products and services owned by the target company. In 2008, Nokia acquired Symbian Limited to gain access to Symbian's open platform for mobile devices, which was key to Nokia's survival against Sony Ericsson.

- Stabilize the earnings stream and mitigate the risk of business failure through diversification of the company's products and services. (While many CEOs believe that diversification is a good thing, shareholders often punish these companies for lack of focus. Shareholders, unlike companies, can easily diversify by buying alternative stocks—they do not need the company to do it for them, and in many cases, they prefer that companies not diversify away from their core focus.)

- Deploy excess cash in a tax-efficient project, since both distributions of dividends and stock redemptions are generally taxable events for shareholders.

- Achieve certain production and distribution economies of scale through vertical integration, which involves the acquisition of a key supplier or customer.

- Exploit residual assets that have been undeveloped or underdeveloped by the target company's retiring or burnt-out management team. Top managers may be ready for retirement, or a key manager may have recently died, leaving the business with certain underutilized assets that can be exploited by an acquiring company.

- Strengthen key business areas, such as research and development or marketing. Sometimes it is more efficient to fill these gaps through an acquisition than to attempt to build the departments internally.

- Penetrate new geographic markets. It may be cheaper to acquire companies that are already doing business in a target market than to create market diversification from scratch. In 2008, InBev acquired Anheuser-Busch for $72 billion, creating the world's largest brewer.

Anheuser-Busch controlled nearly half of the American beer market, and InBev had strong market share in Europe and Latin America. InBev saw the acquisition as an opportunity to penetrate new geographic markets.

- Acquire additional plant or production capacities that can be utilized to achieve economies of scale.

- Take advantage of a bargain. The target company may be available at a distressed price, which tends to pique the interest of growing companies even if they are not necessarily looking for acquisition candidates. This situation often comes about because of a death or divorce affecting the company's founders. For example, in 2008, Bank of America acquired Countrywide at a bargain price because of the distress caused by increasing delinquencies on mortgages but it then took years to work through the regulatory aftermath and the troubled loan portfolios.

- Acquire certain patents, copyrights, trade secrets, or other intangible assets that are available only by means of an acquisition.

In essence, the statement of the objectives should be a reality check, answering these key questions:

- ▶ Why are we doing this?
- ▶ Are we convinced that growth via acquisition makes sense as compared to other growth strategies, such as internal expansion, joint ventures, franchising, licensing, or capital formation?
- ▶ Does this improve our competitive position?
- ▶ Will this enhance shareholder value?
- ▶ If yes, have we identified and evaluated the key value drivers of the proposed transaction (e.g., protectable intellectual property, distribution channel efficiencies, durability of recurring revenue, loyal and dedicated customer base, and so on)?
- ▶ Are we really enhancing our shareholder value and competitive position as a result of this deal?

Step 2: Draft the Plan

The next step is to draft the acquisition plan. The acquisition plan defines the objectives of the buyer, the relevant trends in the target's industry, the method for finding candidates and generating deal flow (especially critical when it is a seller's market and competition for deal flow is intense), the criteria to be used to evaluate candidates, the targeted budgets and timetables for accomplishing the transaction, the projected range of prices, the company's past acquisition track record, the amount of external capital that will be required to accomplish the transaction, and related issues.

One of the key goals of the acquisition plan is to clearly define the characteristics of an ideal target. The field is initially narrowed by choosing acquisitions as a growth strategy over alternatives such as franchising or strategic alliances. It is narrowed again by targeting the industry from which a company to be acquired will be chosen. And it is narrowed further by developing criteria for screening the possible candidates. This narrowing process, in most cases, will yield a small but viable field of attractive candidates that can be approached.

Other benefits to having a well-prepared acquisition plan are:

- ▶ It provides a road map for the company's leadership to follow.
- ▶ It is a way of informing shareholders of key company objectives.
- ▶ It reduces professional and advisory fees by clearly defining objectives.
- ▶ It serves as a screen to filter out deals that don't meet your criteria or long-term objectives.
- ▶ It mitigates the risk of doing a transaction that you'll later regret by anticipating problems and clarifying objectives.
- ▶ It identifies post-closing integration challenges well in advance.
- ▶ It informs sellers of your plans for the company.

In today's marketplace, it is particularly important that the seller (especially when the buyer's stock is a large component of the consideration) understand, accept, and respect the buyer's acquisition strategy and growth plans for the consolidated company. A well-prepared acquisition plan can be a valuable negotiation tool in dealing with the seller's concerns about the value and continued growth of the buyer's stock.

The acquisition plan will also identify:

- ► The targeted *size* of the acquisition candidates.
- ► The *source* of acquisition financing and the amount available.
- ► The *method* for finding candidates (e.g., internal search or use of intermediaries).
- ► The *desired financial returns* and/or *operating synergies* to be achieved as a result of the acquisition.
- ► The minimum and maximum ranges and rates of acceptable *revenues, growth, earnings,* and *net worth* of the seller.
- ► The *impact* of the acquisition on existing shareholders of your company.
- ► The likely *competing bidders* for qualified candidates.
- ► The members of the *acquisition team* and the role of each.
- ► The nature and types of *risks* that the buyer is willing to assume (versus those that are unacceptable).
- ► The desired *geographic location* of the target company.
- ► The desired *demographics* and *buying habits* of the seller's customers.
- ► The plans to retain or replace the *management team* of the target company, even though this policy may vary by candidate; include a section addressing at least your preliminary plans.
- ► Your willingness to consider *turnaround or troubled companies.* Each buyer will have a different tolerance level; some want and prefer the cost savings of buying a fixer-upper company, while others prefer the company to be pretty much intact.
- ► Your tax and financial preferences for *asset versus stock transactions.*
- ► Your openness to *full versus partial ownership* of the seller's entity, or your willingness to consider a spin-off sale, such as purchase of the assets of an operating division or the stock of a subsidiary.
- ► Your interest or willingness to launch an *unfriendly takeover* of a publicly held company or to buy the debt from the largest creditor of a privately held company.

APPLYING THE CRITERIA:
HOW TO NARROW THE FIELD

Once all of the pertinent issues just mentioned have been addressed in the acquisition plan, defining the selection criteria and screening the candidates should be relatively easy. The more typical criteria include some of the following:

- A history of stable financial and growth performance over different market cycles and under different conditions
- A market leader in its industry niche and in its geographic region
- A company with a recognized brand name and established market share
- Products that are not susceptible to obsolescence or rapid technological change
- A strong management team with research and development capability
- Stable and economically favorable relationships with customers, vendors, creditors, and debtors
- Room for growth or excess capacity in manufacturing or production
- A minimum and maximum range of revenue (e.g., from $15 to $25 million)
- A range of cash flow or earnings before interest, taxes, depreciation, and amortization (EBITDA)
- A defined range for the purchase price
- A range for the purchase price addressing a preferred ratio of stock, cash, and earn-out
- Geographical location
- An existing management team that agrees to remain in place for up to a specified number of years

Naturally, unless it's your birthday, you're not likely to find all of these qualifications in every candidate; if you do, there are likely to be multiple bidders. Rather, the buyer must be ready to mix and match—to accept compromise in some areas. But be careful not to overlook too many warts, lest you end up with a deal that you will regret later.

Again, the goal is to compare the acquisition objectives to the strengths and weaknesses of each seller. The acquisition team must have a clear idea of *how* each targeted company will complement the buyer's strengths and/or mitigate its weaknesses. The qualitative and quantitative screening criteria suggested here will help the buying team ensure that the right candidates are selected. They are intended to filter out the wrong deals and mitigate the chances of post-closing regrets and problems.

APPROACHING A COMPANY THAT IS NOT FOR SALE

There's a definite challenge when the ideal candidate is not currently for sale. In these cases, the owner of the company must be approached subtly by a senior member of the buying team and gently informed that the target is of long-run interest to the potential buyer. Here is how that's generally done.

1. Introduce yourself and give information about your company's business, strategic direction, growth rates, financial highlights, and other high-level data. Explain why the target company is a compelling fit with the buyer. This will let the prospective seller know that you are a credible buyer and that you have given serious consideration to the idea of acquiring his company.

2. Request a meeting in order to discuss the strategic fit and alternatives for how the two companies can establish a more formal relationship. Broach the concept of a formal structural relationship (i.e., an acquisition), and outline the rationale for such a transaction.

3. Maintain contact after the meeting, even if the owner insists that the company is not for sale. Call periodically and maintain a level of positive communication. Sometimes it takes years for owners to reach a decision to sell, and while you are not going to sit idly by, some companies may always be good acquisition targets. By maintaining contact, you can develop a relationship with the seller and create an environment of mutual trust and respect.

When, and if, your candidate expresses interest, you will want to act quickly and establish momentum. Set up a meeting to learn the seller's

personal objectives, review the company's operating and financial performance, and identify any concerns or reservations that the seller may
have. Your goal is to get the information you need in order to determine
a preliminary price and to structure a letter of intent that outlines the
key points of the proposed acquisition.

DEALING WITH THE SELLER'S MANAGEMENT TEAM

If you are going to want the seller's key managers to stay on and help
manage the integrated company, from the outset you will need to allay
their concerns about job security and career potential. Most managers
will not believe that you intend to keep them all. It's likely that the best
managers will leave if they feel that their jobs are in jeopardy. Be prepared to answer the following questions:

- "What change can I expect as a result of this transaction?"
- "What is the direction of the combined entity?"
- "Will I still have a job?"
- "Will I continue in my present role?"
- "How will my performance be evaluated?"
- "Will I be better or worse off as a result of this transaction?"
- "What will I be paid?"

Communicating your vision and your performance expectations
early on is critical to obtaining management's commitment. A good
way to do this is to have the seller's current management team play a
role in developing the post-closing integration and communication
plans. Here are five other, more tangible ways of demonstrating your
long-term commitment to the seller's managers, and thereby relieving
any personal career anxieties:

1. Propose salary and wage adjustments, if appropriate, to bring
   compensation up to your company's or industry levels.
2. Establish an incentive bonus plan tied to realistic, attainable
   goals.
3. Provide employee contracts to key members of the management team.

4. Review the seller's benefit plans and assure employees that the transfer will be orderly and fair.
5. Explain any potential structural changes with care and clarity, ensuring that a history of good communication, equity, and trust is established.

In conclusion, the acquisition team's primary focus is to acquire companies that will enhance shareholder value and contribute to the growth and profitability of the combined entity. A well-defined acquisition plan and the rigorous analysis of whether a potential target meets the criteria will help accomplish that goal. The steps set forth in this chapter are a great road map to use, as are the letter of intent and due diligence processes discussed in Chapters 4 and 5.

DIRECTORY OF M&A RESOURCES
FOR PROSPECTIVE BUYERS (AND SELLERS)

International Business Brokers Association (IBBA)
401 North Michigan Avenue
Suite 2200
Chicago, IL 60611
(888) 656-IBBA
www.ibba.org
    [The IBBA also publishes the *M&A Source Membership Directory*, which lists hundreds of mergers and acquisitions professionals and intermediaries. http://www.masource.org/.]

Association for Corporate Growth
71 South Wacker Drive
Suite 2760
Chicago, IL 60606
(877) 358–2220
www.acg.org

International Network of Merger and Acquisition Partners (IMAP)
6000 Cattleridge Drive
Suite 300
Sarasota, FL 34232
(941) 378–5500
www.imap.com

American Society of Appraisers (ASA)
555 Herndon Parkway
Suite 125
Herndon, VA 20170
(800) 272-8258
www.appraisers.org

Directory of M&A Intermediaries
http://www.moneysoft.com/Directory-of-M-A-Intermediaries

Mergers Unleashed
One State Street Plaza
27th Floor
New York, NY 10004
(888) 807-8667
http://www.mergersunleashed.com
　　[Combines the resources of Mergers & Acquisitions Journal and Mergers
& Acquisitions Report.]

Mergers & Acquisitions: The Dealmaker's Journal
1100 Dexter Avenue North
Seattle, WA 98109
(206) 676-3802
http://www.nvst.com/pubs/maj-pub.asp
　　[Founded by M&A expert Stanley Foster Reed in 1965; a division of NVST.]

World M&A Network
1100 Dexter Avenue North
Seattle, WA 98109
(206) 676-3802
http://www.nvst.com/pubs/worldma-pub.asp
　　[A quarterly publication listing hundreds of companies for sale, merger
candidates, and corporate buyers; a division of NVST.]

National Association of Certified Valuation Analysts (NACVA)
Parnell Black, Executive Director
1111 Brickyard Road, # 200
Salt Lake City, UT 84106-5401
(801) 412-7200
http://www.nacva.com

Alliance of Merger and Acquisition Advisors (AMAA)
Mike Nall, Executive Director
150 North Michigan Avenue
Chicago, IL 60601–7553
(312) 856–9530
http://www.amaaonline.com

Middle Market Investment Bankers Association (MMIBA)
Dennis Roberts, Chairman
1111 Brickyard Road, #200
Salt Lake City, UT 84106–5401
(801) 412–7200
www.mmiba.com

4.

The Letter of Intent and Other Preliminary Matters

At this stage of the transaction, both the seller and the buyer (and their respective advisors) have developed a strategic plan and a tentative timetable for completion of the deal, have completed their analysis as to why the transaction is a strong financial and strategic fit for each party, and hopefully have taken the time to understand each other's perspective and the competing as well as aligned objectives.

Buyers may enlist a financial advisor to assist in getting to this stage and helping the buyer ensure it is making decisions consistent with its financial and business goals. Thus, often the first agreement the buyer enters into in preparation of an acquisition is with its financial advisor, traditionally in the form of an *engagement letter*. The terms in an engagement letter must be carefully negotiated to account for the myriad of possible outcomes a buyer could encounter in the early stages of an acquisition. The engagement letter may contain an assortment of fees covering the full range of the transaction, including retainer fees, interim fees, success fees, and termination fees. Thus, the buyer should also build in key provisions to protect itself, similar to the "binding terms" discussed in more detail below. Such provisions include confidentiality, conflicts of interest, exclusivity provisions, and termination provisions (e.g., notice to the advisor if the buyer wants to terminate and the obligation to pay termination fees). These are essential given that at the early stages of a transaction the buyer is interacting with and disclosing information to its financial advisor at an even deeper level than it does with a potential seller.

Eventually the parties reach the point at which the field of available candidates has been narrowed, the preliminary "get to know each other" meetings have been completed, and a tentative selection has been made. After the completion of the presale review, the next step involves the preparation and negotiation of an interim agreement that will guide and govern the conduct of the parties up until closing.

Although there are certain valid legal arguments against the execution of any type of interim document, especially since some courts have interpreted such documents as being binding legal documents (even if one or more of the parties did not initially intend to be bound), it has been my experience that a letter of intent (LOI), which includes a set of binding and nonbinding terms as a road map for the transaction, *is* a necessary step in virtually all mergers and acquisitions. In lieu of a formal LOI, parties may prepare an unexecuted term sheet or, alternatively, enter into definitive agreements directly. I have found, however, that most parties prefer the organizational framework and psychological comfort of knowing that there is some type of written document in place before proceeding further and before significant expenses are incurred. It is also critical to deal with as many of the potential due diligence problems or surprises as possible at this early stage. The ability to resolve problems that may derail a transaction is much stronger at the outset of the deal, *before* each party has incurred significant expenses and becomes more entrenched in its position. The advantages and disadvantages of a letter of intent are discussed in Figure 4-1.

In addition to creating a framework for any potential deal with the prospective buyer, an LOI is a catalyzing event in most deals. Receiving an LOI, even one that has unacceptable terms, gives the investment banker the opportunity to reach out to each of the target buyers and accelerate the "go/no-go" decision. In a normal process, the investment banker strives to keep the potential buyers on a common time frame. However, the first LOI drives the timing of the process and, furthermore, provides a solid framework for more specific price negotiations.

Figure 4-1. Advantages and Disadvantages of
Executing a Letter of Intent

Advantages

➡ Tests the parties' seriousness.

➡ Mentally commits the parties to the sale.

➡ Sets out in writing certain key areas of agreement. Important since there may be a long delay before a definitive purchase agreement is negotiated and executed.

➡ Highlights the remaining open issues, challenges to closing, valuation gaps, and other related matters needing further negotiation.

➡ Discourages the seller from shopping around for a better deal (especially if "no-slip" penalties are included).

Disadvantages

➡ May be considered a binding agreement. It is important to articulate whether or not a letter of intent is meant to constitute an enforceable agreement.

➡ Public announcement of the prospective sale may have to be made due to federal securities law if either company is publicly held.

Finally, if the LOI received is at an acceptable price, the investment banker can now be more aggressive in price negotiations with the other interested parties. There is no event that allows the banker to create an auction more easily than an LOI, and as such, it is a tool that is welcomed, carefully managed, and ultimately used to obtain more value for the seller.

There are many different styles of drafting letters of intent, which vary from law firm to law firm and from business lawyer to business lawyer. These styles usually fall into one of three categories: (1) binding, (2) nonbinding, and (3) hybrids, like the model in Figure 4-2. In general, the type to be selected will depend upon (1) the timing and the scope of the information to be released publicly concerning the transaction (if any), (2) the degree to which negotiations have been definitive and the necessary information has been gathered, (3) the cost to the buyer and the seller of proceeding with the transaction prior to the making of binding commitments, (4) the rapidity with which the parties estimate that a final agreement can be signed, (5) the valuation ranges for the seller's company that have been discussed to date, (6) the degree to which the buyer needs or wants a period of exclusivity (and the degree to which the seller is *willing* to grant an exclusivity period, (7) the relative status of the parties and leverage that both the buyer and seller have, and (8) the degree of confidence each party has in the good faith of the other party and the absence (or presence) of still other parties that are competing for the transaction. In most cases, the hybrid format, which contains *both* binding and nonbinding terms, is the most effective format to protect the interests of both parties and to level the playing field from a negotiations perspective.

Although it is formally executed by the buyer and the seller, a letter of intent is often considered to be an agreement *in principle*. As a result, the parties should be very clear as to whether the letter of intent is a binding preliminary contract or merely a memorandum from which a more definitive legal document may be drafted upon completion of due diligence. Regardless of the legal implications involved, however, by executing a letter of intent, the parties make a psychological commitment to the transaction and provide a road map for expediting more formal negotiations.

In addition, a well-drafted letter of intent will provide an overview of matters that require further discussion and consideration, such as the exact purchase price. Although an exact and final purchase price cannot realistically be established until due diligence has been completed, the seller may hesitate to proceed without a price commitment. Instead of creating a fixed price, however, the letter of intent will typically incorporate a price range that is qualified by a clause or provision setting forth all of the factors that will influence and affect the calculation of a final fixed price, such as balance sheet adjustments, due diligence surprises or problems, a change in the health of the company, or overall market conditions during the transaction period, and sometimes even an "upside surprise" in favor of the seller when a significant *positive* development occurs during the transaction period (e.g., the settlement of litigation, the award of important intellectual property rights, or a big new contract or customer commitment) that had not been included when the valuation range was established. The purchase price may also be affected by the tax implications of the transaction, which is generally a key factor in determining whether the transaction is structured as an asset purchase or stock purchase. The LOI also sets the framework for ancillary agreements to be negotiated later, such as licensing agreements, employment and shareholder agreements, management agreements, and non-competition agreements. Some of these agreements are discussed in more detail in Chapter 7.

PROPOSED TERMS

As you can see from the sample letter of intent in Figure 4-2, the first section addresses certain key deal terms, such as price and method of payment. These terms are usually nonbinding so that the parties have an opportunity to complete the due diligence and analysis and have room for further negotiation, depending on the specific problems uncovered during the investigative process.

Figure 4-2. Sample Letter of Intent

Ms. Prospective Seller
SellCo, Inc.
{address}
Re: *Letter of Intent Between BuyCo, Inc. and SellCo, Inc.*

Dear Ms. Prospective Seller:

This letter ("Letter Agreement") sets forth the terms by which BuyCo, Inc. ("BCI") agrees to purchase all of the issued and outstanding common stock of SellCo, Inc. (the "Company") in accordance with the terms set forth below. BCI and the Company are hereinafter collectively referred to as the "Parties."

Section I of this Letter Agreement summarizes the principal terms proposed in our earlier discussions and is not an agreement binding upon either of the Parties. These principal terms are subject to the execution and delivery by the Parties of a definitive Stock Purchase Agreement and other documents related to these transactions.

Section II of this Letter Agreement contains a number of covenants by the Parties, which shall be legally binding upon the execution of this Letter Agreement by the Parties. The binding terms in Section II below are enforceable against the Parties, regardless of whether or not the aforementioned agreements are executed or the reasons for non-execution.

SECTION I - PROPOSED TERMS

1. Stock Purchase. The Parties will execute a Stock Purchase Agreement, pursuant to which, BCI will purchase _____ shares of the Company's Common Stock (the "Shares"), from the schedule of Shareholders attached hereto for a total purchase price of not less than $_____ for the Company's Common Stock.

2. Employment Agreements. Prior to closing, the Company will enter into an individual employment agreement with _____ and _____ who are employed by the Seller for year-terms at the compensation levels of $_____ and bonus plan eligibility of between $_____ and $_____. The Employment Agreement will contain such other terms and conditions as are reasonable and customary in the type of transaction contemplated hereby.

3. Closing and Documentation. The Parties intend that a closing of the agreements shall occur on or before _____, 20___, at a time and place that is mutually acceptable to the Parties. BCI or its representatives will prepare and revise the initial and subsequent drafts of the necessary agreements.

SECTION II - BINDING TERMS

In consideration of the costs to be incurred by the Parties in undertaking actions toward the negotiation and consummation of the Stock Purchase Agreement and the related agreements, the Parties hereby agree to the following binding terms ("Binding Terms"):

4. Refundable Deposit. BCI will provide a refundable deposit in the amount of $_____ to the Company at the time of the execution of this Letter Agreement. All sums paid hereunder shall be deductible from the purchase price to be paid for the Shares as described in Paragraph 1. In the event that BCI does not complete the purchase of the Shares, the sums payable hereunder shall be referred to BCI (less _____ to be retained by the Seller for its expenses), with interest at the rate of 1.5% above the highest U.S. prime rate published in *The Wall Street Journal* from the date of execution of this Agreement to the date of repayment. In the event that the closing is delayed beyond _____, 20___, BCI will make an additional deposit of $_____ on _____, 20___ and $ _____ on_____, 20___.

5. Due Diligence. The directors, officers, shareholders, employees, agents and other representatives (collectively, the "Representatives") of the Company shall (a) grant to BCI and its Representatives full access to the Company's properties, personnel, facilities, books and records, financial and operating data, contracts and other documents; and (b) furnish all such books and records, financial and operating data, contracts and other documents or information as BCI or its Representatives may reasonably request.

6. No Material Changes. The Company agrees that, from and after the execution of this Agreement until the earlier of the termination of the Binding Terms in accordance with Paragraph 12 below or the execution and delivery of the agreements described herein, the Company's business and operations will be conducted in the ordinary course and in substantially the same manner as such business and operations have been conducted in the past and the Company will notify BCI of any extraordinary transactions, financing, or business involving the Company or its affiliates.

7. No-Shop Provision. The Company agrees that, from and after the execution of this Agreement until the termination of the Binding Terms in accordance with Paragraph 12 below, the Company will not initiate or conclude, through its Representatives or otherwise, any negotiations with any corporation, person, or other entity regarding the sale of all or substantially all of the assets or the shares of the Company. The Company will immediately notify the other Parties regarding any such contact described above.

8. Lock-Up Provision. The Company agrees that, from and after the execution of this Agreement until (a) the consummation of the transactions contemplated in Section I and the execution of definitive agreements thereby, or (b) in the event that definitive agreements are not executed, until the repayment of all amounts advanced hereunder, plus accrued interest, that without the prior written approval of BCI and subject to any anti-dilution provisions imposed hereunder, (x) no shares of any currently issued Common Stock of the Company shall be issued, sold, transferred, or assigned to any party; (y) no such shares of Common Stock shall be pledged as security, hypothecated, or in any other way encumbered; and (z) the Company shall issue no additional shares of capital stock of any class, whether now or hereafter authorized.

9. Confidentiality. Prior to Closing, neither Party nor any of their Representatives shall make any public statement or issue any press releases regarding the agreements, the proposed transactions described herein or this Agreement without the prior written consent of the other Party, except as such disclosure may be required by law. If the law requires such disclosure, the disclosing party shall notify the other Party in advance and furnish to the other Party a copy of the proposed disclosure. Notwithstanding the foregoing, the Parties acknowledge that certain disclosures regarding the agreements, the proposed transactions or this Agreement may be required to be made to each Party's representatives or certain of them, and to any other party whose consent or approval may be required to complete the agreements and the transactions provided for thereunder, and that such disclosures shall not require prior written consent. BCI and its employees, affiliates, and associates will (a) treat all information received from the Company confidentially, (b) not disclose such information to third parties without the prior written consent of the Company, except as such disclosure may be required by law, (c) not use such information for any purpose other than the consideration of the matters contemplated by this Letter of Intent, including related due diligence, and (d) return to the Company any such information if this Agreement terminates pursuant to Paragraph 12 below.

10. Expenses; Finder's Fee. The Parties are responsible for and will bear all of their own costs and expenses incurred at any time in connection with the transaction proposed hereunder up to $_____. Any additional or extraordinary expenses above this amount shall be borne by BCI; provided, however, the Company shall be responsible for any finder's fees payable in connection with the transactions contemplated hereby.

11. Breakup Fee. The Company agrees to pay BCI a breakup fee of $_____ in the event that the sale and purchase of the shares contemplated in Section I is not accomplished by_____, 20___ as a result of the Company's failure or refusal to close pursuant to the terms set forth above and not due to any refusal or delay on the part of BCI to close by that date.

12. Effective Date. The foregoing obligations of the Parties under Section II of this Agreement shall be effective as of the date of execution by the Company, and shall terminate upon the completion of the transactions contemplated in Section I above or, if such transactions are not completed, then at such time as all of the obligations under Section II have been satisfied, unless otherwise extended by all of the Parties or specifically extended by the terms of the foregoing provisions; provided, however, that such termination shall not relieve the Parties of liability for the breach of any obligation occurring prior to such termination.

Please indicate your agreement to the Binding Terms set forth in Section II above by executing and returning a copy of this Agreement to the undersigned no later than close of business on _____, 20___. Following receipt, we will instruct legal counsel to prepare the agreements contemplated herein. The Binding Terms shall become binding on the Company upon the advance of deposit pursuant to Paragraph 4 and the execution of Promissory Note in consideration therefor.

Very truly yours,
/s/ Prospective Buyer
Prospective Buyer, President
BuyCo, Inc.

ACKNOWLEDGED AND ACCEPTED:
SellCo, Inc.

_____   _____
By: Prospective Seller, President   Dated

BINDING TERMS

The sample letter of intent in Figure 4-2 also includes certain binding terms that will *not* be subject to further negotiation. These are certain issues that at least one side, and usually both sides, will want to ensure are binding, regardless of whether the deal is actually consummated. These include:

- **Legal ability of the seller to consummate the transaction.** Before wasting too much time or money, the buyer will want to know that the seller has the power and the authority to close the deal.

- **Protection of confidential information.** The seller in particular, and both parties in general, will want to ensure that all information provided in the initial presentation and during due diligence remains confidential.

- **Access to books and records.** The buyer will want to ensure that the seller and its advisors will fully cooperate in the due diligence process.

- *Breakup or walkaway fees.* The buyer may want to include a clause in the letter of intent to attempt to recoup some of its expenses if the seller tries to walk away from the deal, either because of a change in circumstances or because of the desire to accept a more attractive offer from a different potential buyer. The seller may want a reciprocal clause to cover its own expenses if the buyer walks away or defaults on a preliminary obligation or condition to closing, such as an inability to raise acquisition capital.

- *No-shop/standstill provisions.* The buyer may want a period of exclusivity during which it can be confident that the seller is not entertaining any other offers. The seller will want to place a limit or "outside date" on this provision in order to allow it to begin entertaining other offers if the buyer is unduly dragging its feet.

- *Good-faith deposit—refundable versus nonrefundable.* In some cases, the seller will request a deposit or option fee, and the parties must determine to what extent, if at all, this deposit will be refundable and under what conditions. There are often timing problems with this provision that can be difficult to resolve. For example, the buyer will want the deposit to remain 100 percent refundable if the seller is being uncooperative, or at least until the buyer and its team complete the initial round of due diligence to ensure that there are no major problems discovered that might cause the buyer to walk away from the deal. The seller will want to set a limit on the due diligence and review period, after which point the buyer forfeits all or a part of its deposit. The end result is often a progressive downward scale of refundability as the due diligence and the overall deal reach various checkpoints toward closing. In the event that the buyer forfeits some or all of the deposit and the deal never closes, the buyer may want to negotiate an eventual full or partial refund if the seller finds an alternative buyer within a certain period of time, such as 180 days.

- *Impact on employees.* Perhaps one of the most challenging issues faced by sellers is the decision as to *who* within the company is told *what*, *when*, and *why*. Sellers will typically want to "play their cards close to the vest," whereas buyers, as part of their due diligence perspective, may want access to key executives and employees who are not yet in the loop. From a human capital management perspective, if team members are told too soon, then it may be hard to keep them from running out the door (because of their uncertainty), and if they are told too late, it may lead to resentment and frustration. If the communication of the possible sale is mishandled, then the employees may get the message that their jobs are unimportant or in jeopardy, or both. Supervisory personnel should be briefed first, and all of their questions should be answered so that they can inform their subordinates. After the closing, it is imperative that the top management of the acquiring company meet with the employees of the target company to discuss their post-closing roles, compensation, and benefits. If there will be job cuts, discuss the methods by which this will be determined and whether any training, instruction on résumé-writing skills, or outplacement services will be offered.

- *Key terms for the definitive documents.* The letter of intent will often provide that it is subject to the definitive documents, such as the purchase agreement, and that those definitive documents will address certain key matters or include certain key sections, such as covenants, indemnification, representations and warranties, and key conditions for closing.

- *Conditions to closing.* Both parties will want to articulate a set of conditions or circumstances such that they will not be bound to proceed with the transaction if certain contingencies are not met or if certain events happen after the execution of the letter of intent, such as third-party approvals, regulatory permissions, or related potential barriers to closing. Be sure to articulate these conditions clearly so that there are no surprises down the road.

- *Conduct of the business prior to closing.* The buyer usually wants some guarantee that the general state of the company that it sees today will be there tomorrow. Thus, the seller will be obligated to operate its business in the ordinary course, so that assets, customers, and employees will not start disappearing from the premises; equipment will not be left in disrepair; the company will not fail to pursue new customers; bonuses will not be magically declared; personal expenses will not be paid the night before; and other steps that will deplete the value of the company prior to closing will not be taken. If these things do occur, then the parties should provide a mechanism for adjusting the price based on the relative valuation of the lost contracts, relationships, or human resources. These "negative covenants" help protect the buyer against unpleasant surprises at, or after, closing.

- *Limitations on publicity and press releases.* The parties may want to place certain restrictions on the content and timing of any press releases or public announcements of the transaction, and in some cases may need to follow Securities and Exchange Commission (SEC) guidelines. If either or both of the parties to the transaction are publicly traded, then the general rule is that once the essential terms of the transaction are agreed to in principle, such as through the execution of the letter of intent, there must be a public announcement. The timing and content of this announcement must be weighed carefully by the parties, including an analysis of how the announcement will affect the price of the stock. The announcement should not be made too early, or it may be viewed by the SEC as an attempt to influence the price of the stock.

- *Expenses/brokers.* The parties should identify, where applicable, who shall bear responsibility for investment bankers' fees, finders' fees, legal expenses, and other costs pertaining to the transaction.

COMMON REASONS WHY DEALS DIE
AT AN EARLY STAGE

Obviously, not all deals materialize, and it is useful to know some of the reasons for failure in the early stages. Here are some of the common ones:

- ▶ The seller has not prepared adequate financial statements (e.g., going back at least two years and reflecting the company's current condition).
- ▶ The seller and its team are uncooperative during the due diligence process.
- ▶ The buyer and its team discover a "deal breaker" in the course of the due diligence (e.g., large unknown or hidden actual or contingent liabilities, such as an EPA cleanup matter).

▶ The seller has "seller's remorse," gets "cold feet," or has not properly thought through its after-tax consideration or compensation.

▶ The seller suffers from "don't call my baby ugly" syndrome and becomes defensive when the buyer and its team find flaws (and then focus on them in the negotiation) in the operations of the business, the valuation, the loyalty of the customers, the quality of the accounts receivable, the skills of the personnel, and so on.

▶ A strategic shift (or extenuating set of circumstances) affecting the acquisition strategy or criteria of the buyer occurs (e.g., a change in the buyer's management team during the due diligence process).

▶ The seller is inflexible on price and valuation when the buyer and its team discover problems during due diligence.

For more on this topic, see Chapter 12, "Keeping M&A Deals on Track."

PREPARATION OF THE WORK SCHEDULE

Following the execution of the letter of intent, one of the first responsibilities of the purchaser's legal counsel is to prepare a comprehensive schedule of activities (work schedule) that will serve as a task checklist and assignment of responsibilities. This schedule should be prepared well before the due diligence discussed in Chapter 5 begins. The primary purpose of the schedule is to outline all of the events that must occur and the documents that must be prepared prior to the closing date and beyond. In this regard, purchaser's legal counsel acts as an orchestra leader, assigning primary areas of responsibility to the various members of the acquisition team as well as to the seller and its counsel. Purchaser's counsel must also act as a taskmaster to ensure that the timetable for closing is met. Once all tasks have been identified and assigned, and a realistic timetable for completion has been established, then a firm closing time and date can be preliminarily determined.

Naturally, the exact list of legal documents that must be prepared and the specific tasks to be outlined in the work schedule will vary from transaction to transaction, usually depending on the specific facts and circumstances of each deal, such as (1) whether the transaction is a stock or an asset purchase, (2) the form and terms of the purchase price, (3) the nature of the business being acquired, (4) the nature and extent of the assets being purchased and/or the liabilities being assumed, and (5) the sophistication of the parties and their respective legal counsel.

A sample work schedule for an asset purchase transaction that is not intended to be overly complex or comprehensive is set forth in Figure 4-3.

THE GROWING DEBATE
ABOUT THE ROLE AND USEFULNESS
OF FAIRNESS OPINIONS

The collapse of Enron and the passage of Sarbanes-Oxley have forced boards of directors, particularly those at publicly traded companies, to reassess how they do M&A deals and on what basis they can represent to the shareholders that the deal is fair to all parties. Naturally, the seller's board wants to be able to represent that it is being paid a fair price, and the buyer's board wants to represent to its shareholders that it is not using company resources to overpay for a transaction. If the buyer intends to pay a price that is well above current market conditions, then it had better be prepared to justify its action and defend the reasons for the higher valuation. For decades, directors have sought out "fairness opinions" written by consultants, investment bankers, or accountants that justify the transaction and its price parameters in order to satisfy their duties and obligations to the shareholders. But fairness opinion practices have come under scrutiny as poor analysis, conflicts of interest, and a lack of due diligence to support the opinions have begun to surface. Some boards have tried to correct previously flawed practices by making sure that (1) the author of the fairness opinion is truly independent (i.e., is not affiliated with any party to the deal, either directly or indirectly), (2) the author of the fairness opinion is *not* just "telling the directors what they want to hear" in hopes of obtaining business from the company down the road (the "beholden to management" dilemma), (3) success fees as a component of the compensation paid to the author of the opinion have been removed, and (4) second and third opinions to

Figure 4-3. Work Schedule for an Asset Purchase Transaction

Timetable	Task	Responsible Parties
Six weeks before closing	(1) Letter of intent is signed; board resolutions to authorize negotiations are obtained	Seller and buyer and their counsel
	(2) Due diligence request delivered to seller	Buyer's counsel
Five weeks before closing	(1) Due diligence materials organized and delivered	Seller's counsel
	(2) Review of due diligence materials	Buyer's counsel
	(3) Prepare draft of asset purchase agreement, informational schedules, and exhibits to purchase agreement, employment and consulting agreements, and so on	Buyer's counsel
	(4) Order lien searches on seller's assets to review encumbrances	Buyer's counsel
	(5) Comprehensive review of seller's financial statements	Buyer's accounting firm
Three to four weeks before closing	(1) Review, negotiation, and redrafting of asset purchase agreement (may continue until the night before closing)	Buyer's and seller's counsel
	(2) Preparation and negotiation of opinion(s) of counsel	Buyer's and seller's counsel
	(3) Complete review of all initial due diligence materials and make follow-on requests, where necessary	Buyer's counsel
	(4) Ensure that all board and share-holder approvals have been obtained (as required by state law)	Buyer's and seller's counsel
	(5) Prepare checklist and commence process for all third-party regulatory and contractual approvals (banks, landlords, insurance companies, key customers, and so on)	Buyer's and seller's counsel
Two weeks before closing	(1) Mutual review of press releases or other third-party communications regarding the deal (or sooner if required by the SEC)	Buyer's and seller's counsel
	(2) Prepare schedule of closing documents (including opinions, results of lien searches, compliance certificates, and so on)	Buyer's counsel

Figure 4-3. Work Schedule for an Asset Purchase Transaction **(cont.)**

Timetable	Task	Responsible Parties
One week before and up to closing	(1) Finalize any last-minute negotiations to the asset purchase agreement	Buyer's and seller's counsel
	(2) Obtain closing certificates from state authorities (e.g., good-standing certificates, taxes paid and current, charter and amendments)	Seller's counsel
	(3) Checklist to ensure that all conditions to closing have been met or waived	Buyer's and seller's counsel
	(4) Dry-run closing to identify open issues (highly recommended two or three days before closing)	Buyer and seller
	(5) Closing	All parties
	(6) Resolution of post-closing matters and conditions	All parties

the core fairness opinion have been obtained. The process for selecting the firm to draft the fairness opinion should be competitive and well documented and all potential conflicts should be avoided. The process should be especially rigorous if the transaction is high profile, controversial, or in any way contested, especially if key shareholders of the seller have expressed concern that their shares have been undervalued and/or if the shareholders of the buyer do not understand or agree with the underlying value proposition of the deal as proposed.

5.

Due Diligence

Following the collapse of Enron, WorldCom, and several other major multinational companies, the capital markets experienced the Era of Accountability 1.0, which included the passage of Sarbanes-Oxley (Sarbox) in 2002. Sarbox brought new standards for conduct and governance for public-company boards of directors and officers, new and more stringent reporting requirements, stronger internal controls, and stiffer penalties for noncompliance. It also influenced the focus and depth of M&A due diligence standards, which began to take deeper dives into issues of financial reporting, objectivity, and verification. This is discussed further in the appendix to this chapter.

Less than a short seven years later, we entered the Era of Accountability 2.0. The election of Barack Obama and the Obama administration's commitment to transparency; the role of government in bailouts, including TARP; the failure of banks and automobile companies; the Madoff scandal; the severe global recession; and mistrust of Wall Street collectively contributed to an increase in staffing at the SEC, the expectation of vigorous government enforcement activities in a variety of areas, and the possibility of new generally accepted accounting principles (GAAP) standards. These evolving developments, in turn, are elevating, expanding, and refining the portfolio of due diligence best practices in M&A, financing, and other core business transactions. By 2017, the Era of Accountability had matured and expanded into heightened levels of transparency driven by social media, increased shareholder activism, and boards being held more accountable for botched or ill-fated transactions.

I am not implying that graduation from 1.0 to 2.0 involves a tectonic shift in due diligence best practices. M&A practices and documentation generally are continuing to evolve in small increments. There are occasional exceptions, such as the fairly rapid and widespread move to electronic data rooms. And responses to sweeping legislative and regulatory developments are necessarily fast-paced. The adaptation of acquisition agreements and processes to the preacquisition notification requirements of the U.S. Hart-Scott-Rodino Antitrust Improvements Acts of 1976 is a notable example. Government intervention over the years, triggered in large part by excesses that exploited a flawed regulatory regime, has been so sweeping, fueled by intense and enduring public outrage, that due diligence best practices inevitably will respond to the challenges of a more highly regulated economy in which buyers and sellers must live under the microscope of vigorous government enforcement and intense public scrutiny. This response in large part should encompass a reaffirmation of existing best practices. Accordingly, much of the following discussion emphasizes those practices prevailing in the Era of Accountability 1.0. Although the anticipated changes in practices are likely to be incremental, in the context of ever-expanding government regulation and enforcement activities, the new environment merits a 2.0 designation.

BEST PRACTICES IN DUE DILIGENCE IN THE ERA OF ACCOUNTABILITY 2.0

First, we must embrace the notion that due diligence is both an art and a science, and that it is a process, not an event. Due diligence in this new era requires an increasingly creative and strategic approach, not just a mechanical methodology. Due diligence in M&A requires a deep dive into the history, mission, values, culture, and intangible assets of the company, rather than a mere formalistic review of key contracts and corporate housekeeping documents. Due diligence must be focused on avoiding the "failure" characterization assigned to 30 to 70 percent of all M&A transactions, based on post-closing metrics that include reduced shareholder value.[1] Businesses, large and small alike, that are continuing to cope with the current economic shipwreck surely must avoid foundering again on the rocks of failed M&A endeavors. Lawyers, accountants, investment bankers, industry specialists, and strategic consultants must reaffirm existing best practices and commit themselves to higher and more inquisitive standards of due diligence conduct in the Era of Accountability 2.0.

The due diligence process involves a legal, financial, and strategic review of all of the seller's documents, contractual relationships, operating history, and organizational structure. Due diligence is not just a process; it is also a reality test—a test of whether the factors that are driving the deal and making it look attractive to the parties are real or illusory. Due diligence is not a quest to find the deal breakers; it is a test of the value proposition underlying the transaction to make sure that the inside of the house is as attractive as the outside. Once the foundation has been disassembled, it can either be rebuilt to support a deal that makes sense or left in a disaggregated state so that the buyer avoids the consummation of a transaction that is operationally, financially, strategically, or otherwise imprudent. It is also important to understand that in the Era of Accountability 2.0, due diligence typically will be more expansive and will probe more deeply than ever before. Accordingly, due diligence will take longer and be costlier, especially if the prospective buyer is a public company or a company with plans to go public within the next eighteen months.

A prime example of the need for heightened due diligence is provided by the articulated policy of the U.S. Department of Justice (DOJ) relating to enforcement of the Foreign Corrupt Practices Act (FCPA). At its most basic level, the FCPA prohibits U.S. and certain foreign companies from bribing foreign government officials. A discussion of the many pitfalls a buyer can encounter under the FCPA in acquiring a company that may have violated the FCPA is beyond the scope of this chapter. The FCPA is a strong example because the DOJ has issued written guidance effectively announcing that it is less likely to take

---

1. Robert Mack, Michael Gerrard, and Ned Frey, *An IS Perspective on Mergers and Acquisitions: A Six Stage Handbook* (Stamford, CT: Gartner, 2002).

harsh enforcement action against a company that purchases another company that has violated the FCPA *if* the buyer has (1) conducted extensive FCPA-oriented due diligence, (2) obtained certain representations and warranties from the seller, (3) made voluntary disclosures to the DOJ, and (4) implemented structural compliance safeguards.[2] The DOJ guidance is very fact-specific and therefore is not generically applicable to all buyers facing potential FCPA issues. However, with an ever-increasing number of cross-border acquisitions in the global M&A marketplace, the current environment heightens the need for buyers who are examining certain foreign targets to undertake extensive FCPA due diligence.

Returning to the fundamentals of due diligence, the seller's team must organize the documents and prepare the data room. Although electronic data rooms, which are especially important to cross-border M&A transactions, have improved the efficiency of the due diligence process, the seller still must commit substantial resources to assembling the documents. The buyer's team must be prepared to ask all the right questions as it conducts a detailed analysis of the documents provided and prepares for in-person interviews and follow-on requests. To the extent that the deal is structured as a merger, or where the seller will be taking the buyer's stock as all or part of its compensation, the process of due diligence is likely to be a two-way street as the parties gather background information on each other.

The due diligence work is usually divided between two working teams: (1) the financial and strategic team, which is typically managed by the buyer's management team with assistance from its accountants, and (2) the legal team, which involves the buyer's counsel with appropriate assistance from technical experts such as environmental engineers and export compliance specialists, depending on the nature of the target's business. Throughout the process, both teams compare

---

2. See U.S. Department of Justice, FCPA Opinion Procedure Release No. 2001–01 (May 24, 2001), available at http://www.usdoj.gov/criminal/fraud/fcpa/opinion/2001/0101. html; U.S. Department of Justice, FCPA Opinion Procedure Release No. 2003–01 (January 15, 2003), available at http://www.usdoj.gov/criminal/fraud/fcpa/opinion/2003/0301.html; U.S. Department of Justice, FCPA Opinion Procedure Release 04–02 (July 12, 2004), available at http://www.usdoj.gov/criminal/fraud/fcpa/opinion/2004/0402.html; and U.S. Department of Justice, FCPA Opinion Procedure Release No. 08–02 (June 13, 2008), available at http://www.usdoj.gov/criminal/fraud/fcpa/opinion/2008/0802.html.

notes on open issues and potential risks and problems. The legal due diligence focuses on potential legal issues and problems that may prove to be impediments to the transaction. It also sheds light on how the transaction should be structured and the contents of the transaction documents, such as the representations and warranties. The business due diligence focuses on the strategic and financial issues in the transaction, such as confirmation of the past financial performance of the seller; integration of the human and financial resources of the two companies; confirmation of the operating, production, and distribution synergies and economies of scale to be achieved by the acquisition; and the collection of information necessary for financing the transaction.

Overall, the due diligence process, when done properly, can be tedious, frustrating, time-consuming, and expensive. For example, one FCPA due diligence effort cited in a DOJ opinion encompassed a review of at least four million electronic documents requiring nearly 45,000 hours of mostly lawyer time.[3] Fortunately, many transactions will not require such an extensive effort. Yet, detailed due diligence is a necessary prerequisite to a well-planned acquisition, and it can be quite informative and revealing in its analysis of the target company and its measures of the costs and risks associated with the transaction.

Buyers should expect sellers to become defensive, evasive, and impatient during the due diligence phase of the transaction. Most business owners and executives do not enjoy having their business policies and decisions under the microscope, especially for an extended period of time, and will only tolerate so many rounds of nitpicking. Eventually, the seller is likely to give the prospective buyer an ultimatum: "Finish the due diligence soon or the deal is off." When negotiations have reached this point, it is best to end the examination process soon thereafter to stay focused on a short list of bona fide concerns. Buyers should resist the temptation to conduct a hasty "once-over," either to save costs or to appease the seller. Yet at the same time, they should avoid "due diligence overkill," keeping in mind that due diligence is *not* a perfect process and should not be a tedious fishing expedition. Like any audit, a due diligence process is designed to answer the important questions and provide reasonable assurance that the seller's claims about the business are fair and legitimate.

---

3. U.S. Department of Justice, FCPA Opinion Procedure Release 04–02 (July 12, 2004), available at http://www.usdoj.gov/criminal/fraud/fcpa/opinion/2004/0402.html.

There are, of course, exceptions in which the buyer faces structural constraints on conducting thorough due diligence. These include acquisitions of bankrupt companies under Section 363 of the U.S. Bankruptcy Code. Although companies that are in Chapter 11 proceedings typically provide for some due diligence by prospective buyers who wish to submit bids, the representations and warranties that may be crafted in response to the buyer's due diligence are somewhat less meaningful than in nonbankruptcy transactions because frequently there is no ongoing indemnification obligation on the part of the estate of the bankrupt seller.

In addition to the bankruptcy context, the increasingly common use of auctions managed by investment banks or other financial advisors has affected early-stage due diligence activities. While sellers typically permit interested bidders to examine data room documents and submit follow-on questions, full-scale due diligence generally is not permitted until the seller has selected the winning bidder following a review of the prospective buyers' markups of a proposed acquisition agreement. Buyers frequently propose numerous additional revisions to the acquisition agreement based on their subsequent due diligence, but sellers often impose tight deadlines on the winning bidders and otherwise attempt to limit the due diligence–driven revisions to a bare minimum.

Whatever the type of transaction, there is always the possibility that critical information may slip through the cracks, which is precisely why broad representations, warranties, liability holdbacks, and indemnification provisions should be included in the final purchase agreement, at least in a nonbankruptcy context.[4] These provisions protect the buyer, while the seller negotiates for carve-outs (e.g., a minimum "basket" of liabilities before the buyer may seek reimbursement for undisclosed or unexpected liabilities), exceptions, and limitations on liability that provide post-closing protections. To the extent that the seller is able to negotiate favorable limits on the seller's liability, including the period during

---

4. Representations and warranties may still be important in a bankruptcy context if there is a temporal gap between signing and closing upon receiving bankruptcy court approval. The buyer may be able to terminate the transaction if there is a material breach of an important representation and warranty provision prior to the closing, even if the representation and warranty is often meaningless in terms of giving rise to post-closing indemnification claims. Of course, some Section 363 transactions do involve escrowed funds that are available for a short while to satisfy limited indemnification claims.

which the buyer may assert claims (referred to as the "survival" period for representations and warranties), the indemnification provisions may in fact benefit the seller more than the buyer. Likewise, sophisticated sellers will try to include a disclaimer in the acquisition agreement providing that the buyer is relying only on the representations and warranties in the four corners of the agreement. Such a clause frequently prevents a buyer from bringing fraud claims against the seller.[5]

The nature and scope of all these provisions are likely to be hotly contested in the negotiations. However, buyers should not become so preoccupied with the minutiae and emotion attending these negotiations that they lose sight of the big picture. Remember that the key objective of due diligence is not only to confirm that the deal makes sense (e.g., to confirm the factual assumptions and preliminary valuations underlying the terms by which the buyer negotiates the transaction), but also to determine whether the transaction should proceed at all. The buyer must recognize at all times that there may be a need to terminate negotiations if the risks or potential liabilities in the transaction greatly exceed what is anticipated and there is no effective way to insure against them or otherwise compensate the buyer for assuming such risks and liabilities.

As stated earlier, effective due diligence is both an art and a science. The art is the style and experience to know which questions to ask and how and when to ask them. It is the ability to create an atmosphere of both trust and fear in the seller that encourages full and complete disclosure. In this sense, the due diligence team is on a risk discovery and assessment mission, looking for potential problems and liabilities (the search) and finding ways to resolve these problems prior to closing and to ensure that risks are allocated fairly and openly after the closing.

The science of due diligence is in the preparation of comprehensive and customized checklists of the specific questions to be presented to the seller, in maintaining a methodical system for organizing and analyzing the documents and data provided by the seller, and in quantitatively assessing the risks raised by those problems that are discovered in the process. One of the key areas is detection of the seller's obligations, particularly those that the buyer will be expected or required to assume

---

5. Fraud claims are considered tort actions rather than contract actions and, if successful, allow the buyer to circumvent the negotiated contractual limits on the seller's liability.

after closing (especially in a stock purchase transaction or comparable merger; in an asset purchase, purchased liabilities are specifically defined, subject to a few successor liabilities that cannot be contractually avoided). The due diligence process is designed first to detect the *existence* of the obligations, and second to identify any *defaults or problems* in connection with these obligations that will affect the buyer after closing.

The best way for the buyer to ensure that virtually no stone remains unturned is through effective due diligence preparation and planning. Astute buyers typically employ comprehensive due diligence checklists that are intended to guide the company's management team while it works closely with counsel to gather and review all legal documents that may be relevant to the structure and pricing of the transaction; to assess the potential legal risks and liabilities to the buyer following the closing; and to identify all of the consents, approvals, and notifications that may be required from or to third parties and government agencies. The most common form of third-party consent is that required in connection with existing contracts that cannot be assigned or otherwise transferred without the counterparty's prior approval.

A due diligence checklist, however, should be a guideline, not a crutch. The buyer's management team must take the lead in developing questions that pertain to the nature of the seller's business. These questions will set the pace for the level of detail and adequacy of the review. The key point here is that every type of business has its own issues and problems, and a standard set of questions will rarely be sufficient. Some of the more common mistakes made during the process are set forth in Figure 5-1.

Figure 5-1. Common Mistakes Made by the Buyer
During the Due Diligence Investigation

1. *Mismatch between the documents provided by the seller and the skills of the buyer's review team.* The seller may have particularly complex financial statements or highly technical reports that must be truly understood by the buyer's due diligence team. Make sure that there is a capability fit.
2. *Poor communication and misunderstandings.* The communications between the teams of the buyer and the seller should be open and clear. The process must be well orchestrated.

3. *Lack of planning and focus in the preparation of the due diligence questionnaires and in the interviews with the seller's team.* The focus must be on asking the *right* questions, not just a lot of questions. Sellers will resent wasteful "fishing expeditions" when the buyer's team is unfocused.

4. *Inadequate time devoted to tax and financial matters.* The buyer's (and seller's) CFO and CPA must play an integral part in the due diligence process in order to gather data on past financial performance and tax reporting, unusual financial events, or disturbing trends or inefficiencies.

5. *Lack of reasonable accommodations and support for the buyer's due diligence team.* The buyer must insist that its team be treated like welcome guests, not like enemies from the IRS! Many times, buyer's counsel is sent to a dark room in a corner of the building to inspect documents, without coffee, windows, or phones. It will enhance and expedite the transaction if the seller provides reasonable accommodations and support for the buyer's due diligence team.

6. *Ignoring the real story behind the numbers.* The buyer and its team must dig deep into the financial data and test (and retest) the value proposition as to whether the deal truly makes sense. They must ask themselves, "Does the real value truly justify the price?" The economics of the deal may not hold water once a realistic look at cost allocation, inventory turnover, and capacity utilization is taken into account.

Figure 5-2. Dealing with Due Diligence Surprises

Walk/run away	Purchase agreement amendments and protections (holdbacks, R&Ws, indemnifications, escrows, etc.)
Purchase price adjustments (or terms)	Ignore

RISK

COST

Due diligence surprises can come in varying shapes and sizes, each with varying degrees of severity, as described in Figure 5-2. Also, the current crisis of disengagement is impacting due diligence, as shown in Figure 5-3.

Figure 5-3. The Crisis of Disengagement and Its Impact on Due Diligence

Our global economy is fighting an epidemic of alarming propor-tions. It is *not* cancer, intolerance, racial divides, terrorism, cyber-attacks, hunger, access to clean water, or the technology gap—although, unfortunately, *all* of those social epidemics remain firmly in place. Rather, it is a disease affecting the central nervous system of our economy—and it is destroying creativity, innovation, productivity, profitability, and overall enterprise value. This epidemic is a societal and workplace challenge costing hundreds of billions of dollars a year in the United States—a calamity so large that it could literally reverse the trend of our evolution if not soon corrected. It is the *crisis of disengagement*. And it is having a *direct* impact on corporate venturing, innovation, and the ability of a company to strategically harvest its intangible assets.

For example, in the United States, in the December 2016 update to Gallup's State of the American Workplace, as well as in recent studies by the Conference Board, and many other prominent organizations, researchers have found that fewer than 30 percent of Americans are "somewhat satisfied" with their work and their career paths. The remaining 70 percent are "somewhat or highly dissatisfied," citing inadequate challenge, pay, morale, sense of purpose, or lack of appreciation at the heart of their disdain. Many are bored, which eviscerates productivity and the ability to innovate, and in turn affects the profitability of companies and the ability to remain competitive in the world market.

Readers of this book—whether as intermediaries and investment bankers, principals or executives, corporate development teams, M&A lawyers, accountants and valuation experts—need to understand and embrace this disturbing trend in our workforce and deal with it in a wide variety of ways, from M&A structure, post-closing integration, strategic due diligence, valuation, fairness opinions, etc.—all of which may be affected by varying levels of employee or other types of disengagement.

Gallup 2016 State of the American Workplace Poll

➡ 31.5 percent of U.S. Workforce defines themselves as engaged.

➡ 51 percent are not engaged/disconnected.

➡ 17.5 percent are actively disengaged.

It is hard to imagine that a disengaged workforce that spends the bulk of its time being distracted and dissatisfied will ever be a catalyst for the creativity and productivity in an enterprise or devote itself to driving long-term shareholder or enterprise value. It is equally hard to imagine an employee who feels disconnected and unappreciated spending time thinking about ways to be more efficient in his or her workplace, work with team members, or see new ways to improve the company's current products and services. And it is harder still to imagine a disengaged manager spending the necessary time to figure out how to better engage employees.

Innovation within the organization (also known as *intrepreneurship*) refers to the actions and initiatives that transform organizations through strategic-renewal processes. Firms that consistently demonstrate durable corporate innovation are typically viewed as dynamic entities prepared to take advantage of new business opportunities when they arise, with a willingness to deviate from prior strategies and business models, to embrace new resource combinations that hold promise for new innovations. These companies tend to attract higher valuations in private financing, M&A transactions, strategic investments, and initial public offerings.

There have been numerous articles and books written over the years advocating the importance of "unleashing the entrepreneurial potential" of individuals by removing constraints on entrepreneurial behavior to drive enterprise value (see for example, Gary Hamel's *Leading the Revolution,* Gifford Pinchott's *Intrapreneuring,* and my 2012 book *Harvesting Intangible Assets*). Employees engaging in entrepreneurial behavior are the foundation for organizational innovation. In order to develop a culture of "corporate innovation," organizations must establish a process through which individuals in an established firm pursue entrepreneurial opportunities to innovate without regard to the level and nature of currently available resources. However, keep in mind that, in the absence of proper control mechanisms, firms that manifest corporate-innovation activity may "tend to generate an incoherent mass of interesting but unrelated opportunities that may have profit potential, but that don't move [those] firms toward a desirable future."

Research also shows that engaged workers are more likely to foster a collaborative and innovative atmosphere among fellow employees by reacting positively to creative ideas of others on their team. A good example of this is Google, which fosters a variety of channels to enhance employee engagement through connectivity and the sharing of ideas. Some of the avenues for expression that the company facilities include having Google Cafes, which serve as venues for individuals to interact across their regular team, or Google Moderators, a management tool that was created to allow anyone within the company to posit questions they would like to have answered. Through the Moderator channel, employees can view existing ideas, questions, and suggestions. This generates a symbiotic relationship between innovation and employee engagement creating an inertial atmosphere.

For decades, workers were expected to know their jobs, do their work, keep their heads down, and only "bother" management with questions to avert a crisis. If a problem arises, know how and when to solve it, and don't interfere with the supervisor's valuable time. That mantra needs to shift if we are going to improve engagement in a way that will drive more innovation and upticks in shareholder value. Employees at all levels need to be liberated to ask the "whys?" and the "what ifs?" They need to be able to ask (without retribution or punishment), "Why am I doing my job the way I am doing it?" "Is there a better way?" "What would it take to change and why?" Empowering your teams to ask questions also demonstrates humility by the leadership team by admitting that they don't know all the answers, and it gives permission to the workforce to begin to organize its thinking around the unknowns instead of the knowns, which will foster greater creativity, innovation, and productivity.

There are already a wide variety of human capital challenges in M&A transactions, ranging for a complex web of federal/state/local employment laws and regulations, compliance issues, union laws, retirement and compensation issues, general cultural issues, succession planning, leadership and governance, and the impact of automation and robotics as we begin to contemplate the workplace of the future.

This recently recognized crisis of disengagement raises new and more granular challenges in M&A, private equity, and strategic or venture financings due diligence. Nobody wants (or intends) to invest in or buy a company with a distracted, dysfunctional, or disengaged workforce. And no company will ever reach its full operational potential or maximum enterprise valuation with apathetic and disconnected workers.

Post-closing synergies and integration success are also highly unlikely when one or more of the buyer or seller's human capital assets are grossly underperforming or feeling deeply underappreciated and focused on almost anything but their core tasks at hand. Leadership and governance teams on *both* sides of the transaction as well as their advisors are often either in denial as to the extent of the problem or lack the strategic tools to remedy the key challenges.

Sellers engaged in pre-transaction "mock" due diligence exercises need to be prepared for this new category of due diligence questions surrounding levels of engagement, and buyers and their advisors need to develop strategic due diligence skills around those concerns. Not too far down the road, activist shareholders and other affected third parties could possibly bring legal actions against leaders of buyers and sellers who ignore the importance of employee engagement levels and overall cultural performance in their due diligence and analysis of transactions and where mergers and acquisitions are underperforming on a post-closing bases as a result of this crisis.

What Role Can M&A Principals and Advisors Play?

➡ Strengthen your HR/cultural-related due diligence analytical skills and approaches.
➡ Bring in Subject Matter Experts (SMEs) and specialists as needed.
➡ Focus on these issues in pre–due diligence mock reviews.
➡ Understand the connections between high levels of disengagement and the impact on other aspects of the business model operations (e.g., customer service, innovation, recruitment, brand, social media, etc.).

- ➡ Work with legal counsel with strong L&E skills and strategic understanding of disengagement issues.
- ➡ Closely examine the alignment of reward/compensation systems with workplace performance and engagement.
- ➡ Advise buy-side engagement clients on the risks of acquiring low-engagement companies.
- ➡ Look for disengagement "warning signs" in due diligence on the seller (i.e., dysfunctional leadership, high turnover rates, an excess of negative social media posts on job-related or other websites/platforms, lack of succession planning or obvious turfmanship/protectionism in leadership positions, declining rates of profitability, lack of innovation, etc.).
- ➡ Challenge buyers who think they have the "magic elixir" for curing cultural or employee performance defects on a post-closing basis ("Oh, this won't be a problem once *we* buy them." "Yeah, right!?").

For example, I worked on a deal that involved the purchase of a hockey league in the Midwest. It was easy to prepare the standard due diligence list and draw up questions regarding corporate structure and history, the status of the stadium leases, and team tax returns, and to question the steps that had been taken to protect the team trademarks. The more difficult task was developing a customized list. In my role as legal counsel, I asked my client the question, "If you were buying a sports league, what would you need to review?"

As stated earlier, every type of business has its own issues and problems. The list for this client included player and coaching contracts, stadium signage and promotional leases, league-wide and local-team sponsorship contracts, the immigration status of each player, team and player performance statistics, the status of contracts with each team's star players, scouting reports and drafting procedures, ticket sales (including walk-up, advance, season, group tickets, and coupons) for each team and game, promotional agreements with equipment suppliers and providers of game-day merchandise, food and beverage concession contracts, the status of each team's franchise agreement, commitments made to cities for future teams, and unique per-team advertising rates for dasher boards (the signs for advertising that surround the rink).

When done properly, due diligence is performed in multiple stages. First, all the basic data are gathered and specific topics are identified. Follow-up questions and additional data gathering can be performed in subsequent rounds of due diligence; they must be custom-tailored to the target's core business industry trends and unique challenges.

The legal due diligence checklist in the following section is intended to guide the company's management team while it works closely with counsel to gather and review all legal documents that may be relevant to the structure and pricing of the transaction; to assess the potential legal risks and liabilities to the buyer following the closing; and to identify all of the consents and approvals, such as an existing contract that can't be assigned without consent, which must be obtained from third parties and government agencies.

Following the high-level suggestions in this overview of M&A due diligence best practices will not ensure that the parties to a transaction have successfully negotiated the rapids of the Era of Accountability 2.0. However, compliance with the best practices will go a long way toward keeping their transaction from joining the ranks of failed M&A deals that have plagued the economy in recent years.

LEGAL DUE DILIGENCE

In analyzing the company for sale, the buyer's team carefully reviews and analyzes the following legal documents and records, where applicable.

I. Corporate Matters

A. Corporate records of the seller

- Certificate of incorporation and all amendments
- Bylaws as amended
- Minute books, including resolutions and minutes of all directors' and shareholders' meetings
- Current shareholders list (certified by the corporate secretary), annual reports to shareholders, and stock transfer books
- A list of all states, countries, and other jurisdictions in which the seller transacts business or is qualified to do business

- Applications or other filings in each state listed in (5), for qualification as a foreign corporation and evidence of qualification
- Locations of business offices (including overseas)

B. Agreements among the seller's shareholders
C. All contracts restricting the sale or transfer of shares of the company, such as buy/sell agreements, subscription agreements, offeree questionnaires, or contractual rights of first refusal; all agreements for the right to purchase shares, such as stock options or warrants; and any pledge agreements by an individual share holder involving the seller's shares

II. Financial Matters

A. Copies of management and similar reports or memoranda relating to the material aspects of the business operations or products
B. Letters of counsel in response to auditors' requests for the preceding five years
C. Reports of independent accountants to the board of directors for the preceding five years
D. Revolving credit and term loan agreements, indentures, and other debt instruments, including, without limitation, all documents relating to shareholder loans
E. Correspondence with principal lenders to the seller
F. Personal guarantees of the seller's indebtedness by its shareholders or other parties
G. Agreements by the seller where it has served as a guarantor for the obligations of third parties
H. Federal, state, and local tax returns and correspondence with federal, state, and local tax officials
I. Federal filings regarding the Subchapter S status of the seller (where applicable)
J. Any private placement memorandum (assuming, of course, that the seller is not a Securities Act of 1934 "reporting company") prepared and used by the seller (as well as any document used in lieu of a private placement memorandum, such as an investment profile or a business plan)

K. Financial statements of the seller, which should be prepared in accordance with GAAP, for the past five years, including:

- Annual (audited) balance sheets
- Monthly (or other available) balance sheets
- Annual (audited) and monthly (or other available) earnings statements
- Annual (audited) and monthly (or other available) statements of shareholders' equity and changes in financial position
- Any recently prepared projections for the seller
- Notes and material assumptions for all statements described in K (1) to (5)

L. Any information or documentation relating to tax assessments, deficiency notices, investigations, audits, or settlement proposals

M. An informal schedule of key management compensation (listing information for at least the ten most highly compensated management employees or consultants)

N. Financial aspects of overseas operations (where applicable), including the status of foreign legislation, regulatory restrictions, intellectual property protection, exchange controls, methods for repatriating profits, foreign manufacturing, government controls, import/export licensing and tariffs, and so on

O. Projected budgets, accounts receivable reports (including a detailed aging report, turnover, bad debt experience, and reserves), and related information

III. Management and Employment Matters

A. All employment agreements
B. Agreements relating to consulting, management, financial advisory services, and other professional engagements
C. Copies of all union contracts and collective bargaining agreements
D. Equal Employment Opportunity Commission (EEOC) and any state equivalent compliance files
E. Occupational Safety and Health Administration (OSHA) files, including safety records and workers' compensation claims
F. Employee benefit plans (and copies of literature issued to employees describing such plans), including the following:

- Pension and retirement plans, including union pension or retirement plans
- Annual reports for pension plans, if any
- Profit-sharing plans
- Stock option plans, including information concerning all options, stock appreciation rights, and other stock-related benefits granted by the company
- Medical and dental plans
- Insurance plans and policies (including errors and omissions policies and directors' and officers' liability insurance policies)
- Any Employee Stock Ownership Plan (ESOP) and trust agreement
- Severance pay plans or programs
- All other benefit or incentive plans or arrangements not covered by the foregoing, including welfare benefit plans

G. All current contract agreements with or pertaining to the seller and to which directors, officers, or shareholders of the seller are parties, and any documents relating to any other transactions between the seller and any director, officer, or shareholders, including receivables from or payables to directors, officers, or shareholders

H. All policy and procedures manuals of the seller concerning personnel; hiring and promotional practices; compliance with the Family Leave Act; drug and alcohol abuse policies; AIDS policies; sexual harassment policies; vacation and holiday policies; expense reimbursement policies; and so on

I. The name, address, phone number, and personnel file of any officer or key employee who has left the seller within the past three years

IV. Tangible and Intangible Assets of the Seller

A. List of all commitments for rented or leased real and personal property, including location and address, description, terms, options, termination and renewal rights, policies regarding ownership of improvements, and annual costs

B. List of all real property owned, including location and address, description of general character, easements, rights of way, encumbrances, zoning restrictions, surveys, mineral rights, title insurance, pending and threatened condemnation, hazardous waste pollution, and so on

C. List of all tangible assets

D. List of all liens on all real properties and material tangible assets

E. Mortgages, deeds, title insurance policies, leases, and other agreements relating to the properties of the seller

F. Real estate tax bills for the real estate of the seller

G. List of patents, patents pending, trademarks, trade names, copyrights, registered and proprietary Internet addresses, franchises, licenses, and all other intangible assets, including registration numbers, expiration dates, employee invention agreements and policies, actual or threatened infringement actions, licensing agreements, and copies of all correspondence relating to this intellectual property

H. Copies of any survey, appraisal, engineering, or other reports relating to the properties of the seller

I. List of assets that may be held on a consignment basis (or that may be the property of a given customer), such as machine dies, molds, and so on

V. Material Contracts and Obligations of the Seller

A. Material purchase, supply, and sale agreements currently outstanding or projected to come to fruition within twelve months, including the following:

- List of all contracts relating to the purchase of products, equipment, fixtures, tools, dies, supplies, industrial supplies, or other materials having a price under any such contract in excess of $5,000
- List of all unperformed sales contracts

B. Documents incidental to any planned expansion of the seller's facilities

C. Consignment agreements

D. Research agreements

E. Franchise, licensing, distribution, and agency agreements

F. Joint-venture agreements

G. Agreements for the payment or receipt of license fees or royalties and royalty-free licenses

H. Documentation relating to all property, liability, and casualty insurance policies owned by the seller, including for each policy a summary description of:

- Coverage
- Policy type and number
- Insurer/carrier and broker
- Premium
- Expiration date
- Deductible
- Any material changes in any of the foregoing since the inception of the seller
- Claims made under such policies

I. Agreements restricting the seller's right to compete in any business

J. Agreements for the seller's current purchase of services, including, without limitation, consulting and management

K. Contracts for the purchase, sale, or removal of electricity, gas, water, telephone, sewage, power, or any other utility service

L. List of waste dumps, disposal, treatment, and storage sites

M. Agreements with any railroad, trucking, or other transportation company or courier service

N. Letters of credit

O. Copies of any special benefits under contracts or government programs that might be in jeopardy as a result of the proposed transaction (e.g., small business or minority set-asides, intra-family transactions or favored pricing, internal leases or allocations, and so on)

P. Copies of licenses, permits, and government approvals applied for or issued to the seller that are required in order to operate the businesses of the seller, such as zoning, energy requirements (natural gas, fuel, oil, electricity, and so on), operating permits, or health and safety certificates

Note: This section is critical and will be one key area of the negotiations as discussed in Chapter 11. Therefore, it is suggested that the buyer and its advisory team request copies of *all* material contracts and obligations of the seller and then organize them as follows:

Schedule of All Contracts and Obligations of Seller That Are to Be Assumed by Buyer After Closing*	Status of Each Contract or Obligation	To What Extent Will Third-Party Consents Be Required for the Assignment or Assumption of These Contracts or Obligations?
	Sample Responses	*Sample Responses*
A. _____	Current	Not required
B. _____	Received notice of default on _____, 20___; cured on _____, 20___	Consent to assignment requested _____, 20___, and obtained _____, 20___
C. _____	Notice of default received; default not yet cured!	Consent to assumption required but not yet requested

* For example, contracts that have a reaming term in excess of six months.

VI. Litigation and Claims, Actual and Contingent

A. Opinion letter from each lawyer or law firm prosecuting or defending significant litigation to which the seller is a party, describing such litigation

B. List of material litigation or claims for more than $5,000 against the seller asserted or threatened with respect to the quality of the products or services sold to customers, warranty claims, disgruntled employees, product liability, government actions, tort claims, breaches of contract, and so on, including pending or threatened claims

C. List of settlement agreements, releases, decrees, orders, or arbitration awards affecting the seller

D. Description of labor relations history

E. Documentation regarding correspondence or proceedings with federal, state, or local regulatory agencies

Note: Be sure to obtain specific representations and warranties from the seller and its advisors regarding any knowledge pertaining to potential or contingent claims or litigation.

VII. Miscellaneous

A. Press releases (past two years)

B. Résumés of all key members of the management team

C. Press clippings (past two years)

D. Financial analyst reports, industry surveys, and so on
E. Texts of speeches by the seller's management team, especially if reprinted and distributed to the industry or the media
F. Schedule of all outside advisors, consultants, and so on, used by the seller over the past five years (domestic and international)
G. Schedule of long-term investments made by the seller
H. Standard forms used (purchase orders, sales orders, service agreements, and so on)

The buyer's acquisition team and its legal counsel gather data to answer the following ten legal questions during the legal phase of due diligence:

1. What legal steps will need to be taken to effectuate the transaction (e.g., is director and stockholder approval needed, or are there share transfer restrictions or restrictive covenants in loan documentation)? Has the appropriate corporate authority been obtained to proceed with the agreement? What key third-party consents (e.g., FCC, DOJ, lenders, venture capitalists, landlords, or key customers) are required?

2. What antitrust problems, if any, are raised by the transaction? Will filing with the Federal Trade Commission (FTC) be necessary under the premerger notification provisions of the Hart-Scott-Rodino Act?

3. Will the transaction be exempt from registration under applicable federal and state securities laws under the "sale of business" doctrine?

4. What significant legal problems or issues are affecting the seller now or are likely to affect the seller in the foreseeable future? What potential adverse tax consequences to the buyer, the seller, and their respective shareholders may be triggered by the transaction?

5. What are the potential post-closing risks and obligations of the buyer? To what extent should the seller be held liable for such potential liabilities? What steps, if any, can be taken to reduce these potential risks or liabilities? What will it cost to implement these steps?

6. What are the impediments to the assignability of key tangible and intangible assets of the seller company that are desired by the buyer, such as real estate, intellectual property, favorable contracts or leases, human resources, or plant and equipment?

7. What are the obligations and responsibilities of the buyer and the seller under applicable environmental and hazardous waste laws, such as the Comprehensive Environmental Response Compensation and Liability Act (CERCLA)?

8. What are the obligations and responsibilities of the buyer and the seller to the creditors of the seller (e.g., bulk transfer laws under Article 6 of the applicable state's commercial code)?

9. What are the obligations and responsibilities of the buyer and the seller under applicable federal and state labor and employment laws (e.g., will the buyer be subject to successor liability under federal labor laws and as a result be obligated to recognize the presence of organized labor and therefore be obligated to negotiate existing collective bargaining agreements)?

10. To what extent will employment, consulting, confidentiality, or noncompetition agreements need to be created or modified in connection with the proposed transaction?

BUSINESS AND STRATEGIC DUE DILIGENCE

At the same time, as legal counsel is performing its legal investigation of the seller's company, the buyer assembles a management team to conduct business and strategic due diligence. The level and extent of this general business and strategic due diligence will vary, depending on the experience of the buyer in the seller's industry and its familiarity with the target company. For example, a financial buyer who is entering a new industry and has no prior experience with the seller should conduct an exhaustive due diligence—not only on the seller's company, but also on any relevant trends within the industry that might directly or indirectly affect the deal. In contrast, a management buyout by a group of industry veterans who have been with the seller for an extended period of time will probably require only a minimum amount of business or strategic due diligence; in this case, the focus will be on legal due diligence and the assessment and assumption of risk.

In conducting the due diligence from a business perspective, the buyer's team is likely to encounter a wide variety of financial problems and risk areas when analyzing the seller. These typically include an undervaluation of inventory, overdue tax liabilities, inadequate management information systems, related-party transactions (especially in small, closely held companies), an unhealthy reliance on a few key customers or suppliers, aging accounts receivable, unrecorded liabilities (e.g., warranty claims, vacation pay, claims, and sales returns and allowances), or an immediate need for significant expenditures as a result of obsolete equipment, inventory, or computer systems. Each of these problems poses different risks and costs for the acquiring company, and these risks must be weighed against the benefits to be gained from the transaction. Note that in view of the significant upheaval in the global economy following the credit crisis and ripple effect events, any type of due diligence will have to include the heightened scrutiny that is demanded by the new order of due diligence best practices.

For the buyer who is just getting to know the seller's industry, the following two basic questions should be asked:

1. How would you define the market or markets in which the seller operates? What steps will you take to expedite your learning curve for trends within these markets? What third-party advisors are qualified to advise you on key trends affecting this industry?

2. What are the factors that determine success or failure within this industry? How does the seller stack up? What are the image and reputation of the seller within the industry? Does it have a niche? Is the seller's market share increasing or decreasing? Why? What steps can be taken to enhance or reverse these trends?

The following checklist is designed to provide the acquisition team with a starting point for analysis of the seller. It helps to level the playing field in the negotiations, since the seller usually starts with greater expertise regarding its industry and its business. Here are some examples (this checklist is not intended to be exhaustive) of the topic areas and specific questions that should be addressed in due diligence on a given seller:

The Seller's Management Team

1. Has the seller's organization chart been carefully reviewed? How are management functions and responsibilities delegated and implemented? Are job descriptions and employment manuals, among other similar documents, current and available?

2. What is the general assessment of employee morale at the lower echelons of the corporate ladder? To what extent are these rank-and-file employees critical to the seller's long-term health?

3. What are the future growth prospects for the principal labor markets that the seller depends on for attracting key employees? Are employees with the necessary skills generally available? How are the seller's employees recruited, evaluated, trained, and rewarded?

4. What are the background and experience of the seller's key management team? What is the reputation of this management team within the industry? Has there been high turnover among the seller's top management? Why or why not? Who are the seller's key professional advisors and outside consultants?

5. What are the basic management styles, practices, and strategies of the seller's current team? What are the strengths and weaknesses of the management team? To what extent has the seller's current management engaged in long-term strategic planning, developed internal controls, or structured management and marketing information systems?

Operations of the Seller

1. What are the seller's production and distribution methods? To what extent are these methods protected, either by contract or by proprietary rights? Have copies of the seller's brochures and reports describing the seller and its products and services been obtained?

2. To what extent is the seller operating at its maximum capacity? Why? What are the significant risk factors (e.g., dependence on raw materials or key suppliers or customers) affecting the seller's production capacity and ability to expand? What are the significant costs of producing the seller's goods and services? To what extent are the seller's production and output dependent on economic cycles or seasonal factors? *Note:* Obtain a breakdown of major sales by specific product and specific customer categories in order to fully assess the seller's financial performance, dependence on key customers, or product line susceptibility to risk.

3. Are the seller's plant, equipment, supplies, and machinery in good working order? When will these assets need to be replaced? What

are the annual maintenance and service costs for these key assets? At what levels are the seller's inventories? What are the break-even production efficiency and inventory turnover rates for the target company and how do these compare with industry norms?

4. Does the seller maintain production plans, schedules, and reports? Have copies been obtained and analyzed by the buyer? What are the seller's manufacturing and production obligations pursuant to long-term contracts or other arrangements? What long-term (post-closing) obligations or commitments for the purchase of raw materials or other supplies or resources have been made?

5. What is the status of the seller's inventories (e.g., the amount and balance in raw materials and finished goods in relation to production cycles and sales requirements)? What is the condition of the inventory? To what extent is it obsolete?

Note: Be sure to get a breakdown and an analysis of all expenses (e.g., amounts, trends, and categories) in order to assess the profitability of the seller's business, as well as to determine where post-closing expense savings can be obtained or economies of scale achieved.

Sales and Marketing Strategies of the Seller

1. What are the seller's primary and secondary markets? What is the size of these markets, and what is the seller's market share within each market? What strategies are in place to expand this market share? What are the current trends affecting either the growth or the shrinkage of these particular markets? How does the seller segment and reach these markets?

2. Who are the seller's direct and indirect competitors? What are the respective strengths and weaknesses of each competitor? In what principal ways do companies within the seller's industry compete (e.g., price, quality, or service)? For each material competitor, the buyer should seek to obtain data on the competitor's products and services, geographic location, channel of distribution, market share, financial health, pricing policies, and reputation within the industry.

3. Who are the seller's typical customers? What demographic data have been assembled and analyzed? What are the customers' purchasing

capabilities and patterns? Where are these customers principally located? What political, economic, social, or technological trends or changes are likely to affect the demographic makeup of the seller's customer base over the next three to five years? What are the key factors that influence the demand for the seller's goods and services?

4. What are the seller's primary and secondary distribution channels? What contracts are in place in relation to these channels? How could these channels or contracts be modified or improved? How will these channels overlap or conflict with the buyer's existing distribution channels?

5. What sales, advertising, public relations, and promotional campaigns and programs are currently in place at the seller's company? To what extent have these programs been effectively monitored and evaluated?

Financial Management of the Seller

1. Based on the financial statements and reports collected in connection with the legal due diligence, what key sales, income, and earnings trends have been identified? What effect will the proposed transaction have on these aspects of the seller's financial performance? What are the various costs incurred in connection with bringing the seller's products and services to the marketplace? In what ways can these costs be reduced or eliminated?

2. What are the seller's billing and collection procedures? How current are the seller's accounts receivables? What steps have been (or can be) taken to expedite the collection procedures and systems? How credible is the seller's existing accounting and financial control system?

3. What is the seller's capital structure? What are the seller's key financial liabilities and debt obligations? How do the seller's leverage ratios compare to industry norms? What are the seller's monthly debt-service payments? How strong is the seller's relationship with creditors, lenders, and investors?

Figure 5-4 discusses a number of potential due diligence problems. A way for the buyer to ensure that the seller has been forthright in disclosing all material obligations and liabilities (whether actual or contingent) is to prepare an affidavit. An affidavit like the one in Figure 5-5 provides additional protection against misrepresentation or material omissions by the seller, its lawyers, and its auditors. The affidavit can be customized to a particular transaction and include the specific concerns that may arise during the transaction and afterward.

Figure 5-4. Common Due Diligence Problems and Exposure Areas

There is a virtually infinite number of potential problems and exposure areas for the buyer that may be uncovered in the review and analysis of the seller's documents and operations. The specific issues and problems will vary based on the size of the seller, the nature of its business, and the number of years that the seller (or its predecessors) has been in business.

➡ "Clouds" in the title to critical tangible (real estate, equipment, inventory) and intangible (patents, trademarks, and so on) assets. Be sure that the seller has clear title to these assets and that they are conveyed without claims, liens, and encumbrances.

➡ Employee matters. There are a wide variety of employment or labor law issues or liabilities that may be lurking just below the surface but will not be uncovered unless the right questions are asked. Questions designed to uncover wage and hour law violations, discrimination claims, OSHA compliance, or even liability for unfunded persons under the Multiemployer Pension Plan Amendments Act should be developed. If the seller has recently made a substantial workforce reduction (or if you as the buyer are planning post-closing layoffs), then the requirements of the Worker Adjustment and Retraining Notification Act (WARN) must have been met. The requirements of WARN include minimum notice of sixty days prior to wide-scale terminations.

➡ The possibility of environmental liability under CERCLA or related environmental regulations.

➡ Unresolved existing or potential litigation. These cases should be reviewed carefully by counsel.

➡ A seller's attempt to "dress up" the financial statements prior to sale. Often this is an attempt to hide inventory problems, research and development expenditures, excessive overhead and administrative costs, uncollected or uncollectible accounts receivable, unnecessary or inappropriate personal expenses, unrecorded liabilities, tax contingencies, and other such issues.

Figure 5-5. Affidavit Regarding Liabilities

State of _____ }

                       } ss.

County of _____ }

Prospective Seller, being of lawful age and being first duly sworn upon her oath states:

1. I am the sole shareholder of the S Corporation, which trades under the name "SellerCo," and I have full right to sell its assets as described in the Bill of Sale dated _____. Those assets are free and clear of all security interests, liabilities, obligations, and encumbrances of any sort.

2. There are no creditors of SellerCo, or me, or persons known to me who are asserting claims against me or the assets being sold, which in any way affect the transfer to Prospective Buyer of the trade name SellerCo, its goodwill, and its assets, including the equipment as set forth in the Bill of Sale dated _____. I agree to pay all gross receipt and sales taxes and all employment taxes of any sort due through closing. I am current in regard to these taxes and all other taxes, and there are no pending disputes as to any of my taxes or the taxes of SellerCo.

3. There are no judgments against SellerCo or me in any federal or state court in the United States of America. There are also no replevins, attachments, executions, or other writs or processes issued against SellerCo or me. I have never sought protection under any bankruptcy law nor has any petition in bankruptcy been filed against me. There are no pending administrative or regulatory proceedings, arbitrations, or mediations involving SellerCo or me, and I do not know and have no reasonable ground to know of any proposed ones or any basis for any such actions.

4. There are no known outstanding claims by any employees of SellerCo or me, and I expressly recognize that no claims of, by, or on behalf of any employees arising prior to closing are being transferred to Prospective Buyer.

5. There are no and have been no unions that have been or are involved in any business that I own, and particularly, SellerCo. Furthermore, there currently is no union organizational activity under way in any business that I own, and particularly, SellerCo.

6. There are and have been no multi-employer pension plans or other pension or profit-sharing plans involved in any business that I own, and particularly, SellerCo.

7. I have always conducted SellerCo according to applicable laws and regulations.

8. From the time when the purchase agreement was executed through closing, I have conducted the business called SellerCo only in the usual and customary manner. I have entered into no new contracts and have assumed no new obligations during that time period.

9. I shall remain fully liable for payment of all bills, accounts payable, or other claims against SellerCo or me created prior to closing. None of them are being transferred to Prospective Buyer.

10. I hereby warrant and represent to Prospective Buyer that all statements in paragraphs one through nine of this Affidavit are true and correct.

11a. I agree to indemnify and hold harmless Prospective Buyer in respect to any and all claims, losses, damages, liabilities, and expenses, including, without limitation, settlement costs and any legal, accounting, and other expenses for investigating or defending any actions or threatened actions, reasonably incurred by Prospective Buyer in connection with:

  i. Any claims or liabilities made against Prospective Buyer because of any act or failure to act of myself arising prior to closing in regard to SellerCo; or

  ii. Any breach of warranty or misrepresentation involved in my sale of SellerCo to Prospective Buyer.

11b. As to claims or liabilities against Prospective Buyer arising prior to closing in connection with SellerCo, or any claim arising at any time in regard to any profit-sharing or pension plan started prior to closing involving SellerCo, or any breach of warranty or other material misrepresentation made by me, I agree that Prospective Buyer has the option to pay the claim or liability and deduct the amount of it from any money owed to me, after giving me reasonable notice of the claim and reasonable opportunity to resolve it. This right of setoff expressly applies to any damages Prospective Buyer suffers as a result of any breach of any warranty I have given to Prospective Buyer. Prospective Buyer's right of setoff against any money owed me shall not be deemed his exclusive remedy for any breach by me of any representations, warranties, or agreements involved in the sale of SellerCo to him, all of which shall survive the closing and any setoff made by Prospective Buyer.

12. I agree to execute any further documents to complete this sale.

Prospective Seller
Subscribed and Sworn to before me this _____day of
_____, 20____.

Notary Public
My Commission Expires: _____

Note: Proper use of this affidavit depends on the exact type of purchase agreement used.

Figure 5-6. The Emergence of Virtual Data Rooms

It appears that the age of bad hotel rooms, expensive travel costs, and bad donuts in classic due diligence data rooms is slowly but surely being replaced with "virtual data rooms," or VDRs. Virtual data rooms use existing computer software and Internet technology to provide a secure online format for reviewing and organizing due diligence information. The documents are easier to search and index when they are already online, and the use of a VDR prevents "water cooler rumor mills" about what the guys in suits are doing in the corner conference room. The VDR does require the company's IT department to be involved early and often in the overall selling process. The VDR also better facilitates the review of certain types of data that are easier to review online and in electronic form, such as CAD drawings, video files, patent filings, and architectural drawings. Are VDRs growing in acceptance? It appears so. IntraLinks (www.intralinks.com), a leading provider of VDR software and systems, handled 50 transactions in 2001, 450 in 2004, and predicts being a technology provider to 1,500 transactions in 2005. In January of 2009, it was reported that IntraLinks had facilitated 55,000 projects and transactions and had had six consecutive years of double-digit growth. By 2016, virtual data rooms had hosted hundreds of thousands of transactions and Intralinks alone was used by 3.1 million professionals on transactions valued at over $13 trillion dollars.

Significant portions of the due diligence process have shifted online, as shown in Figure 5-6; however, these technology tools should be used as an asset and not a crutch. There is still no substitute for problem-specific due diligence being done on a face-to-face basis, where interactivity, follow-on questions, body language, and voice inflection can be very enlightening and revealing.

CONCLUSION

Due diligence must be a cooperative and patient process involving both the buyer's and the seller's teams. Any attempts to hide or manipulate key data will only lead to problems down the road. Material misrepresentations or omissions can (and often do) lead to post-closing litigation, which is expensive and time-consuming for both parties. Another mistake in due diligence that sellers often make is to forget the human element. I have worked on deals where the lawyers were sent into a dark room in the corner of the building, without any support or even coffee; on other deals, we were treated like royalty, with full access to support staff, computers, telephones, food, and beverages. It is only human for the buyer's counsel to be a bit more cooperative in the negotiations when the seller's team is supportive and allows counsel to do his job.

Post-Sarbanes-Oxley
Due Diligence Checklist

In the 1990s, acquirers rarely had the opportunity to conduct extensive, time-consuming due diligence. Buyers were seldom granted exclusivity periods, and the typical auction might have allowed the potential buyer only a day or two in the data room (which sometimes had a no-copy rule) and a few hours of management interviews. After the Enron scandal and a few others hit the American corporate world, the Public Company Accounting Reform and Investor Protection Act of 2002, also known as the Sarbanes-Oxley Act (Sarbox), was enacted, which changed the way in which businesses were conducted and corporate governance was practiced. Sarbox lays out a government-mandated disclosure process that is monitored by auditors, certified by top-level executives under penalty of prison, and reviewed by the SEC. It addresses corporate responsibility, the creation of a public-company accounting oversight board, auditor independence, and enhanced criminal sanctions. The effect of Sarbox has been to compel investment banks, regulators, shareholder groups, plaintiffs' lawyers, and other parties to analyze companies with a focus on the broad mandates of Sarbox.

Sarbox does not apply only to large publicly traded corporations; privately held companies can also be subject to Sarbox. Lenders and customers can each require a company to adopt Sarbox-style procedures. A company's accountants and its directors' and officers' (D&O) insurance carrier can also prompt a company to do so.

THE DISCLOSURE REQUIREMENTS

Potential acquirers must be aware of the main federal corporate disclosure requirements: Regulation S-K, SFAS No. 5, and Sarbox.

Regulation S-K

Regulation S-K, issued by the SEC, acts as an instruction manual for public companies filing their annual, quarterly, and interim reports. The important provisions are as follows:

1. Item 101 requires reporting companies to describe their businesses, products, and competition as well as report on their financial position by industry segments. Companies must discuss transactions outside of the ordinary course of business, R&D activities, intellectual property, backlog, foreign operations, and the anticipated costs and effects of environmental compliance—both current and projected.

2. Item 103 calls for companies to disclose any large non-routine legal proceedings to which they are a party, and even some routine matters that exceed certain thresholds. Also, Item 103 requires a company's management to discuss known trends, events, and uncertainties that could have a material effect on its business.

3. Item 402 calls for a detailed review of the company's executive compensation, employee contracts, benefits, options, and so on.

4. Item 404 focuses on related-party transactions. Material contracts are to be included as exhibits to the periodic filings, so many times credit agreements, joint venture agreements, and even real estate leases are on the public record.

SFAS No. 5

Statement of Financial Accounting Standards No. 5, Accounting for Contingencies, issued by the Financial Accounting Standards Board, deals with disclosing loss contingencies. Observing SFAS No. 5 is part of complying with generally accepted accounting principles and is a key element in the audit letter process. It requires a company to establish a loss contingency in its financial statements if:

1. Available information indicates that it is probable that the company has suffered a loss.
2. The amount of that loss can be reasonably estimated.

Sarbanes-Oxley

Sarbox introduces stringent disclosure requirements for companies. The main disclosure requirements that a potential acquirer must keep in mind are as follows:

1. Section 302 of Sarbox requires the chief executive officer and the chief financial officer of a company to personally certify certain items about the annual or quarterly report being filed. In summary, they must certify that:

- ▸ They have read the report.
- ▸ The report fairly presents the company's financial condition and results of operations.
- ▸ To their knowledge, the report contains no untrue statements or omissions of material fact that would make the statements misleading.
- ▸ They are responsible for and have evaluated the company's disclosure controls and procedures, and its internal controls over financial reporting.

2. Under Section 906 of Sarbox, senior officers can be subject to potential criminal liability if they falsely, knowingly, or willfully make an inaccurate Section 302 certification. These provisions together obligate the buyer's CEO and CFO to certify the financial statements and internal disclosure controls of the combined company as of the end of the first quarter post-acquisition. In major acquisitions, this can be an impossible task if substantial due diligence was not done prior to the closing.

3. Under Section 404, a company has to establish and maintain adequate internal control structures and processes to allow for accurate financial reporting. In the company's annual report, senior executives need to assess and report on the effectiveness of these internal control structures and processes. Furthermore, the company's auditors must provide an independent report on management's assessment.

Taken together, these measures require reporting companies (and companies otherwise observing these requirements) to:

- ▸ Review their liability assessment and reporting practices and, if necessary, adopt new ones.

- ► Regularly obtain and evaluate insurance company risk assessments for the company's properties.
- ► Include environmental matters in their Item 303 Management Discussion and Analysis.
- ► Discuss pending and threatened litigation and regulatory enforcement actions in their periodic reports.
- ► Disclose and value contingent liabilities in their financial statements, including those related to legal, operational, warranty, and environmental issues.
- ► Implement and periodically evaluate Section 404 internal controls and procedures.
- ► Perform the actions called for by their internal controls and procedures, including maintaining internal records, establishing milestones for regularly evaluating known problem areas, searching out new problem areas, and providing reports up and down the management chain.
- ► Have all of the above reviewed, evaluated, and certified by senior management.
- ► Have all of the above formally reviewed and audited by their accountants.

Among other things, audit committees must enact whistle-blowing procedures to report questionable accounting or auditing practices. The buyer should also compare the target's internal controls with its own to identify any deficiencies or differences. This will enable the buyer to prepare integration steps to harmonize both sets of control procedures after closing.

In particular, acquiring companies need to:

- ► Expand their review of publicly available information to include the EPA Enforcement and Compliance History (ECHO) list and periodic reports filed by the target with the SEC.
- ► Specifically inquire about their target's internal review processes and procedures.
- ► Review the target's internal operational, real estate, intellectual property, insurance, litigation, and environmental policies.

- ► Examine the internal committees charged with monitoring and assessing the target's Sarbox compliance, including getting a list of committee members and their functions.
- ► Consider whether other internal procedures might touch on managerial, financial, and operational issues (for example, as part of the target's accounting and legal functions).
- ► Inquire about what is generally known as the disclosure controls committee, a general oversight committee that may gather and evaluate information generated by the internal review structure.
- ► Obtain all minutes, reports, memoranda, and valuations generated by these internal procedures.
- ► Review the work papers and reports generated by the target's auditors while assessing the company's internal controls.

As a result of Sarbanes-Oxley, the duties of the audit committee have substantially increased. A review of committee minutes often uncovers potentially important issues. How the committee has resolved these issues may indicate its effectiveness and independence. The process used by the target's audit committee to select its outside auditor, as well as the target's relationship with its outside auditor, should also be examined. Comparing the amount of money spent on nonaudit services with the amount spent on the audit itself may suggest the relative importance of each to the auditor. If nonaudit services are significant, the buyer should consider potential exposure to bias that could affect the integrity of the audit.

GAAP practices often allow for discretion, and to the extent that the target's accounting practices differ from the buyer's, the differences need to be harmonized. The buyer should recognize the potential impact that this may have on the combined company's earnings. For example, buyers should pay attention to the target's policies for accounting for contingent liabilities. If the buyer's accounting practices are more conservative (i.e., if they will result in greater reserves), the impact of this must be understood and taken into account in the buyer's evaluation.

CHECKLIST OF ITEMS POST-SARBOX

Thus, Sarbox and the SEC rules promulgated thereunder have profoundly affected important aspects of M&A practice in a number of ways, including the nature and scope of the due diligence process and the terms and conditions under which the transaction is affected. In conducting due diligence and in crafting appropriate representations and warranties in deal documents—particularly with respect to closing conditions and material adverse effect or change (MAE or MAC) clauses—public-company buyers must consider the following Sarbox-related items:

❑ 1. **Does the seller maintain effective disclosure controls and procedures?**

- ❑ Have the disclosure controls and procedures been followed consistently in crafting the seller's public disclosures?
- ❑ Does the seller have a disclosure committee, and, if so, what function has it played in reviewing the seller's public disclosures? What is the role of the general counsel? What is the outside auditor's role in the process? Some buyers will insist on having their outside auditors evaluate the seller's financial statements and communicate with the seller's outside auditors, without the seller's management present. Access to the seller's outside auditors will be a critical part of the due diligence process.
- ❑ Does the audit committee or another independent committee of the board of directors oversee the effective operation of the seller's disclosure controls and procedures? What do the minutes of the relevant committee meetings reflect, if anything, in this regard?

❑ 2. **Does the seller maintain effective internal control over financial reporting?**

- ❑ Many companies have had to include a management report on internal control for the first time in their 2004 10-Ks in accordance with Sarbox Section 404 and the SEC's implementing rules; hence, the question has arisen whether the report of the buyer's management must encompass the seller's internal control, even if the seller's operations may not be fully integrated into those of the buyer. The SEC staff has acknowledged that it might not always be possible to conduct an assessment of a seller's internal control over financial reporting within the period between the consummation of the merger and the date when the buyer's management must make its own assessment of internal control for the combined company. Question 3 of the SEC staff's June 2004 FAQs on internal control allows the buyer's management to defer reporting on the seller's internal control, but only if the buyer's management refers in its 404 report to a discussion in its Form 10-K explaining the basis for the limited scope of management's assessment—that is, why the 404 report excludes the seller's business. Additionally, the staff indicates in this FAQ that the period in which management may omit an assessment of an acquired business's internal control over financial reporting from its own internal control assessment may not extend beyond one year from the date of acquisition. Nor may such assessment be omitted from more than one annual management report on internal control over financial reporting.

❏ Notwithstanding the accommodation from the SEC staff, can the seller's management give a "clean" internal control assessment? This must be determined during the due diligence process and provided for in the seller's representations and warranties.

❏ If the seller is a public company, is it likely to receive a "clean" audit from its independent auditor on the seller's internal control over financial reporting? (As noted, this assessment is required, beginning in the 2004 fiscal year, from many companies' management under Section 404 of Sarbox.) Companies that report to the SEC on a calendar-year basis, and their outside auditors, already should be assessing the effectiveness of existing financial reporting controls with a view toward remediation where necessary or appropriate. We understand that the Big Four accounting firms have been signaling to audit clients that they may have material control weaknesses that could preclude the auditor from issuing a clean report as of the close of the December 31 fiscal year-end. (Nor could management conclude that the company's internal control was effective, in the event of a material weakness.)

❑ If the seller has any internal control problems, how will they be corrected, and, even if they are corrected, is there sufficient potential liability exposure on the part of the buyer to warrant abandonment of the deal? What sort of disclosure will be made, at a minimum, in the seller's pre-closing 10-Qs and 10-Ks regarding possible control deficiencies identified during the due diligence process?

❑ Have the CEO and the CFO of public sellers provided the required SEC certifications under Sections 302 (relating to both disclosure controls and procedures and internal control over financial reporting) and 906 of Sarbox?

☐ 3. **Are there any issues relating to the seller's financial statements that are significant enough to interfere with the ability of the buyer's CEO and CFO to certify SEC reports in the future?**

❑ Have there been any recent waivers of or amendments to the seller's code of ethics under Section 406 of Sarbox (applicable to the seller's CEO, CFO, and other senior financial officers)? If the seller's stock is listed on a national stock exchange or quoted in NASDAQ, has the seller established the broad-based ethics code called for by the exchange or NASDAQ under Sarbox-induced revisions to self-regulatory organization (SRO) governance listing standards? Is there any evidence that either or both codes are not being enforced?

❑ Have there been any concerns or allegations regarding auditor independence; for example, have activist institutions withheld votes from audit committee members because of a perception of excessive non-audit fees paid to the outside auditor?

❑ Has the seller's audit committee fulfilled its enhanced oversight role under Sarbox? Note likely requests from buyers for access to audit committee meeting minutes, whistle-blower procedures and documentation of complaints, and preapproval policies.

❑ Have there been any recent whistle-blower complaints received by the audit committee, and, if so, how were they handled and by whom? The buyer may request access to logs and other documentation relating to the treatment of such complaints, at least where they pertain to accounting and auditing matters and/or possible CEO/CFO ethics code breaches.

❑ If the seller's stock is listed on the NYSE, AMEX, or NASDAQ, are the seller's corporate governance practices sufficient under the enhanced governance listing standards adopted by these markets under Sarbox?

❑ If any of the seller's directors will serve on the buyer's board, are there any independence issues from the buyer's perspective?

❑ Are there any loans or extensions of credit to the seller's executive officers and directors in violation of Section 402 of Sarbox?

6.

The Board's Role In M&A

Boards of directors are playing an increasing and critical role in M&A transactions in 2017 and beyond. Boards must embrace key principles of due diligence, buy vs. build analysis, financial analysis, and risk assessment as primary factors in their decision-making and evaluation process, both for M&A as well as other capital investment proposals. Transactions should help drive shareholder value and be aligned with both short-term and long-term strategic objectives. They should be accretive not dilutive to the market price of the company's shares as well as to the company's brand, reputation, and to consumer perception of its core products and services. Transactions must be structured and implemented in a manner where they will be able to withstand second-guessing and searching by an increasing pool of shareholder activists and by courts who seem increasingly more willing to play "Monday morning quarterback" in their analysis of transactions. Screens and filters need to be in place to ensure that risk is avoided and strategic objectives are met. Analysis must be conducted to predict and mitigate any post-closing litigation risk or costly post-closing integration challenges. The new corporate governance paradigm and state of the law is that boards can and will be held accountable and responsible for misguided strategies and/or transactions that are not carefully assessed and evaluated.

Boards and company leaders must embrace and understand the notion that there is no more complicated transaction than a merger or acquisition. The issues raised are broad and complex, from valuation and deal structure to tax and securities laws. It seems that virtually every board member executive in every major industry faces a buy-or-sell decision at some point during her tenure as leader of the company. In fact, it is estimated that some executives spend as much as one-third of their time considering merger-and-acquisition opportunities and other structural business decisions. The strategic reasons for considering such transactions are also numerous, from achieving economies of scale to mitigating cash-flow risk via diversification to satisfying shareholder hunger for steady growth and dividends. The federal government's degree of intervention in M&A transactions varies from administration to administration, depending on the issues and concerns of the day.

Recent years have witnessed a significant increase in merger-and-acquisition activity within a wide variety of industries that are growing rapidly and evolving overall, such as health care, information technology, education, and software development, as well as in traditional industries such as manufacturing, infrastructure, consumer products, and food services. Many developments reflect an increase in strategic buyers and a decrease in the amount of leverage, implying that these deals were being done because they made sense for both parties. That was far from the case with the highly leveraged, financially driven deals of the late 1980s.

Boards of companies in small- to middle-market segments need to understand the key drivers of valuation since they are often able to focus their operating goals to maximize the potential valuation range. Therefore, it is important to know that the valuation of the target company directly correlates with the following characteristics:

1. Strong revenue growth
2. Significant market share or strong niche positions
3. A market with barriers to entry by competitors
4. A strong management team
5. Strong, stable cash flow

6. No significant concentration in customers, products, suppliers, or geographic markets

7. Low risk of technological obsolescence or product substitution

Successful mergers and acquisitions are neither an art nor a science but a *process*. In fact, regression analysis demonstrates that the
number-one determinant of deal multiples is the growth rate of the
business. The higher the growth rate, the higher the multiple of cash
flow the business is worth.

For example, boards on *both* the buy-side and sell-side of the transaction need to understand that when a deal is improperly valued one
side wins big while the other loses big. By definition, a transaction is a
failure if it does not create value for shareholders. The easiest way to fail,
therefore, is to pay too high a price. To be successful, a transaction must
be fair and balanced, reflecting the economic needs of both buyer and
seller, and must convey real and durable value to the shareholders of
both companies. Achieving this involves a review and analysis of financial statements, a genuine understanding of how the proposed transaction meets the economic objectives of each party, and recognizes the
tax, accounting, and legal implications of the deal.

A transaction as complex as a merger or acquisition is fraught with
potential problems and pitfalls on *both* sides of the table. Many of these
problems arise either in the preliminary stages, such as when the parties force a deal that shouldn't really be done (i.e., some couples were just
never meant to be married). Other times, inadequate, rushed, or misleading due diligence results in mistakes, errors, or omissions; risks are
not properly allocated during the negotiation of definitive documents;
or it becomes a nightmare to integrate the companies after closing.
These pitfalls can lead to expensive and protracted litigation unless an
alternative method of dispute resolution is negotiated and included in
the definitive documents.

The board can and should play a key role in overseeing the M&A deal
team and C-level executives in making sure that valuations are accurate and being assessed properly, that due diligence is complete, and
that the integration that follows a deal does not undermine the company's very reason for doing the deal to begin with. When boards fail to
play an active role in the deal process, a company can wind up entering
into a transaction that it later regrets. Classic mistakes include a lack of

adequate planning, an overly aggressive timetable to closing, a failure to really look at possible post-closing integration problems, or, worst of all, that projected synergies turn out to be illusory. By engaging in the M&A process early and often, developing a strategy and process, and carefully overseeing the role of the executive team, a board can make sure that a company does not make any of these classic mistakes.

SPECIFIC BOARD RESPONSIBILITIES

Generally, proposing, planning, and implementing M&A transactions are the responsibility of a company's executive team. With the board's oversight, it is the executive team that will develop the acquisition plan that leads to M&A transactions. But that does not mean that the board won't play an integral role in the M&A process; the board must act in a way that is consistent with its fiduciary duties as caretakers and gate-keepers of the company's tangible and intangible assets. An engaged board will develop the company's overall strategic direction and might determine that growth should be driven through acquisition. In the alternative, it might determine that the best way for a company to maximize value to shareholders is to sell itself or certain of its key assets. The board must understand that its decision-making process, the depth and breadth of the information it considered to make its decision, and the reasonableness of the board's actions will all be under the microscope as viewed by shareholders, stakeholders, regulations, activists, and possibly even the courts.

It is in this environment that the company's executive team will develop a specific acquisition strategy, which might lead to the identification of M&A targets, perhaps with the help with an investment bank or other advisors. The board will also identify and assess key risks, supervise and test the premises of a proposed transaction, and insure that the M&A transaction being proposed by the company's executive team will be in the best interests of the company and ultimately drive shareholder value. If the company wishes to sell, the board will give its input into that approach as well as evaluate various offers and determine whether a deal being offered is fair and maximizes value for shareholders. See Figure 6-1.

Figure 6-1. The Board and M&A

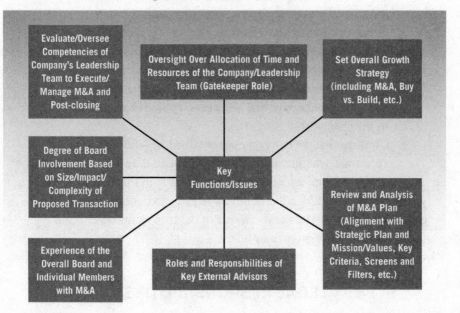

The board's role in the context of M&A can be broken into its macro roles and micro roles. In the macro, the board should:

- ▶ Embrace and meet its various fiduciary obligations. This will be addressed further in the next section.
- ▶ Oversee the company's management as it negotiates the contours of a particular deal.
- ▶ Test and confirm the economic premise of the proposed transaction—namely, perform its own analysis of the management's justification for doing the deal to see if it reaches the same conclusion.
- ▶ Confirm the value proposition that the deal offers to the company's shareholders.
- ▶ Confirm that management has taken necessary steps to mitigate the risk of the transaction and reduce the chances of conflict and litigation later on.
- ▶ Assist management in addressing the fear, uncertainties, and doubts of employees and company teams.
- ▶ Confirm that management is planning the post-closing integration adequately.

In the micro, the board should:

▶ Confirm compliance regarding timing and scope of disclosure of the transaction to various constituencies particularly
with an eye toward prevention of any insider trading.

▶ Consult with the executive team regarding the due diligence
process to make sure that all necessary steps have been taken
to mitigate post-closing risk.

▶ Confirm that the company has obtained key third-party
approvals, whether regulatory or contractual. In some instances,
the board may actually assist the company in this respect.

▶ Review the allocation of purchase price to confirm that allocation of the risks and rewards of the transaction is fair and
reasonable relative to upside.

LEGAL RESPONSIBILITIES

The board's responsibilities with respect to M&A go well beyond providing strategic advice and oversight. The board's obligation to drive
shareholder value results from its fiduciary duties to the company. Fiduciary duties are legal obligations, which fall into two broad general categories: the duty of care and the duty of loyalty. When directors violate these
duties, courts may impose monetary liability upon them or may invali-
date or enjoin their actions. The key starting point for understanding the
nature and scope of these duties and how they dictate the board's role in
M&A is considering what actions and decisions a court will not disturb.

Under the business judgment rule, directors are presumed to have
made a business decision on an informed basis, in good faith, and in
honest belief that their actions were taken in the best interest of the company. And when they do in fact act in this manner, directors will not
have their decisions second-guessed by a court, even if the decision turns
out to be a bad one. That is, directors' fiduciary duties do not bar them
from taking business risks, and courts generally are not in the business
of substituting their business judgment for that of directors, or otherwise
engaging in substantive evaluations of business decisions or outcomes.

So, when will a court disturb a business decision made by a board
of directors or impose liability on such decision makers? When the
directors act in a manner contrary to the presumptions of the business

judgment rule—that is, when they fail to act on an informed basis, in good faith, or in honest belief that their actions are in the best interest of the company. These are issues that judges and lawyers are in a position to scrutinize; business expertise is not necessary. The focus of the judicial review, therefore, is on the *process* undertaken by the board, particularly whether that decision-making process was materially flawed or inadequate, or whether it was tainted or driven by personal interests instead of by the company's interests. These concepts are embodied in the directors' duties of care and loyalty.

Duty of Care

When making a decision, directors must actively gather material information regarding the company's affairs and then act upon that information with the diligence, care, and skill necessary to make a rational business decision. Board members are entitled to rely primarily on the data provided by officers and professional advisors, provided that they have no knowledge of any irregularity or inaccuracy in the information. But they cannot act in a grossly negligent manner. That is, they risk breaching their duty of care when they remain willfully ignorant of material information or, even when in possession of such information, rush a decision so they cannot reasonably and responsibly evaluate the options. I've even seen cases in which board members were held personally responsible for misinformed decisions if their duty of care was not taken seriously.

In the context of selling the company, the duty of care means that the board must "undertake reasonable efforts to secure the highest price realistically achievable given the market for the company."[1] This standard is actually tougher than the one courts employ when applying the business judgment rule to ordinary board decisions, which as noted above only requires that the board act in an informed manner, in good faith, and with the assumption that its actions are in the best interests of the company. Because in the context of M&A the board has "Revlon duties," when looking at a board's actions in a sale, the court will take a substantive look at what a board did to get the highest reasonable price.

---

1. *In re Netsmart Technologies, Inc. Shareholder Litigation*, 2007 WL 1576151 (Del. Ch.)

Because the board has these Revlon duties, it should develop a process whereby it will maximize shareholder value, which drills down into fair pricing, fair dealing, and a strong plan for post-closing integration and value maximization. While not a requirement under Revlon, the board may engage in an auction process to fetch the highest price for the company. It also might mean that once the company receives an offer, the board should actively seek additional offers to make sure that the company is getting the best deal possible. In any event, the board should be well educated on various devices it can employ to make sure the company is getting the best deal. Furthermore, the board should carefully document its role in the M&A process and the various steps it took to maximize the sale price so that it can demonstrate that it undertook such reasonable efforts.

Consider how the Delaware Chancery Court viewed the possible sale of Netsmart Technologies, Inc. Its decision in *In re Netsmart Technologies, Inc., Shareholders Lit.* criticized Netsmart's board's decision to only consider private equity firms as potential buyers to the exclusion of strategic buyers. The court also criticized the board's failure to keep minutes of an important meeting where this decision was made. This emphasizes the point that process and recordkeeping are important if a board is not going to breach its fiduciary duties during the M&A process.

Recent Delaware cases have established that, in a limited set of circumstances, the business judgment standard may apply in the context of M&A. In *In re MFW Shareholders Litigation* (Del. Ch. May 29, 2013, referred to as MFW), the Delaware Chancery Court held that the board satisfies its duty when reviewing a going-private transaction with a controlling stockholder if the merger receives the approval of either (i) a special committee of directors independent of the controlling stockholder that is fully empowered to decline the transaction and such committee relies on its own advisors and satisfies the duty of care in negotiating the sale price or (ii) a majority of the stockholders not affiliated with the majority stockholder, provided that such stockholders are uncoerced in their vote and fully informed.

Another recent Delaware Chancery Court case, *In re Volcano Corporation Stockholder Litigation*, demonstrates that the MFW logic can apply to other situations as well. In Volcano, the court determined that the tendering of shares by a majority of fully informed, uncoerced, disinterested stockholders essentially has the same effect as a majority vote of unaffiliated stockholders, effectively cleansing the transaction in question and causing the transaction to be subject to review in accordance with the business judgment.

Duty of Loyalty

Each director must exercise his or her powers in the interest of the corporation and not in his or her own interest or that of another person or organization. The duty of loyalty has a number of specific applications: The director must avoid any conflicts of interest in dealings with the corporation and cannot extract personal benefits from the corporation that are not shared by all of the shareholders. The director must not personally usurp what is more appropriately an opportunity or business transaction to be offered to the corporation. For example, say an officer or director of the company was in a meeting on the company's behalf and a great opportunity to obtain the distribution rights for an exciting new technology was offered. It would be a breach of this duty to try to obtain those rights for himself and not first offer them to the corporation. Further, the director cannot act in bad faith and for a purpose other than advancing the best interests of the corporation. For example, the director cannot knowingly cause the corporation to violate the law, cannot consciously disregard his obligation to oversee the corporation's activities and thereby sanction misconduct by the corporation and its employees, and cannot waste corporate assets.

The board's duty of loyalty impacts its role in M&A in numerous ways. Essentially it means that a board member's decisions can only be driven by a desire to maximize shareholder value. A director would be violating this duty of loyalty if she supported a deal that benefited a company in which she had a stake solely because the deal would benefit her directly or indirectly. It would also be a breach of the duty of loyalty if she determined that one buyer of the company was better than another because that buyer promised her a bigger role after the sale. In short, directors cannot put their own interests before the company's.

To the extent that "interested" directors play too large of a role on a board, the board risks losing the presumption of the business judgment rule, meaning that courts will scrutinize the decisions made by a board deemed not to be impartial with respect to a particular matter. To that end, in the context of considering M&A transactions (or other situations in which one or more directors could be deemed to have misaligned interests), interested directors should consider recusing themselves from discussing and voting on relevant transactions. The board could also form a special committee comprised of only outside directors to control the sale process in order to avoid any potential conflicts of interest.

Several recent Delaware cases have highlighted how the duty of loyalty impacts financial advisors in M&A transactions. The recent Del Monte, El Paso, and Rural Metro decisions in the Delaware Chancery Court have shown that courts are also concerned about disloyal financial advisors. But these cases implicate boards as well. Under this recent case law, boards have a responsibility to oversee financial advisors and be on the lookout for potential conflicts of interests (e.g., a bank favoring buyers who will seek financing from that bank). In other words, the board must adhere to its Revlon duties throughout the sale process, not just at the approval stage, and the disloyalty of a financial advisor can lead to board liability.

Boards need to always take their fiduciary duties very seriously, but this is particularly true in the context of M&A and related transactions, especially those that may be cross-border in nature. In order to do so, a diligent board may wish to hire independent counsel to advise it of its duties in the context of the particular situation the company is in. Boards should remain diligent in their oversight role and always play the role of "constructive skeptic" when political transactions and their alleged value propositions are presented for debate and appeal.

In conclusion, boards on *both* sides of any transaction will have the best chance to avoid bad deals with bad consequences—and the litigation that often follows them—if they remain steadfast in their focus on core principles of stewardship and on their key fiduciary duties, develop and encourage a sound M&A process, and are diligent about keeping records of their decisions and actions.

7.

An Overview of Regulatory Considerations

INTRODUCTION

There is a wide variety of regulatory considerations in a merger or acquisition, with most of them falling into one of two categories: (1) *general* regulatory issues affecting all types of transactions, and (2) *industry-specific* regulatory issues that affect only certain types of transactions in certain industries. The general regulatory considerations include issues such as antitrust, environmental, securities, and employee benefits matters, which are discussed in this chapter. There are also industry-specific regulatory issues, with federal and/or state regulators exercising rights of approval over those transactions that involve a change in ownership or control, or that may have an anticompetitive effect on a given industry. Any transaction in the broadcasting, health-care, insurance, public utilities, transportation, telecommunications, financial services, or even defense contracting industries should be analyzed carefully by legal counsel to determine what level of government approval may be necessary in order to close the transaction. Regulatory agencies such as the Federal Communications Commission (FCC) and the Pension Benefit Guaranty Corporation (PBGC) have broad powers to determine whether a proposed transaction will be in the best interests of the consuming general public or, in the case of the PBGC, the employees and retirees of a given seller.

In certain regulated industries, these government approvals are needed in order to effectuate the transfer of government-granted licenses, permits, or franchises. These may range from the local liquor board approving the transfer of a liquor license in a small restaurant acquisition to the need to obtain FCC approval for the transfer of multibillion-dollar communication licenses, such as the transaction between Verizon Wireless and Alltel.

ENVIRONMENTAL LAWS

Prior to the 1970s, sellers normally had little or no legal obligation to disclose information concerning the presence or use of potentially hazardous substances on their premises, nor to report the release of such substances into the environment to the potential buyers of their business. What obligations did exist were imposed by state or local governments regulating public nuisances or engaging in emergency planning.

In the 1970s and early 1980s, as the federal government passed new laws concerning health and the environment, it created new obligations to report on the presence, use, and release of hazardous substances under certain circumstances. The Clean Water Act (CWA), the Toxic Substances Control Act (TSCA), the Resource Conservation and Recovery Act (RCRA), and the Comprehensive Environmental Response, Compensation, and Liability Act (CERCLA or Superfund) all contained provisions requiring notification of government authorities in the event of chemical releases and other emergencies. In addition, TSCA and regulations promulgated pursuant to the Occupational Safety and Health Administration (OSHA) required chemical manufacturers and others to compile and report information on the presence and use of certain chemicals on their premises. Each of these laws had a unique, limited scope—for example, covering some substances but not others—and the result was a patchwork of different but sometimes overlapping reporting requirements.

In 1986, Congress enacted the Emergency Planning and Community Right-to-Know Act (EPCRA), found in Title III of the Superfund Amendments and Reauthorization Act of 1986 (SARA). Subchapter I of EPCRA creates a framework for state and local emergency response planning, and in that setting imposes on companies two types of reporting obligations: (1) the obligation to provide information about the presence of extremely hazardous substances so as to facilitate emergency planning, and (2) the obligation to notify authorities immediately in the event of a release. Subchapter II of EPCRA requires companies to file additional reports on the presence of hazardous substances at their facilities, and also to report on the periodic release of toxic chemicals. Unlike the information required by other federal laws, much of the information that is reported under EPCRA is available to the public.

Not only did EPCRA not completely supersede other federal reporting provisions, but it also did not preempt state law. Several states have passed right-to-know or other reporting and disclosure laws, the most aggressive being California's Proposition 65. However, because EPCRA's reporting requirements are fairly extensive and because they are implemented largely by the states themselves, the importance of state reporting laws has generally been diminished.

In 1990, Congress amended the Clean Air Act of 1970 (CAA), revising section 112. The CAA regulates any emissions, either stationary or mobile. This revision imposed significant enhanced air quality standards for emissions of hazardous air pollutants, whereas prior to 1990, the CAA only mandated a risk-based program with very few standards.

Any company that makes, uses, or otherwise is involved with potentially hazardous substances may be required under federal law to notify authorities of a release of such a substance into the environment. In many cases, a company's obligations will be satisfied by reporting under EPCRA and CERCLA, but in some cases the CWA, TSCA, RCRA, or CAA might be applicable. This complex web of federal and state environmental laws creates legal issues for both the buyer and the seller in a proposed merger or acquisition, usually surrounding the problem of allocating liability for environmental problems under federal laws such as RCRA and CERCLA and state laws that address hazardous waste discharge and disposal. The seller should have its legal counsel obtain an environmental audit from a qualified consulting firm prior to the active recruitment of potential buyers in order to assess its own liability under federal and state laws. Nonetheless, it is very likely that the buyer and its counsel will want to do their own independent review and assessment of the seller's sites, insurance policies, and possible areas of exposure.

The issue of potential liability under federal and state environmental laws is typically one of the broadest areas of coverage requested by buyers under the representations and warranties, such as those set forth in Figure 7-1.

Figure 7-1

(a) Hazardous Material. Other than as set forth in *Schedule*, (i) no amount of substance that has been designated under any law, rule, regulation, treaty, or statute promulgated by any governmental entity to be radioactive, toxic, hazardous, or otherwise a danger to health or the environment, including, without limitation, PCBs, asbestos, petroleum, urea-formaldehyde, and all substances listed as hazardous substances pursuant to the Comprehensive Environmental Response, Compensation, and Liability Act of 1980, as amended, or defined as a hazardous waste pursuant to the United States Resource Conservation and Recovery Act of 1976, as amended, and the regulations promulgated pursuant to said laws (a "Hazardous Material"), and (ii) no underground or aboveground storage tanks containing Hazardous Material, are now or at any time have been present in, on, or under any property, including the land and the improvements, groundwater, and surface water thereof, that Seller has at any time owned, operated, occupied, or leased. *Schedule* identifies all underground and aboveground storage tanks, the proper closure or removal of such tanks, and the capacity, age, and the contents of such tanks, located on property owned, operated, occupied, or leased by TCI.

(b) Hazardous Materials Activities. Seller has not arranged for the transport of, stored, used, manufactured, disposed of, released or sold, or exposed its employees or others to Hazardous Materials or any product containing a Hazardous Material (collectively, "Seller's Hazardous Materials Activities") in violation of any rule, regulation, treaty, or statute promulgated by any governmental entity.

(c) Environmental Permits and Compliance. Seller currently holds all environmental approvals, permits, licenses, clearances, and consents (the "Environmental Permits") necessary for the conduct of Seller's Hazardous Material Activities and the business of Seller as such activities and business are currently being conducted. All Environmental Permits are in full force and effect. Seller (i) is in compliance in all material respects with all terms and conditions of the Environmental Permits and (ii) is in compliance in all material respects with

all other limitations, restrictions, conditions, standards, prohibitions, requirements, obligations, schedules, and timetables contained in the laws, rules, regulations, treaties, or statutes of all governmental entities relating to pollution or protection of the environment or contained in any regulation, code, plan, order, decree, judgment, notice, or demand letter issued, entered, promulgated, or approved thereunder. To the best of Seller's knowledge after due inquiry, there are no circumstances that may prevent or interfere with such compliance in the future. *Schedule* includes a listing and description of all Environmental Permits currently held by Seller. For purposes of this Agreement, knowledge of Seller includes the knowledge of the persons who, as of the Closing Date, were its officers, directors, and stockholders (including the trustees, officers, partners, and directors of stockholders that are not natural persons).

(d) Environmental Liabilities. No action, proceeding, revocation proceeding, amendment procedure, writ, injunction, or claim is pending or, to the best knowledge of Seller, threatened against Seller or the business of Seller concerning any Environmental Permit, Hazardous Material, or the Seller's Hazardous Materials Activity or pursuant to the laws, rules, regulations, treaties, or statutes of any governmental entity relating to pollution or protection of the environment. There are no past or present actions, activities, circumstances, conditions, events, or incidents that could involve either Seller or any person or entity whose liability Seller has retained or assumed, either by contract or by operation of law, in any environmental litigation, or impose upon Seller (or any person or entity whose liability Seller has retained or assumed, either by contract or by operation of law) any material environmental liability including, without limitation, common law tort liability.

FEDERAL SECURITIES LAWS

Mergers and acquisitions among small and growing privately held companies do not generally raise many issues or filing requirements under the federal securities laws, specifically the Securities Act of 1933 and Exchange Act of 1934. Privately held companies may utilize the 1933 SEC private placement exemption, commonly known as Regulation D

Safe Harbors. Privately held companies, however, may be subject to the obligations of the 1933 Act if the transaction involves a public offering. Regulation D sets the standards in determining whether a transaction involves a public offering. In addition, where one or both of the companies are publicly traded and therefore have registered their securities under the Securities Act of 1933, a host of reporting obligations are triggered.

■ *10-Q and 10-K reports.* The Exchange Act of 1934 imposed periodic reporting requirements on issuers of securities. A discussion of the proposed transaction may need to be included in either or both of the acquiring company's and the target's quarterly and annual filings with the SEC. The acquiring company will usually be obligated to include the information in its scheduled SEC reports if the acquisition is deemed to be "significant." A significant acquisition is typically defined as one where the target's assets or pretax income exceeds 10 percent of the acquiring company's assets or pretax income.

■ *Registration statements.* If the acquiring company plans to issue new securities as part of the consideration to be given to the target's shareholders, then a registration statement should be filed with the SEC. For a negotiated merger or acquisition transaction, the registration statement filed with the SEC is a form S-4, which contains details relating to the share distribution, amounts, terms, and other information related to the consolidation. Additionally, a prospectus must be provided to shareholders who will receive the securities, detailing specific disclosure requirements based on the business and financial affairs of the issuer.

■ *Proxy information.* If the proposed transaction must be approved by the shareholders of either the acquiring company or the target, then the SEC's special proxy rules and regulations must be carefully followed.

■ *Tender offers.* When a buyer of a publicly held company elects to make a tender offer directly to the shareholders of the target, rather than negotiating through management, then the filing requirements in the Williams Act must be followed. This includes the filing of the SEC's Schedule 13D whenever the purchaser becomes the beneficial owner of more than 5 percent of the target's equity securities, which gives notice of the buyer's intentions to both the SEC and the target company's officers and directors.

- *Antifraud Liability.* The 1933 and 1994 Acts create liability for fraud in the offer, purchase, or sale of securities. Both parties must be careful, and should consult with counsel to ensure avoiding any material misrepresentation or omissions of material facts in connection with the sale.

FEDERAL ANTITRUST LAWS

The central concern of federal government policy is with those acquisitions that increase the danger that companies in a particular market will have *market power*—the power to raise prices or limit production free from the constraints of competition. This danger increases when a market is dominated by a few large firms with substantial market shares. Federal antitrust laws prohibit any acquisition of stock or assets that tends to substantially lessen competition. Acquisitions of the stock or assets of a competitor or potential competitor ("horizontal acquisitions") are most likely to raise antitrust concerns, especially if they occur in markets that are already dominated by a few firms. Acquisitions involving companies in a supplier–purchaser relationship ("vertical acquisitions") can also raise antitrust concerns, but in general, vertical transactions are less of a concern from an antitrust perspective.

The DOJ and the FTC may seek to halt, delay, or modify the terms of those acquisitions that they consider likely to significantly lessen competition. Furthermore, the Hart-Scott-Rodino Act generally requires that the FTC and the DOJ be given advance notification of mergers and acquisitions involving companies and transactions above a specified minimum size, the details of which are discussed here.

Horizontal Acquisitions

The principal responsibility for enforcing antitrust laws with respect to business combinations continues to be exercised by the DOJ and the FTC. These agencies have jointly issued their own set of merger guidelines to help businesses assess the likelihood that their specific business transactions may be challenged under the federal antitrust laws.

These federal agencies will consider a number of factors in assessing the legality of acquisitions involving companies competing in the same geographic market and offering competing products or services to generally the same targeted customers. However, the respective market shares of the combining companies, as well as the degree of "market concentration," continue to be the starting point for the government's analysis. Transactions that result in the combined company having a large share of the relevant market may raise antitrust concerns.

Because of the importance of market concentration, the definition of the relevant geographic and product market is critical. Among other things, the guidelines take into account reasonable product substitutes, production facilities that may be easily converted to making a particular product, and entry barriers. Once the market is defined, the guidelines seek to measure the extent to which the proposed transaction increases market concentration. While various tests are available, the guidelines measure concentration using the Herfindahl-Hirschman Index (HHI). The HHI is calculated by adding the squares of the individual market shares of all competitors in the market. For example, a market consisting of four competitors, each of which has a 25 percent share of the market, has an HHI of 2,500 ($25^2 + 25^2 + 25^2 + 25^2 = 2,500$). Under the guidelines, markets with HHIs below 1,500 are presumed to be unconcentrated, HHIs between 1,500 and 2,500 are presumed to be moderately concentrated, and HHIs over 2,500 are presumed to be highly concentrated. The competitive significance of particular acquisitions is then examined in terms of both the level of the market's HHI following the acquisition and the extent to which the acquisition increases the HHI. In general, the higher the increase in the post-merger HHI, the higher the probability the DOJ and FTC will raise potential anticompetitive concerns.

In addition to market shares and market concentration, federal enforcement agencies consider the degree of ease of entry into the market. The presence of barriers that would prevent a new competitor from entering a market—such as patents, proprietary technology, know-how, and high "sunk" capital investments—increases the likelihood that the agencies will seek to block the transaction. However, if the agencies conclude that it would be relatively easy for new competitors to enter a market within a relatively short time if prices rose to noncompetitive levels, it is unlikely that they will consider a merger in that market to be anticompetitive, even though it produces a high post-acquisition HHI. Other factors that will be given varying degrees of weight under the guidelines are changing market conditions that might undermine the significance of market shares, such as rapidly changing technology; the financial condition of a company, which might affect its future competitive significance; characteristics of a product that make price collusion difficult or unlikely; and efficiencies resulting from the combination.

Vertical Acquisitions

Acquisitions involving suppliers and their customers could raise questions under the antitrust laws. Courts, as well as earlier federal enforcement policies, have expressed concerns that such acquisitions could foreclose access by competitors to necessary suppliers or distribution outlets. The foreclosure effect was measured by reference to the share of the market held by the supplier company and the share of purchases of the product made by the customer company. Current federal enforcement policy is somewhat skeptical about claims that vertical acquisitions produce anticompetitive effects. It limits the inquiry primarily to the question of whether such an acquisition is likely to create unacceptable barriers to entry by making it necessary for any new entrant to enter at both the supplier and purchaser levels in circumstances where it is difficult to do so, and thus insulates concentrated markets at either level from new competition.

Hart-Scott-Rodino Act

The premerger notification requirements of the Hart-Scott-Rodino Act (H-S-R) can have an important impact on an acquisition timetable. Under H-S-R and the regulations issued under it by the FTC, acquisitions involving companies and transactions of a certain size cannot be consummated until certain information is supplied to the federal enforcement agencies and until specified waiting periods elapse.

The premerger notification program was established to avoid some of the difficulties that antitrust enforcement agencies encounter when they challenge anticompetitive acquisitions after they occur. The enforcement agencies have found that it is often impossible to restore competition fully because circumstances change once a merger takes place; furthermore, any attempt to reestablish competition is usually costly for both the parties and the public. Prior review under the premerger notification program has created an opportunity to avoid these problems by enabling the enforcement agencies to challenge many anticompetitive acquisitions before they are consummated.

The Hart-Scott-Rodino Antitrust Improvements Act requires that persons contemplating proposed business transactions that satisfy certain size criteria report their intentions to the antitrust enforcement agencies before consummating the transaction. If the proposed transaction is reportable, then both the acquiring business and the business that is being acquired must submit information about their respective business operations to the Federal Trade Commission and to the Department of Justice and wait a specified period of time before consummating the proposed transaction. During that waiting period, the enforcement agencies review the antitrust implications of the proposed transaction. Whether a particular transaction is reportable is determined by application of the act and the premerger notification rules (see Figure 7-2).

Figure 7-2. Hart-Scott-Rodino Act Reporting Rules

On January 25, 2005, the Federal Trade Commission announced that it had authorized the publication of a Federal Register Notice, required by the 2,000 amendments to the act, revising the notification thresholds and limitations in the act and rules. The new rules and regulations regarding increased notification thresholds took effect on March 2, 2005, and the new rules and regulations amending the reporting rules for unincorporated entities took effect on April 6, 2005.

Size of Transaction

There are two basic tests to determine whether a transaction will be reportable. The first test is known as the "size of transaction" test. The minimum required value for any reportable transaction is $53.1 million (as adjusted), and this value is adjusted on an annual basis based upon changes in the GNP during the previous year. The size of transaction test is satisfied if, after consummation of the transaction, the acquiring person will hold voting securities or assets of the acquired person valued at $53.1 million (as adjusted) or more. Rather than amend the rules annually, each dollar threshold will be listed "as adjusted," which term is defined in the HSR rules. Certain of the exceptions and exemptions to the reporting requirements are discussed in paragraphs (a) and (d) under "Miscellaneous."

Size of Persons

The second test is known as the "size of person" test. This test applies only to transactions that are valued at between $53.1 and $212.3 million (as adjusted). Deals that exceed $212.3 million (as adjusted) are reportable without regard to the size of the parties. If a transaction falls within the $53.1 to $212.3 million (as adjusted) range, in order for the transaction to be reportable, one party must have at least $106.2 million (as adjusted) in annual net sales and/or assets. Total assets and total annual net sales of a person are determined by reference to the last regularly prepared balance sheet and annual income statement. When calculating the total assets and net sales, all entities that are controlled by such person must be included.

Filing Fee

As of late 2017, the fees for filing a premerger notification with the FTC and DOJ are staggered as follows:

➡ Deal value in excess of $80.8 million but less than $161.5 million—$45,000
➡ Deal value at least $161.5 million but less than $807.5 million—$125,000
➡ Deal value $807.5 million or more—$280,000

The regulations provide for such fees to be paid by the acquiring person; however, parties often agree to share such fees.

WAITING PERIODS

The parties to a reportable transaction may not consummate the transaction until the statutory waiting period detailed in the H-S-R Act has expired. The waiting period begins on the date that the FTC and DOJ receive the completed notification forms. The waiting period will end on the thirtieth day following such receipt (for cash tender offers and bankruptcy transactions, the waiting period is fifteen days). If any waiting period would expire on a Saturday, Sunday, or legal holiday, the waiting period shall extend to the next regular business day. Parties can request "early termination" of the waiting period at the time of filing at no additional cost, but it is not guaranteed (although early termination is granted in most cases). When early termination is granted, it is usually within two weeks of the initial filing. It is important to note, however, that early terminations are reported in the Federal Register, listed on the FTC website, and listed in the FTC's public reference room; therefore, parties seeking to maintain the nonpublic nature of a transaction should not request early termination.

During the waiting period, a transaction raising competitive concerns will be reviewed by only one of the agencies—assigned to either the DOJ or the FTC through a clearance procedure. Prior to the expiration of the waiting period, either the FTC or the DOJ can issue a "second request" for additional documents and information, but second requests are not common.

The issuance of a second request extends the waiting period until thirty days after the date when the parties certify that they have substantially complied with the second request (the extension for cash tender offers and bankruptcy transactions is ten days). Responding to a second request will often take between sixty and ninety days, depending on the size of the companies, the number of product markets, and the amount of material to be reviewed. During this time, the responsible agency will be evaluating the relevant markets and interviewing suppliers, customers, and competitors to learn more about the anticompetitive effects of the transaction.

As a general matter, the act and the rules require both parties to file notifications under the premerger notification program if the following conditions are met:

1. One person has sales or assets of at least $161.5 million.
2. The other person has sales or assets of at least $16.2 million.
3. As a result of the transaction, the acquiring person will hold a total amount of stock or assets of the acquired person valued at more than $80.8 million, or, in some stock transactions, even if the stock held is valued at $15 million or less, if it represents 50 percent or more of the outstanding stock of the issuer being acquired and the issuer is of a certain size.
4. As a result of the transaction, the acquiring person will hold a total amount of stock or assets of the acquired person valued at more than $200 million, regardless of the sales or assets of the acquiring persons.

The first step in determining reportability is to determine what voting securities, assets, or combination of voting securities and assets are being transferred in the proposed transaction. Then you must determine the value of the voting securities and/or assets or the percentage of voting securities that will be "held as a result of the transaction." Calculating what will be held as a result of the transaction is complicated and requires the application of several complex rules. The securities held as a result of the transaction include both those that will be transferred in the proposed transaction and certain assets of the acquired person that the acquiring person has purchased within certain time limits. If the value of the voting securities exceeds $200 million and no exemptions apply, the parties must subsequently file notification and observe the waiting period before closing the transaction. If the value of the voting securities exceeds $80.8 million, but is $323 million or less, the parties must utilize the "size of person" test.

The first step in determining the "size of person" test is to identify who the "acquiring person" is and who the "acquired person" is. These technical terms are defined in the rules and must be applied carefully. In an asset acquisition, the acquiring person is the buyer and the acquired person is the seller. The rules require that a person who is proposing to acquire voting securities directly from shareholders, rather than from the issuer itself, serve notice on the issuer of those shares to make sure that the acquired person knows about its reporting obligation.

Once you have determined who the acquiring and acquired persons are, you must determine whether the size of each person meets the act's minimum size criteria. This "size of person" test generally measures a company based on the company's last regularly prepared balance sheet. The size of a person includes not only the business entity that is making the acquisition and the business entity whose assets are being acquired or that issued the voting securities that are being acquired, but also the parent of either business entity and any other entities that the parent controls. If the value of the voting securities exceeds $80.8 million, but is $323 million or less, the "size of person" test is met, and no exemptions apply, the parties must subsequently file notification and observe the waiting period.

In some instances, a transaction may not be reportable even if the size of person and size of transaction tests have been satisfied. The act and the rules set forth a number of exemptions, describing particular transactions or classes of transactions that need not be reported despite the fact that the threshold criteria have been satisfied. For example, the acquisition of assets in the ordinary course of a person's business, such as new goods and current supplies, may be exempt. The acquisition of voting securities of a foreign issuer may be exempt if the foreign company's sales into the United States were $50 million or less.

Once it has been determined that a particular transaction is reportable, each party must submit its notification to the Premerger Notification Office of the Federal Trade Commission and to the Director of Operations of the Antitrust Division of the Department of Justice. In addition, each acquiring person must pay a filing fee to the Premerger Notification Office for each transaction that it reports. The filing fee is $45,000, $125,000, or $280,000 depending on the value of the securities held as a result of the acquisition.

LABOR AND EMPLOYMENT LAW

There is a wide variety of federal and state labor and employment law issues that must be addressed by the buyer and its counsel as part of its overall due diligence on the seller's business. This includes a comprehensive review of the seller's employment practices and manuals to ensure historical compliance with the laws governing employment discrimination, sexual harassment, drug testing, wages and hours, and so on, as well as its compliance with the Family and Medical Leave Act (FMLA), the Americans with Disabilities Act (ADA), and the Worker Adjustment and Retraining Notification Act (WARN), which governs plant closings and retraining requirements.

Where applicable, it will also be necessary to review collective bargaining agreements, with a particular focus on the buyer's duty to bargain with the union as a "successor" employer.

The buyer must be aware of the wide range of potential ERISA liability issues that it may confront if the employee benefit plans established by the seller are not properly structured or funded. The buyer must also develop a strategy for the integration of the seller's plan(s) into its own, which may involve transferring plan assets in whole or in part or the utilization of surplus plan assets. There are many different types of employee benefit plans, including a "qualified" plan (which currently provides certain favorable tax consequences, such as deductions for plan contributions and deferral of income for plan participants) and unqualified plans (such as deferred compensation arrangements, which currently do not provide favorable tax consequences). Retirement plans generally are either "defined-contribution plans" or "defined-benefit plans." Defined-contribution plans include profit-sharing plans with or without a 401(k) feature, thrift or savings plans, money purchase pension plans, target benefit plans, stock bonus plans, employee stock ownership plans, simplified employee pensions (SEP), savings incentive match plans for employees (SIMPLE plans), and certain funded executive compensation plans. A defined-benefit plan is a retirement plan other than a defined-contribution plan. The traditional defined-benefit pension plan is one in which the employer takes financial responsibility for funding an annuity payable over an employee's life or as a joint and survivor annuity to the employee and his spouse.

Employee benefit plans can represent one of the largest potential liabilities of a business enterprise. The types of employee benefit plans involving the greatest potential liabilities are defined-benefit pension plans, post-retirement medical and life insurance benefits, and deferred compensation programs for executives. In many cases, the liability for an employee benefit plan shown on the financial statements may not be an adequate portrayal of the true liability. A buyer is well advised to have an actuary compute the value of the employee benefits, both retirement plans and retiree medical plans, in order to be sure that the balance sheet provision is adequate.

The treatment of employee benefit plans in corporate acquisition, merger, and disposition situations has taken on greater and greater importance since the passage of ERISA in 1974. The importance of employee benefit plans grows with each new development in the benefits arena, including the Multiemployer Pension Plan Amendments Act of 1980 (MEPPAA), Deficit Reduction Act of 1984 (DRA), Retirement Equity Act of 1984 (REA), Omnibus Budget Reconciliation Act of 1986 (OBRA), Consolidated Omnibus Budget Reconciliation Act of 1986 (COBRA), Single Employer Pension Plan Amendments Act of 1986 (SEPPAA), Tax Reform Act of 1986 (TRA 86), Omnibus Budget Reconciliation Act of 1987 (OBRA 87), Technical and Miscellaneous Revenue Act of 1988 (TAMRA), Omnibus Budget Reconciliation Act of 1989 (OBRA 89), Omnibus Budget Reconciliation Act of 1990 (OBRA 90), Tax Extension Act of 1991 (TEA '91), Unemployment

Compensation Amendments of 1992 (UCA), Omnibus Budget Reconciliation Act of 1993 (OBRA 93), Unemployment Compensation Act of 1992 (UCA), Retirement Protection Act of 1994 (RPA), Small Business Job Protection Act of 1996 (SBJPA), Health Insurance Portability and Accountability Act of 1996 (HIPAA), Taxpayer Relief Act of 1997 (TRA '97), Internal Revenue Service Restructuring and Reform Act of 1998 (IRSRRA), Tax Relief Extension Act of 1999 (TRE '99), Community Renewal Tax Relief Act of 2000 (CRTRA), Economic Growth and Tax Relief Reconciliation Act of 2001 (EGTRRA), Consolidated Appropriations Act of 2001 (CAA), Sarbanes-Oxley Act of 2002 (Sarbox), Job Creation and Worker Assistance Act of 2002 (JCWAA), Medicare Prescription Drug, Improvement, and Modernization Act of 2003, and the Pension Funding Equity Act of 2004 (PFEA), Statements 87, 88, and 106 132R of the Financial Accounting Board (SFAS 87, 88, and 106 132R), Worker Retiree and Employer Recovery Act of 2008 (WRERA), American Recovery and Reinvestment Act of 2009 (ARRA), Trouble Assets Relief Program under the Emergency Economic Stabilization Act of 2008 (TARP), and Patient Protection and Affordable Care Act of 2010 (PPACA).

Employee benefit plans can be the source of major off–balance sheet liabilities that have to be dealt with by the parties to the transaction. In some cases, employee benefit plans will dictate whether the transaction will be structured as a sale of stock or a sale of assets. In a few cases, employee benefit plans may result in the deal falling through. In still other situations, employee benefit plans can be utilized to accomplish the transaction.

Generally, employee benefit plan considerations do not dictate the structure of a corporate acquisition. There are, however, a few exceptions. A seller that faces a potentially large withdrawal liability with respect to a multiemployer pension plan may insist on a sale of stock rather than a sale of assets. On the other hand, a buyer that does not want to inherit a burdensome plan from the seller may insist on a sale of assets. In the case of a sale of assets, the buyer is not generally obligated to assume the plans of the seller. This decision will depend on the nature of the plans, their funding status, their past history of compliance with the laws, and the nature of the adjustment in the purchase price with respect to the plans.

The biggest difficulty related to employee benefit liabilities in a merger or acquisition is to determine the appropriate adjustment of the purchase price. Since the liabilities involve actuarial calculations, they are totally dependent upon the assumptions as to interest rates and life expectancies, the selection of mortality tables, and other factors that will affect the ultimate liability under the plan. The parties have to agree on these assumptions or on a method of arriving at these assumptions in order to calculate whether the plan is overfunded or underfunded. One such method for a pension plan would be to value the plan's liabilities using the PBGC's assumptions for terminated pension plans. While the PBGC rates are not the most favorable rates in the marketplace, they do represent the rates that will be utilized to determine whether the plan is underfunded in the event that the plan should terminate. Another approach is to value the liability on an ongoing basis rather than on a termination basis.

The most important aspect of the acquisition process for the buyer is to start its investigation of the employee benefit plans early and to do as thorough a job as possible. The buyer should be especially concerned with identifying items that are hidden liabilities. Obviously, a buyer should review the plans and their summary plan descriptions. Annual form 5500s for the last three years should be examined by professionals. To the extent that there are actuarial reports for the plans, the buyer should examine copies of them and make sure that they reflect any recent plan amendments increasing benefits. Collective bargaining agreements should also be examined to determine whether they provide for benefit increases that were not contemplated in the most recent actuarial report. With respect to welfare plans, buyers should determine whether they are obligated to provide for increases pursuant to "maintenance of benefit provisions" in collective bargaining agreements. If a union-negotiated plan bases benefits on the compensation of the employees, the buyer should check to see if large wage increases have been negotiated. Finally, the buyer should review any post-retirement medical or life insurance benefits provided by the seller.

The definitive Purchase Agreement should contain detailed and explicit provisions with respect to the handling of employee benefits. If responsibility for a benefit program has to be divided between the buyer and the seller, it is easier to have a fair division of the responsibility if it is negotiated in advance. Buyers rarely get significant concessions from sellers after the deal has closed. A set of sample representations and warranties to cover these issues is set forth in Figure 7-3.

Figure 7-3

(a) *Definitions*.

(i) "Benefit Arrangement" means, whether qualified or unqualified, any benefit arrangement, obligation, custom, or practice, whether or not legally enforceable, to provide benefits, other than salary, as compensation for services rendered, to present or former directors, employees, agents, or independent contractors, other than any obligation, arrangement, custom, or practice that is an Employee Benefit Plan, including, without limitation, employment agreements, severance agreements, executive compensation arrangements, incentive programs or arrangements, rabbi or secular trusts, sick leave, vacation pay, severance pay policies, plant closing benefits, salary continuation for disability, consulting, or other compensation arrangements, workers' compensation, retirement, deferred compensation, bonus, stock option, ESOP or purchase, hospitalization, medical insurance, life insurance, tuition reimbursement or scholarship programs, employee discount arrangements, employee advances or loans, any plans subject to Section 125 of the Code, and any plans or trusts providing benefits or payments in the event of a change of control, change in ownership, or sale of a substantial portion (including all or substantially all) of the assets of any business or portion thereof, in each case with respect to any present or former employees, directors, or agents.

(ii) "Seller Benefit Arrangement" means any Benefit Arrangement sponsored or maintained by Seller or with respect to which Seller has or may have any liability (whether actual, contingent, with respect to any of its assets or otherwise), in each case with respect to any present or former directors, employees, or agents of Seller as of the Closing Date.

(iii) "Seller Plan" means any Employee Benefit Plan for which Seller is the "plan sponsor," as defined in Section 3(16)(B) of ERISA, or any Employee Benefit Plan maintained by Seller or to which Seller is obligated to make payments, in each case with respect to any present or former employees of Seller as of the Closing Date.

(iv) "Employee Benefit Plan" has the meaning given in Section 3(3) of ERISA.

(v) "ERISA" means the Employee Retirement Income Security Act of 1974, as amended, and all regulations and rules issued thereunder, or any successor law.

(vi) "ERISA Affiliate" means any person that, together with Seller, would be or was at any time treated as a single employer under Section 414 of the Code or Section 4001 of ERISA and any general partnership of which either Seller is or has been a general partner.

(vii) "Pension Plan" means any Employee Benefit Plan described in Section 3(2) of ERISA.

(viii) "Multiemployer Plan" means any Employee Benefit Plan described in Section 3(37) of ERISA.

(ix) "Welfare Plan" means any Employee Benefit Plan described in Section 3(1) of ERISA.

(b) *Schedule* contains a complete and accurate list of all Seller Plans and Seller Benefit Arrangements. With respect, as applicable to Seller Plans and Seller Benefit Arrangements, true, correct, and complete copies of all the following documents have been delivered to Buyer and its counsel: (A) all documents constituting the Seller Plans and Seller Benefit Arrangements, including but not limited to, insurance policies, service agreements, and formal and informal amendments thereto, employment agreements, consulting arrangements, and commission arrangements; (B) the most recent Forms 5500 or 5500 C/R and any financial statements attached thereto and those for the prior three years; and (C) the most recent summary plan description for the Seller Plans.

(c) Neither Seller nor any ERISA Affiliate maintains, contributes to, or is obligated to contribute to, nor has either Seller or any ERISA Affiliate ever maintained, contributed to, or been obligated to contribute to any Pension Plan or Multiemployer Plan. Neither Seller nor any ERISA Affiliate has any liability (whether actual or conditional, with respect to its assets or otherwise) to or resulting from any Employee Benefit Plan sponsored or maintained by a person that is not a Seller or any ERISA Affiliate. Neither Seller nor any ERISA Affiliate has or has ever had any obligations under any collective bargaining agreement. The Seller Plans and Seller Benefit Arrangements are not presently under audit or examination (nor has notice been received of a potential audit or examination) by the IRS, the Department of Labor, or any other governmental agency or entity. All group health plans of each Seller and their ERISA Affiliates have been operated in compliance with the requirements of Sections 4980B (and its predecessors) and 5000 of the Code, and each Seller has provided, or will have provided before the Closing Date, to individuals entitled thereto all required notices and coverage under Section 4980B with respect to any "qualifying event" (as defined therein) occurring before or on the Closing Date.

(d) *Schedule 3.19(d)* hereto contains the most recent quarterly listing of workers' compensation claims of the Sellers for the last three fiscal years.

8.

Structuring the Deal

There is a virtually infinite number of ways in which a corporate merger or acquisition may be structured. There are probably as many potential deal structures as there are qualified and creative transactional lawyers and investment bankers. The goal is *not* to create the most complex structure, but rather to create a structure that fairly reflects the goals and objectives of the buyer and the seller. Naturally, not all of the objectives of each party will be met each time—there will almost always be a degree of negotiation and compromise.

Virtually all structures, even the most complex, are at their roots basically either mergers or acquisitions, including the purchase or consolidation of either stock or assets. (The basic alternative structures are shown in Figure 8-1.) The creativity often comes in structuring the deal to achieve a particular tax or strategic result or to accommodate a multistep or multiparty transaction. This chapter will look at some of the typical structures as well as a few alternative types of transactions, such as spin-offs, shell mergers, and employee stock ownership plans (ESOPs).

Figure 8-1. The Basic Alternative Structures

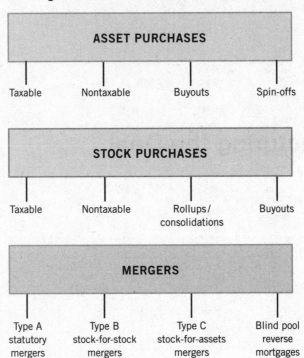

At the heart of each transaction are the following key issues that will affect the structure of the deal:

- ▶ How will tangible and intangible assets be transferred to the purchaser from the seller?
- ▶ At what price will they be transferred, and on what terms?
- ▶ How will issues discovered during due diligence affect the price, terms, or structure of the deal?
- ▶ What liabilities will be assumed by the purchaser? How will risks be allocated among the parties?
- ▶ What are the tax implications for the buyer and the seller?
- ▶ What are the long-term objectives of the buyer?
- ▶ What role will the seller have in the management and growth of the underlying business after closing?
- ▶ To what extent is the buyer fully "arm's length"—or is the transaction closer to a management or employee buyout? If so, how will that affect due diligence and deal structure?

▶ To what extent will third-party consents or government filings or approvals be necessary?

▶ What post-closing arrangements will be made for the key management team of the seller (who may not necessarily be among the selling owners of the company)?

▶ Does the buyer currently have access to all of the consideration to be paid to the seller, or will some of these funds need to be raised from debt or equity markets?

There is a wide variety of corporate, tax, and securities law issues that affect the final decision as to the structure of any given transaction. Each issue must be carefully considered from a legal and accounting perspective. However, at the heart of each structural alternative are the following basic questions:

▶ Will the buyer be acquiring the *stock* or the *assets* of the target?

▶ In what form will the consideration from the buyer to the seller be paid (e.g., cash, notes, securities, or some other form)?

▶ Will the purchase price be fixed, contingent, or payable over time on an installment basis?

▶ What are the tax consequences of the proposed structure for the acquisition (see the discussion later in the chapter)?

STOCK VS. ASSET PURCHASES

Perhaps the most fundamental issue in structuring the acquisition of a target company is whether the transaction will take the form of an asset or a stock purchase. Each form has its respective advantages and disadvantages, depending on the facts and circumstances surrounding each transaction. The buyer and seller should consider the following factors in determining the ultimate form of the transaction.

Stock Purchases

The Buyer's Perspective: Advantages

1. Tax attributes carry over to the buyer (e.g., net operating loss and credit carryforwards).

2. Many of the restrictions imposed on sales of assets in loan agreements and potential sales tax are avoided.
3. This structure preserves the right of the buyer to use the seller's name, licenses, and permits.
4. There are no changes in the corporation's liability, unemployment, or workers' compensation insurance ratings.
5. Nontransferable rights or assets (e.g., licenses, franchises, or patents) can usually be retained by the buyer.
6. This structure provides continuity of the corporate identity, contracts, and structure.

The Seller's Perspective: Advantages

1. The seller is taxed only on the sale of stock.
2. All obligations (i.e., disclosed, not disclosed, unknown, and contingent) and nontransferable rights can be transferred to the buyer.
3. Any gain or loss is usually capital in nature.
4. If stock held by individuals is IRC Section 1244 stock and is sold at a loss, the loss is generally treated as ordinary.
5. This structure may permit sellers to report gains from the sale of stock on an installment basis.
6. The transaction does not leave the seller with the problem of disposing of assets that were not bought by the purchaser.

The Buyer's Perspective: Disadvantages

1. There is less flexibility to cherry-pick key assets of the seller.
2. The company may be liable for unknown, undisclosed, or contingent liabilities (unless adequately protected in the purchase agreement).
3. There is no step-up in basis (i.e., the seller's historical tax basis is carried over to the buyer).
4. This structure normally does not terminate existing labor union collective bargaining agreement(s) and generally results in the continuation of employee benefit plans.
5. Dissenting shareholders have a right of appraisal for the value of their shares, with the right to be paid the appraised value or remain a minority shareholder.

The Seller's Perspective: Disadvantages

1. The offer and sale of the company's securities may need to be registered under certain circumstances.
2. The seller cannot pick and choose the assets to be retained.
3. The seller may not use the corporation's net operating loss and credit carryforwards to offset a gain on the sale.
4. A loss on the sale of stock may not be recognized by a corporate shareholder that included the company in its consolidated income tax return.

Asset Purchases

The Buyer's Perspective: Advantages

1. The buyer can be selective as to which assets of the target will be purchased.
2. The buyer is generally not liable for the seller's liabilities unless they are specifically assumed under the contract.
3. There is a step-up in the basis of the assets acquired equal to the purchase price, allowing higher depreciation and amortization deductions.
4. Buyers are generally free of any undisclosed or contingent liabilities.
5. This structure normally results in termination of labor union collective bargaining agreement(s), and employee benefit plans may be assumed or terminated.
6. Buyers may elect new accounting methods.

The Seller's Perspective: Advantages

1. Sellers maintain their corporate existence.
2. Ownership of nontransferable assets or rights (e.g., licenses, franchises, or patents) is usually retained.
3. The corporate name and goodwill can generally be maintained.
4. The corporation's tax attributes (e.g., net operating loss and credit carryforwards) are retained.

The Buyer's Perspective: Disadvantages

1. There is no carryover of the seller corporation's tax attributes (e.g., net operating loss and credit carryforwards).

2. If it is a bargain purchase, there is a step-down in the basis of assets.
3. Nontransferable rights or assets (e.g., licenses, franchises, or patents) cannot be transferred to buyers.
4. The transaction is more complex and costly in terms of transferring specific assets and liabilities (i.e., a new title to each asset transferred must be recorded, and state sales tax may apply).
5. The lender's consent may be required to assume liabilities.
6. The corporation's liability, unemployment, or workers' compensation insurance ratings can be lost.

The Seller's Perspective: Disadvantages

1. There may be double taxation if the corporation is also liquidated.
2. The transaction generates various kinds of gain or loss to sellers based on the classification of each asset as capital or ordinary.
3. The transaction is more complex and costly in terms of transferring specific assets and liabilities (i.e., a new title to each asset transferred must be recorded, and state sales tax may apply).
4. The bill of sale must be comprehensive, with exhibits attached, in order to ensure that no key assets are overlooked and as a result are not transferred to the buyer.
5. A variety of third-party consents will typically be required to transfer key tangible and intangible assets to the buyer.
6. The seller will be responsible for liquidation of the remaining corporate "shell" and distribution of the proceeds of the asset sale to its shareholders, which may result in double taxation unless a Section 338 election is made.
7. Asset acquisition requires compliance with applicable state bulk sales statutes, as well as state and local sales and transfer taxes.

TAX AND ACCOUNTING ISSUES AFFECTING THE STRUCTURE OF THE TRANSACTION

In a given merger or acquisition, there are a wide variety of tax and accounting issues that must be considered and understood as part of the negotiation and structuring of the transaction. These issues will affect the valuation and pricing as well as the structure of the deal and may be a condition precedent to closing. This section will provide an overview of the basic tax and accounting issues to be addressed in a merger or acquisition; however, it will be limited to a summary because the tax laws are very complex and are constantly changing. You should discuss the accounting issues with the certified public accountant (CPA) who will serve as a part of the acquisition team.

Mergers and acquisitions may be completely tax free, partially tax free, or entirely taxable to the seller. Figure 8-2 illustrates some types of transactions that are taxable and tax free. Each party and its advisors will have its own, often differing, views on how the transaction should be structured from a tax perspective, depending on the nontax strategic objectives of both buyer and seller in the transaction and the respective tax and financial position of each party. In some cases, the tax consequences will be the primary driving force in the transaction, whereas in other cases the tax consequences are secondary or even a nonissue. In addition to the taxable aspects of the structure of the transaction, there will be a wide variety of other tax issues to be considered, such as the tax basis of the assets acquired, the impact of the imputed interest rules on the transaction, and the tax aspects of any deferred consideration and/or incentive compensation to the seller.

Figure 8-2. Taxable vs. Nontaxable Deals

Taxable

Purchase of *stock* for cash, promissory notes, or other non-equity consideration

Purchase of *assets* for cash, promissory notes, or other non-equity consideration

Taxable transactions generally anticipate that the seller will have little or no continuing equity participation in the acquired company

Nontaxable

An exchange of the *buyer's stock* for the seller's stock

An exchange of the *buyer's stock* for all or substantially all of the seller's assets

Nontaxable transactions generally anticipate a continuing, direct, or indirect equity participation in the acquired company by the seller or its shareholders

It is relevant to highlight an example that illustrates the degree to which tax considerations can be an impediment to a transaction. In one situation, the CEO of the seller had negotiated a "carve-out" with his board and received some of the new combined company's stock as personal income. That income, however, created more than a million dollars in cash tax liability. This tax liability presented a significant challenge to getting the deal done. The CEO, who deserved credit for the deal, now had a strong incentive to prevent the deal from happening. Navigating tax liability issues, like the one in this example, is a critical step in successful deal closure.

The general tax-related goals of the seller usually include:

▶ Deferring the taxation of the gain realized on the sale of the business to a future date (for example, if the seller acquires the buyer's securities, and these appreciate in value, the seller generally need not pay taxes on these gains until these securities are sold)

▶ Classifying the income that is recognized as *capital gain* and not as *ordinary income*

▶ Ensuring that *cash is available to pay taxes* as they become due, and to avoid the "double tax" (taxation at both the corporate and the shareholder level)

Again, the strategic objectives must be balanced against the tax consequences. If the seller has an immediate need for liquidity or has no desire to receive the buyer's securities (the seller may not accept the buyer's post-closing vision and plans for the combined entities), then it will be difficult to achieve nontaxable status.

Over the years, changes in the federal tax laws have chipped away at the buyer's motivations for having the transaction characterized as tax-free. The buyer's ability to carry over favorable tax attributes of the seller has been diminished to such a degree that the buyer's use of its own securities as consideration to pay the seller often has more to do with preservation of cash than it does with the applicable tax laws.

If the transaction is taxable, then the tax basis will be "stepped up," or increased to equal the fair market value of the consideration paid to the seller. If the transaction is nontaxable, the buyer is able to carry over the seller's tax basis to its own financial statements. If the buyer would prefer to carry these assets on the balance sheet at the stepped-up tax basis (for example, if the buyer is paying much more than the seller's tax basis), or if the buyer would prefer not to issue securities to the seller to prevent dilution of ownership, then the buyer should opt for a taxable transaction. Based on our experience, resolving the tax issues between the parties effectively is critically important. This issue has a direct impact on the price of the transaction and each party's perception of the fair value.

Most corporate acquisitions will be deemed to be taxable transactions if they are structured as a purchase of either stock or assets in exchange for cash, promissory notes, or other forms of non-equity consideration. Nontaxable transactions usually fall more into the category of a merger in that they involve an exchange of the target company's stock or assets for the purchaser's equity securities or those of a subsidiary created by the purchaser, coupled with some direct or indirect continuing relationship between the buyer and the seller and their respective shareholders. These nontaxable transactions must fall within one of several reorganization categories contained in IRS Code Section 368.

Tax-Free Reorganizations

If the parties choose to structure the transaction as a tax-free reorganization, then the requirements set forth here must be followed.

The three principal forms of tax-free reorganizations under the Internal Revenue Code are (1) Type A statutory merger, (2) Type B stock-for-stock merger, and (3) Type C stock-for-assets merger.

1. **Type A reorganizations.** A Type A reorganization is a statutory merger or consolidation under state law. No express limitations are imposed on the type of consideration that can be used in the transaction or on the disposition of assets prior to the merger. This is a very flexible

acquisition device that permits shareholders to receive property, including cash, in addition to stock of the acquiring corporation.

2. **Type B reorganizations.** A Type B reorganization is an acquisition of one corporation by another, in exchange solely for all or part of its voting stock or that of its controlling company. Immediately after the acquisition, the acquiring corporation must have control (at least 80 percent of the total combined voting power of all classes of stock and at least 80 percent of the total number of shares of all other classes of stock) of such other corporation (whether or not the acquiring corporation had control immediately before the acquisition). Counsel to the buyer, however, must be particularly sensitive to any cash payment, such as a finder's fee or the payment of appraisal rights to dissenting shareholders.

3. **Type C reorganizations.** A Type C reorganization is an acquisition of one corporation by another, in exchange solely for all or part of its voting stock (or that of its parent) and "substantially all" of the properties of that corporation. The transferor corporation must distribute the stock, securities, and other properties it receives from the acquiring corporation, as well as any retained assets, as part of the plan of reorganization.

The tax aspects of the proposed transaction are among the most important issues to be addressed by the acquisition team. These laws are complex and are constantly changing. Therefore, knowledgeable advisors should be carefully consulted.

Accounting Issues

The pooling-of-interests method of merger accounting ended on June 30, 2001, almost without fanfare. Before that time, companies, especially financial firms and those in the high-technology and pharmaceutical industries, often chose pooling as a way of avoiding the long-term earnings dilution caused by the amortization of goodwill against earnings. Goodwill was defined as the excess of the cost of an acquired entity over the net of the amounts calculated for assets acquired and liabilities assumed.

The objections to the elimination of pooling have been muted to a large degree because of the new rules for treating acquired goodwill and intangibles in a purchase acquisition. Instead of the old approach of amortization of goodwill over a period of up to forty years, companies now must subject the acquired goodwill to a complex annual "impairment test" aimed at determining whether there has been a decline in the value of that goodwill. Write-offs are required only if the value has been impaired. The impact will be initially positive because amortization of the goodwill is no longer automatically required.

The Financial Accounting Standards Board's (FASB) approach, adopted in Statement 142, Goodwill and Other Intangible Assets, in July 2001, is more complicated than amortization. Under these FASB goodwill and intangible-asset measurement standards, companies generally must perform an impairment test yearly for each reporting unit. This is a two-step test that first determines whether the book value of the acquired assets of the reporting unit exceeds the unit's so-called fair value—typically measured through discounted cash flow estimates. If fair value is lower than book value, the company then must determine whether the fair value of the unit's goodwill is less than the goodwill's book value, which would necessitate an impairment loss being recognized. Since companies do not know in what year goodwill may become impaired, financial personnel may be challenged to predict earnings internally to a greater degree. Further, tension concerning the FASB's new criteria for determining whether some acquired intangible assets, like patents, should be recognized separately from goodwill, and perhaps amortized over the asset's perceived life span, is created as a result of the new rules.

Although there are dozens of ways to structure a transaction, the core five structures are described in Figure 8-3.

ONE-STEP VS. STAGED TRANSACTIONS

Another key issue regarding the structure of the deal is whether the entire transaction will be completed in one step or whether it will occur over a series of steps. The parties may want to get to know each other better before considering a full-blown merger, or there may be some contingencies affecting the value of the company that are driving the buyer, or even the seller, to want to slow things down and consider a preliminary transaction as the first step. It is also plausible that the seller believes that the long-term value of the company may be much higher, and as a result would prefer to keep "some of his chips still on the table."

Figure 8-3. The Five Basic Structural Alternatives

• •

1. Asset Purchase

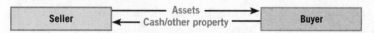

This is often the simplest of structures with the buyer purchasing a set of selected assets from the seller in exchange for cash or other assets.

• •

2. Stock Purchase

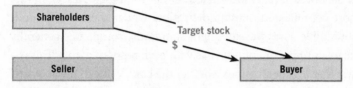

The shareholders of the seller sell their shares to the buyer in exchange for cash or other assets.

• •

3. Statutory Merger

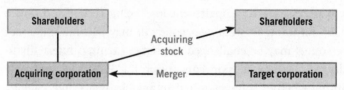

The statutory merger is a nontaxable acquisition in which one corporation completely absorbs another by virtue of a merger under state corporate law.

• •

4. Stock-for-Stock Acquisition

The acquiring company exchanges its voting stock for the stock of the acquiring company.

• •

5. Stock-for-Assets Acquisition

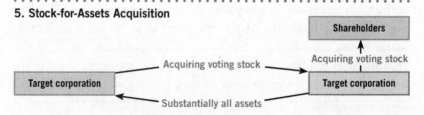

This is generally a nontaxable transaction where the acquiring company exchanges only its voting stock (or that of its parent) for substantially all of the assets of the target corporation.

For example, from the buyer's perspective, there may be certain government approvals needed that affect the seller's valuation, such as the approval of the Food and Drug Administration (FDA) for a new line of pharmaceutical or medical devices. These approvals may be two years away, and if they are not obtained, would significantly affect the value of the seller's business. In such a case, the buyer may want to consider an alternative and more preliminary initial structure, such as a strategic alliance (as a first step toward a merger) or a technology licensing agreement (as a first step toward an acquisition). There may even be certain shares exchanged to allow cross-ownership, or the buyer may want to purchase a minority interest in the seller with an option to purchase the balance within six months after obtaining FDA approval.

Alternatively, the seller may have certain reservations about the buyer or may want to see certain contingencies met before it commits to selling 100 percent of its business. The buyer may be waiting for some key third-party approval or event to take place, before which the seller may be reluctant to commit, such as the buyer's being in the process of filing for approval of an initial public offering (IPO) of its securities. If these securities are to serve as part of the seller's compensation, then it may be wise to wait to ensure that there will be a secondary market (and hence liquidity) for the shares before moving forward. In such cases, the parties would enter into a letter of intent, but there would typically be a clause that allows the seller to walk away from the deal if the offering is unsuccessful.

Some transactions are multistaged for strategic reasons, and some may be structured to be one stage with the possibility of being multistaged if certain post-closing contingencies are not met.

METHOD OF PAYMENT

The way in which the seller will be paid is quite clearly one of the most important aspects of structuring the deal. The method of payment for the acquisition of stock or assets ordinarily involves a balancing of business and tax considerations. Often a particular fact or set of circumstances will outweigh the others and determine the method of payment. Although the personal, strategic, and tax needs of all parties must be considered, there is a wide variety of forms of payment that should be considered before a final decision is made. These include cash, marketable securities, parcels of real estate, the rights to intangible assets (licenses, franchises, and so on), secured and unsecured promissory notes, the common and preferred securities of the purchaser or its affiliates (often with the promise that these securities will one day be publicly traded), earn-outs, consulting and employment agreements, royalty and license agreements, or even the exchange of another business. All of these tools should be considered in structuring the elements of the purchase price.

For example, a seller who is concerned about the financial and/or business viability or the creditworthiness of a buyer will demand payment in cash for the assets or stock being sold. Alternatively, a seller who is reluctant to dispose of an interest in a business completely or who wishes to defer taxes to a later taxable year may be willing to take the buyer's stock and/or take back a promissory note as part of the consideration. Tax considerations may also dictate the form of payment. From a buyer's perspective, debt is often preferable to stock, since interest may be tax deductible. For example, in a leveraged acquisition, the business assets acquired are expected to generate sufficient cash flow to pay off the debt incurred to acquire the assets.

Another key factor that has had a significant impact on the nature of deals and the method of payment is the state of the capital markets. For example, during the global financial crisis of late 2008, credit markets tightened significantly, and private equity firms developed cold feet over their investments, in particular, in capital-locking projects. The significant write-downs that financial institutions had to take as a result of the subprime mortgage crisis that followed the bursting of the housing bubble resulted in an evaporation of liquidity as such institutions tightened borrowing terms in order to guard their remaining capital, thus making debt financing difficult to secure. Things have improved from 2010 to 2017, but some conservatism in lending is still prevalent as bad memories from the financial meltdown remain. Thus, even though a leveraged acquisition might be ideal considering other factors, the crisis prevailing today is likely to force a Plan B that is less ideal.

Cash

It is often said that "cash is king." This is particularly true in the current financial situation in the M&A sector. Although at first blush, most sellers envision an all-cash deal as the preferred route, they must consider a wide variety of payment methods, some of which may result in a much greater total price in the long run. There are certain circumstances, however, when an all-cash transaction makes sense, such as when the seller suspects that the buyer will be unable to honor the types of consideration mentioned previously, as they may depend on the buyer's long-term viability and credibility. From a buyer's perspective, an all-cash transaction can be internally financed, financed by raising equity or in conjunction with a private equity fund, financed through the cash flow of the combined companies and/or the acquired company, or even financed through asset-based lending, to be collateralized by the business assets or stock acquired.

Debt

If the creditworthiness of the buyer is high, then sellers may be willing to accept promissory notes from the buyer as part of the consideration. These promissory notes may be secured by the assets of the buyer, by the seller's assets, or not at all, or they may be guaranteed by the buyer's principals. It is also possible that the notes will be subordinated to a senior commercial lender if the buyer borrows money from a bank as part of its capital to acquire the seller's business.

Stock

The securities of the buyer may constitute all or part of the payment to the seller for the business assets or stock. In some situations, common stock of the buyer or a newly formed subsidiary (or even a new class of preferred stock) will be issued to encourage a seller to maintain an economic interest in the ongoing viability of the business assets or stock being sold. Under this type of payment structure, a seller can participate as a shareholder in any future growth in value or profits derived from the combined entities and is thus motivated to ensure the success of the business.

Convertible Securities

Convertible debt securities often enable buyers and sellers to obtain the benefits of both the stock and the debt forms of payment. From a seller's perspective, convertible debt securities provide downside protection and a fixed return while offering the opportunity to reap the benefits of growth in value or profits derived from the combined entities. From a buyer's perspective, they provide the tax advantages of interest deductions while enabling the buyer to avoid payments of principal at maturity should such an instrument be converted into equity.

Contingent Payments

Often buyers and sellers will be unable to agree on the determination of the value of the assets or stock being sold or may want to reserve the right to adjust the terms of the transaction in light of changes in circumstances or expectations. *Contingent consideration* provides for additional payments based on factors such as revenue targets, cash flow goals, or synergies achieved.

Similarly, the parties to an acquisition may provide for the repayment of cash or other consideration through the use of escrows or other security arrangements, upon the occurrence of specified contingencies.

NONTRADITIONAL STRUCTURES AND STRATEGIES

There are a wide variety of nontraditional deal structures and acquisition strategies that are not as straightforward as a stock or asset purchase, such as spin-offs, rollups, leveraged buyouts, and employee stock ownership plans. These deal structures are often a smaller slice of an overall corporate restructuring, but they nevertheless have grown and become a significant part of the annual merger and acquisition activity.

However, as stated earlier, the recent downturn in financial markets has led to a decrease in the availability of the financing required for such nontraditional structures. For example, leveraged buyout activity has been reduced significantly as a result of the credit crunch. This has led to an overall marked decrease in M&A activity through such nontraditional sources.

An Introduction to Spin-Offs

Spin-offs are transactions that are designed to divest noncore operating divisions or assets (or divisions that have matured to the point of deserving or requiring stand-alone status) into their own independent operating company. Although some respectable companies have been created as a result of spin-offs, it has also been said, "You don't spin off your crown jewels for no reason." Many spin-offs have been criticized by the IRS as trying to dump liabilities into spin-off entities, which then have balance sheets laden with debt and a core focus with limited potential.

In 2008 through 2010, there was a significant uptick in public spin-offs and divestitures as companies scrambled to raise cash, cut costs, and streamline their operations by shedding certain business units and focusing on their core competencies. According to a 2008 study by Thomson Reuters, forty-nine spin-offs were accomplished by public companies in 2008, up from thirty-one in 2007. And 2009 set a record of over sixty spin-off transactions. From 2010 to 2016, spin-offs stabilized and leveled off a bit, but still featured notable transactions such as the spin-off of the MGM Growth properties LLC by MGM Resorts International. These transactions can be complex, and careful thought must be given to the viability of the spun-off entity after it leaves the mother ship. Employee anxiety is likely to be high: Many will worry about job security, access to resources, corporate culture, and compensation. It is also critical to address the terms and conditions of any ongoing relationship between the spin-off entity and its previous parent, such as sharing of key technology, customers, or resources, as well as resolution of any conflicts of interest. Another trend is to spin off governance and decision making without spinning off ownership—the not-quite-spin-off spin-off—as Caterpillar did in the fall of 2009 with several of its operating divisions.

To qualify for favorable tax treatment, the transaction must meet the rigorous Internal Revenue Service business-purpose test designed to ensure that a spin-off has a valid business reason. Among the purposes that are acceptable to the IRS are that a deal will help with access to capital markets, debt-financing prospects, competitive position, management direction, or retention of key employees.

Leveraged Buyouts

A leveraged buyout (LBO) is a transaction in which capital borrowed from a commercial lender is used to fund a large portion of the purchase. Generally, the loans are arranged with the expectation that the earnings of the business will easily repay the principal and interest. The LBO potentially has great rewards for the buyers, who, although they frequently make little or no investment, own the target company free and clear after the acquisition loans are repaid from the earnings of the business. LBOs are often arranged to enable the managers of subsidiaries or divisions of large corporations to purchase a subsidiary or division that the corporation wants to divest, a transaction known as an MBO, or management buyout.

The LBO transaction will generally take one of two basic forms: the sale of assets or the cash merger. Under the cash merger format, the acquired company disappears through a merger into the acquiring company and its shareholders receive cash for their shares. Under the sale of assets format, on the other hand, the operating assets become part of the buying company, but the selling company will generally be given the option of either receiving cash or continuing to hold its shares in the selling company. A variation of the LBO transaction is the use of paid in kind (PIK) notes to finance LBOs. PIK notes allow borrowers to make interest payments with securities instead of cash. This structure allows the borrower to take out a loan and choose whether it wants to make interest payments as due or in aggregate at the end of the loan period (at a higher fee).

At the heart of the LBO transaction are the dynamics of financing the acquisition by employing the assets of the acquired company as a basis for raising capital. Large unused borrowing capacity is the characteristic that typically enables a purchaser to use the seller's assets to borrow the purchase price. Specific factors that may exist to enhance borrowing capacity are (1) large amounts of excess cash and cash equivalents, such as certificates of deposit and other short-term paper, (2) a limited amount of current debt, (3) a demonstrated ability to achieve substantial earnings over a number of years, (4) substantial undervalued assets, which, when taken individually, have a market value in excess of the depreciated value at which they are carried on the seller's balance sheets, sometimes called "hidden equity," (5) subsidiaries with operations in unrelated industries that have large amounts of excess properties that can be readily liquidated for cash without detriment to ongoing operations, and (6) the potential for "hidden cash flow" for the purchaser arising from income sheltered by depreciable property, the basis of which is readjusted upward as a consequence of the sale. Because of the complexities and uncertainties associated with arranging financing of this nature, the purchase agreement should provide that the purchaser's obtaining the financing is a condition precedent to the purchaser's obligations under the agreement.

Consolidations/Rollups

Another major structural trend or strategy that became popular during the 1990s and has continued to be popular as of 2017 in select industries and market conditions is the consolidation, or "rollup." Under such a strategy, the buyer is a holding company that has targeted an industry that may be ripe for consolidation within a given region or market niche. The rollup strategy may be horizontal or vertical in nature, but it typically involves the aggressive acquisition of competitors in a given market to achieve operating efficiencies, synergies, and market dominance. Obviously, antitrust laws are an issue (see Chapter 7), and some acquisitions will be friendly and some hostile. The consideration paid to the seller is usually the securities of the buyer. It is best to devise a plan and a compensation strategy that provide an incentive for the current management to stay in place and build up the value of their equity in the consolidated entity. The rollup buyer must look at each deal to see how the target fits into its overall strategy and to determine the impact of the given acquisition on the earnings, valuation, and taxes of the consolidated entities. If the consolidator (the buyer in a rollup strategy) is public or close to an initial public offering, it must also consider the reaction of Wall Street, the business media, and the investment bankers to each transaction.

Some rollup companies are the result of certain private equity or venture capital firms picking target industries, hiring management teams to manage the consolidation process, and then financing the deals with their own capital resources. The well-managed rollup companies have a specific strategic focus and rigid criteria for evaluating deals and are not just haphazardly accumulating companies to build an asset base or a revenue stream through consolidation. These better-managed companies are constantly searching for cross-marketing opportunities and operating efficiencies by and among their operating divisions as well as ancillary yet related products and services that can be added to the menu. From the seller's perspective, if you are approached by a consolidator who is offering you primarily its own securities in order to "join the team," be sure to realize that most of your upside in the deal is tied to the buyer's ability to execute its business and consolidation plan successfully. Make sure that you understand and agree with the buyer's strategy and vision and that you are clear as to your role on a post-closing basis.

Selling to Your Staff ESOPs as an Acquisition/Exit Strategy for Sellers

An employee stock ownership plan (ESOP) is an alternative available to sellers for disposing of their business that offers certain tax advantages to both seller and lender. There is a wide range of small and middle-market companies that cannot find a suitable buyer (or that choose to "sell" the company to their employees) and therefore create an ESOP to buy all or substantially all of the company using deferred compensation. There are two general categories of ESOPs:

1. **Leveraged ESOP.** This type of ESOP uses borrowed funds (either directly from the company or from a third-party lender based on the company's guaranty, with the securities of the employer as collateral) to acquire the employer's securities. The loan will be repaid by the ESOP from employer and employee contributions, as well as any dividends that may be paid on the employer's securities.

2. **Nonleveraged ESOP.** This type of ESOP involves a stock bonus plan (or a contribution stock bonus plan with a money purchase pension plan) that purchases the employer's securities using funds from the employer that would have been paid as some other form of compensation (that *were not* provided by a third-party lender).

General Legal Considerations in Structuring an ESOP

ESOPs, like all types of deferred compensation plans, *must* meet certain requirements set forth by the IRS as summarized here. Failure to meet these requirements will result in the contributions by the sponsoring employer *not* being tax deductible. To ensure that you're in compliance with IRS regulations, when creating your ESOP, you must:

■ Establish a trust in order to make contributions. The trust must be for the exclusive benefit of the participants and their beneficiaries.

- *Not* discriminate in favor of officers, major shareholders, or highly compensated employees, particularly regarding the allocation of assets and income distribution. A good rule of thumb is that at least *70 percent of all non-highly compensated employees must be covered* by the plan.

- Benefit no fewer than the lesser of (1) fifty employees or (2) 40 percent or more of the employees of the plan sponsor.

- Invest primarily in the securities of the sponsoring employer. Although there are no strict guidelines, it is assumed that at least 50 to 60 percent of the ESOP portfolio will consist of the employer's securities at any given time.

- Vest in compliance with one of the minimum vesting schedules set forth by the IRS. The plan must adopt either (1) five-year "cliff" vesting (the employee is vested after five years of service) or (2) seven-year "scheduled" vesting (20 percent is fully vested after three years, increasing by 20 percent per year until 100 percent vesting is reached after seven years).

- Establish voting requirements that conform to those set forth by the IRS. Under the Internal Revenue Code, voting rights may be vested in the trust's fiduciary, except under certain circumstances where rights must be passed through to the plan's participants. Generally, passing through becomes an issue when the vote will involve mergers, consolidations, reorganizations, recapitalizations, liquidations, major asset sales, and the like. Voting rights "in toto" may be passed through to employees, however, at the discretion of the employer in structuring the plan. Failure to fully pass through these rights may raise personnel and productivity problems (if the employees do not feel like true owners and as a result are cynical about the ESOP), thereby defeating a major incentive for adopting the ESOP.

- Comply with IRS rules regarding the distribution of ESOP benefits and assets. The plan must provide for a prompt (within one year) distribution of benefits to the participants following *retirement*, *disability*, or *death*. The nature and specific timing of the distribution will depend in part on the *cause* for the employee's separation from service with the company as well as whether the sponsoring employer is closely held as opposed to publicly traded.

- Base the employer's contributions on a specific percentage of payroll, such as a money purchase pension plan, or on some other formula, such as a percentage of profits, as is the case with some profit-sharing plans. This form provides for maximum flexibility in that contributions are at the complete discretion of the employer. Each year the employer simply makes a determination of the appropriate amount of contribution. It should be noted that the plan provides for a minimum contribution sufficient to permit the plan to pay any principal and interest due with respect to a loan used to acquire the employer's securities. The employer's contribution may be made in cash or other property, including the employer's securities. In the event that the employer contributes its own securities, it may obtain a so-called cashless deduction. The employer is entitled to deduct the fair market value of the securities so contributed, and the contribution involves no cash outlay by the employer.

- Provide "adequate consideration" in connection with the purchase of the employer's stock in an ESOP. This requires that some method for valuation of the shares must be available. For publicly traded companies, this is generally not a problem, since the prevailing market price is a sufficient indication of value. For privately held companies, however, value must be determined by the fiduciaries of the plan, acting in good faith. This will generally require an *independent appraisal* by a qualified third-party appraisal firm, initially upon the establishment of the ESOP, and at least annually thereafter. (The cost and impact of such an appraisal on a closely held company should be considered before adopting an ESOP plan.)

Key Legal Documents in the Establishment of an ESOP

A wide variety of legal documents must be prepared in connection with the organization and implementation of an ESOP by a seller. These documents must be prepared by counsel, however, only after input has been received from all key members of the company's ESOP team (e.g., financial and human resources staff, accountants, investment bankers, commercial lenders, the designated trustee, the designated appraisal firm, and so on). The preliminary analysis that should be conducted *prior to* the preparation of the documents should include:

- ▶ The impact on dilution, ownership, control, and earnings of the company
- ▶ The type of securities to be issued (common versus preferred)
- ▶ The tax deductibility of contributions and related tax issues
- ▶ Registration of the securities, where required, under federal and state securities laws
- ▶ Employee motivation and productivity improvement analysis
- ▶ Current and future capital requirements and growth plans for the company
- ▶ Interplay of the ESOP with other current or planned employee benefit plans within the company
- ▶ The timetable for planning, organization, and implementation of the ESOP

ESOP Documentation

Once these and other factors have been considered, and strategic decisions have been made, counsel may be instructed to prepare the necessary documentation. In a leveraged ESOP, the documents may include (1) the ESOP plan, (2) the ESOP trust agreement, which may be combined with the plan, (3) ESOP loan documentation, such as the loan agreement or note guaranty (the initial set of documents may be from the commercial lender to the sponsoring employer, with a "mirror-image" loan being made by the employer to the ESOP), (4) the ESOP stock purchase agreement (where stock is purchased from the employer or its principal shareholders), (5) corporate charter amendments and related board resolutions, and (6) legal opinion and valuation reports.

The primary issues to be addressed by each of these documents are as follows:

The ESOP Plan (Where the Trust Agreement Is Self-Contained)

1. Designation of a name for the ESOP
2. Definition of key terms ("Participant," "Year of Service," "Trustee," and so on)
3. Eligibility to participate (standards and requirements)
4. Contributions by employer (designated amount or formula, discretionary)

5. Investment of trust assets (primarily in employer securities, along with plans for diversification of the portfolio, purchase price for the stock, rules for borrowing by the ESOP, and so on)
6. Procedures for release of the shares from encumbrances (formula as the ESOP obligations are paid down)
7. Voting rights (rights vested in trustee, special matters triggering employee voting rights)
8. Duties of the trustee(s) (accounting, administrative, appraisal, asset management, recordkeeping, voting obligations, preparation of annual reports, allocation and distribution of dividends, and so on)
9. Removal of trustee(s)
10. Effect of participants' retirement, disability, death, and severance of employment
11. Terms of the put option (for closely held companies)
12. Rights of first refusal upon transfer
13. Vesting schedules

ESOP Stock Purchase Agreement

1. Appropriate recitals
2. Purchase terms for the securities
3. Conditions to closing
4. Representations and warranties of the seller
5. Representations and warranties of the buyer
6. Obligations prior to and following the closing
7. Termination
8. Opinion of counsel
9. Exhibits, attachments, and schedules

Figure 8-4. Structuring the Offer to Meet the Needs of Both Parties in an ESOP Transaction

Seller's Needs

1. Price
2. Form of consideration (cash, stock, notes, and so on)
3. Continuing employment or involvement
4. Important qualitative concerns
5. "Hidden" agenda

Buyer's Needs

1. Control
2. Return on investment
3. Minimal cash equity
4. Retention of key managers
5. Structured to meet lenders' needs

Tools to Bridge the Gap

1. Cash is king (try to limit net worth)
2. Unsecured, subordinated long-term notes with low fixed interest rates
3. Employment and consulting contracts
4. Non-compete agreement
5. Earn-outs

9.

Valuation and Pricing
of the Seller's Company

Price is the paramount issue in a merger and acquisition transaction. Beyond anything else, it determines the amount of value that is transferred to the seller in exchange for ownership of the business that is for sale. It is the number-one concern for both buyers and sellers, and it ultimately determines whether or not a transaction can be consummated. It is also always critical to distinguish between price and terms. The price could be very favorable to a seller but be crippled by alternative terms that make the transaction unpalatable, costly, and risky. There are several established and traditional valuation methods used to estimate the price range within which a business will be sold. The actual price, however, is ultimately determined by what companies are willing to pay, which will be as much a function of market conditions as it is of economic formulas.

Although a formal valuation of the seller's business is a vital component of the buyer's analysis of the proposed transaction, it is important to realize that valuation is not an exact science, nor will valuation alone typically drive the terms and pricing of the transaction. There are numerous acceptable valuation methods, and in most situations, each will yield a different result. Unfortunately, no method will answer the question: "How much is the business actually worth?" That question can be answered only through the receipt and negotiation of term sheets. The reality is that the market determines the price, and valuation, while an important exercise, is only indicative of what the market has paid for similar companies in the past. That said, there is clearly utility in the exercise of valuation because both buyers and sellers use these tools to gain insight into whether their perception of value is likely to intersect the other party's perception of value.

In late 2017, at the time this manuscript went to print, valuations in a variety of industries had reached alarming highs. Was this the "new normal" or were we on the cusp of another market bubble? Many felt that traditional EBITDA-based valuation methodologies had become extinct and failed to recognize other variables and metrics that drive shareholder value, while skeptics felt strongly that financial performance still trumped other intangibles. Should Apple have paid over $3 billion for Beats? Should Microsoft have paid over $25 billion for LinkedIn? Should Facebook have paid $1 billion for Instagram?

Even non-public-, non-M&A- driven valuations seemed frothy. In the spring of 2017, ride-hailing company Lyft Inc. (a clear number two in the market compared to Uber) fetched a recent financing round that valued it at $7.5 billion and included some pretty smart investors, including Alibaba, General Motors, and Andreessen Horowitz, notwithstanding operating losses. Note that market leader Uber had been valued at $70 billion in its most recent round of capital raising.

Where the "right" valuation should be in these times of uncertainty is hotly debated among pundits, experts, investment bankers, and buyers and sellers. Low interest rates give way to elevated profit margin. The Trump administration's promises of tax cuts and regulatory reform may further drive market valuations if they come to fruition. But beyond the Beltway, new metrics are being recognized and reinforced that will change how companies are valued—in the context of M&A or otherwise—as we enter the age of robotics, AI, big data, brand loyalty, customer experience, autonomous vehicles, drones, and other technological phenomena that will directly and indirectly influence valuation in the decades ahead of us. See Figure 9-1.

Figure 9-1. The Stunning Value of Digital Companies

An incredible $2.8 trillion—this is the market capitalization of five of the six largest companies in the United States, Amazon, Apple, Alphabet/Google, Facebook, and Microsoft. Three of them are younger than twenty-five, two of them barely forty-five years old—and all are located on the U.S. West Coast. To put that into context: The combined market value of the thirty companies listed in Germany's DAX 30 is a mere $1.1 trillion, and the most valuable company there, SAP with $100 billion value, turned forty-five this year. Almost every other significant player in the German market was founded a hundred or more years ago. As of late 2017, Apple had readied a market capitalization of more than $900 billion, making it the first global company to be just a few steps away from a $1 trillion valuation.

And another digital company is rising fast in valuation. Tesla—yes, Tesla is a digital company, not so much a car company—surpassed GM and Ford recently in market capitalization, and now is approaching the market cap of BMW, the top German car company.

THE FUTURE OF EBITDA

We often talk about EBITDA (earnings before interest, taxes, depreciation, and amortization) multiples as the key price determiner. EBITDA is a metric or formula that essentially values a company based on its historical and likely future cash flow. When the markets are robust, you hear stories of companies in the hottest industries commanding EBITDA multiples of eight, ten, and even twelve times their earnings. In a softer market and in weaker industries, buyers may be lucky to get one and a half or two times their earnings. In other industries, such as technology, biotech, and software, the EBITDA multiple may not be the best formula for determining a company's true value, and the multiplier may be based on gross sales, number of customers, contracts, or some other key economic variable.

To sell a company at the higher end of the EBITDA multiple range prevailing in the market, you will need to demonstrate to the buyer a series of value drivers that can substantiate and support a higher price. These value drivers vary from company to company, but they can generally include a strong management team (that will commit to staying in place after the closing), a loyal customer base, dedicated and profitable distribution channels, a culture of innovation and creativity with a robust new product or service pipeline, a deep inventory of protectable intellectual property, a global market presence, demand trends that appear strong in the future, and an overall competitive advantage that appears to be sustainable over the medium- to long-term.

Conversely, it is critical to conduct an analysis of any possible value leakage and to fill those holes well before any potential buyers conduct their strategic due diligence. Failure to maximize value and take corrective pre-transactional action on problems that are likely to be identified by a buyer and that will influence price and terms could not only cost you millions of dollars in an EBITDA calculation, but also subject you to legal action for failure to meet your fiduciary obligations toward the minority shareholders of your company. Another mistake that is often made is the failure to harvest or recognize key intangible assets that will be valuable to a buyer after closing. The variables driving a leakage in value can include gaps in the management team, tax and regulatory problems, pending litigation, disgruntled channel and strategic partners, accounting and financial statement issues, hasty due diligence preparation, and a seller's willingness to accept "tougher than market" deal terms because it is perceived to be desperate or overanxious to sell the company. The prevalence of value leakage is more common than you might think: The idea that sellers would purposely or negligently drop critical strategic balls that would otherwise have fetched them millions more in purchase price seems counterintuitive, but in a fall 2007 KPMG survey of corporate sellers and private equity fund managers, nearly 50 percent said that they failed to maximize value in their latest sale or portfolio divestiture and, even more alarmingly, two-thirds of the respondents said that they were not likely to correct the practices that led to the acknowledged undervaluation over the next five years.

To determine the value of a company, several key questions must be addressed: To whom is the asset valuable? In what context is the asset worth paying for? Before we get into the specifics of how businesses are valued, it is important to understand how prices are set in the real world.

A QUICK INTRODUCTION TO PRICING

The key question in pricing is: "How do I, the seller, extract as much value from the buyer as possible?" The obvious answer is: "Get as much as the business is worth to the buyer!" Although this would certainly maximize the price paid, there are certain real-world constraints that prevent this from happening. First, people generally do not advertise how much something is worth to them. A man who is dying of thirst will value a glass of water far more than someone who has just drunk a glass of water; however, unless the potential water customers are willing to identify their situation, the water vendor may be able to charge only a single price. Similarly, just as a computer is worthless to someone who does not have electricity, worth a small amount to a three-year-old child, and potentially worth millions to a technology entrepreneur, it is impossible to charge a single price and capture all of the value provided to each of the three potential computer customers.

In the real world, this problem is addressed through versioning, where vendors force customers to identify the segment in which they belong by providing different options that appeal to each segment differently. For the child, a basic kid's computer is all that is necessary. The technology entrepreneur, on the other hand, will probably prefer a more high-end computer and will pay a substantially different price as a result. Similarly, a Tiffany's diamond, while often the same quality as diamonds sold at other retail locations, commands a 30 to 50 percent premium because the Tiffany's brand is attached.

There are several key lessons from the world of pricing:

- ▶ Each potential buyer will value a business differently.
- ▶ Getting the buyer to identify itself (or its intentions) helps determine what good should be offered and how that good will be valued.
- ▶ Cost is often not relevant in determining market value (i.e., the price of bottled water is not at all related to the cost of the water, which is ostensibly free).
- ▶ A single set price will exclude certain buyers from bidding and will not ensure that the maximum price is paid.
- ▶ An auction pricing format is generally believed to be the best way for a seller to maximize the price paid by the buyer. There are several different auction formats, each with generally the same principles: (1) A competitive process ensures that the price offered is near the maximum price that any individual buyer is willing to pay, (2) the "winner" pays more than all the other bidders are willing to pay, and (3) the

"winner" generally pays just a little bit more than what the second-highest bidder was willing to pay.

When this format is applied to businesses, there are several key differences. First, no business buyer likes to participate in an auction, as these buyers understand the principle and the expected outcome, and second, it is generally very difficult to ensure that each potential bidder adheres to the same process and schedule as the other bidders. Nevertheless, the concept of an auction is a valuable tool for a seller and should be simulated, as much as is reasonably possible, during a sales process.

Finally, an auction, while great for maximizing the price that is actually paid, still does not help inform the buyer or seller of what the likely outcome of the auction process will be. For that, we turn to a more traditional valuation exercise.

VALUATION OVERVIEW

The valuation of a business may be done by the seller prior to entertaining prospective buyers, by a buyer who identifies a specific target, by an investment banker or other intermediary involved in the transaction process, or by all parties during negotiations to resolve a dispute over price. The fair market value of a business is generally defined as the amount at which property would change hands between a willing seller and a willing buyer when neither is under compulsion and both have reasonable knowledge of the relevant facts. However, this is often an unrealistic scenario, as buyers and sellers are forced to consider "investment" or "strategic" value beyond a street analysis of fair market value.

Determining Strategic Value

In the context of a proposed acquisition, a proper valuation model will evaluate what the seller's business would look like under the umbrella of the prospective buyer's company (i.e., create a forward-looking "pro forma" financial model). The first step is to normalize current operating results to establish net free cash flow. Next, it is important to examine "what-if" scenarios to determine how specific line items would change under various circumstances. This exercise identifies a range of strategic values based on the projected earnings stream of the seller's company under its proposed new ownership. The greater the synergy, the higher this earnings stream and the higher the purchase price.

To arrive at this strategic value, large amounts of financial data and general information on many aspects of the seller's business are required, such as the quality of management or overlapping functions within both businesses. The valuation exercise will attempt to assess how the value of the target company will be affected by any changes in the operations or foundation of the company as a result of the proposed transaction, such as a loss of key customers or key managers.

A thorough valuation should also examine the seller's intangible assets when determining strategic value. The list of intangible assets should include items such as customer lists, brands, intellectual property, patents, license and distributorship agreements, regulatory approvals, leasehold interests, and employment contracts. The greater the extent to which the seller can supply specifics on its intangibles, since certain intangibles may not be readily apparent, the more likely it is that they will enhance the valuation.

The Basic Methods of Valuation

There are three main approaches to valuation: comparable company and comparable transaction analysis, asset valuation, and discounted cash flow (DCF) valuation. The first approach identifies companies that are comparable to the one in question and looks at their performance ratios (e.g., value as a ratio of revenue) as guidance in valuing the business in question. The second approach is relevant to businesses with high levels of fixed assets and involves valuing the measurable pieces of the business in order to determine the value of the whole. The final approach looks at the amount of cash that the business is likely to produce each year going forward, then discounts those future cash flows to present value (i.e., today) terms.

Of the three main methods of valuation, no single method will provide a price that cannot be questioned. The methods are useful in that they provide points from which to start and supply a range of reasonable values grounded in reasonable assumptions and actual facts. In the end, it is vital to remember that the value or price of a company is largely dependent on the true motivations and goals of the key players involved, as well as on the transaction's timing.

Comparable Company and Comparable Transaction Analysis. The notion of comparable worth pertains to the use of performance and price data of publicly and privately held companies in order to estimate the value of a similar business. The premise of comparable company analysis is that by examining publicly held companies that operate in the same or a similar industry, one can infer how shareholders would value the target company if it were publicly traded. Since market theory holds that publicly traded companies are valued "fairly" given all available information, then any public business that is similar to the target would be valued using similar metrics. This is not to say that "since our company is a large retailer, we are worth the same as other large retailers," but rather, that the relative value of a large retailer as a percentage of sales may be a good way to value a private retailer. Similarly, comparable transaction analysis is done by identifying transactions involving privately held companies with operations similar to those of the target. By examining the consummated transaction value in relation to the relevant company metric, a value for the target can be inferred.

The justification for this method lies in the premise that potential buyers will not pay more for the target company than what they would spend for a similar company that trades publicly or that has been sold in a recent transaction. The challenge of this approach is that the comparison is good only to the extent that the companies chosen for the analysis are truly comparable to the target. Obviously, the companies should be as similar to the target as possible, particularly with regard to product offering, size of revenue base, and growth rate.

Once a preliminary range of valuations based on this method has been determined, it is often necessary to adjust the price for situations specific to the target company. If, for example, the target company has profits that are consistently above industry averages because of an unusually low cost structure, then the value of the target firm must be adjusted upward from the comparables in order to account for that competitive advantage. In the example just mentioned, the buyer must be able to see and understand the justification for the target company's being valued higher than the comparable analysis dictates or she will not be willing to pay the premium.

In some cases, a comparable analysis may not be possible or may yield unrealistic results. If the target company is closely held, comparable company or transaction analysis may be difficult or impossible, as the metrics necessary to make crucial judgments may not be available.

In addition, the goals of financial reporting for a publicly held company can be quite different from those for a private company. While a publicly held company's management strives to show high earnings on its financial reports in order to attract investors, a closely held private company's management may be a sole entrepreneur or small group that wishes to minimize the earnings shown on its financial reports in order to minimize the tax burden. While both goals are legitimate, the key financial ratios of a target company that is closely held may vary widely from those of similar public companies in the industry.

Asset Valuation Method. If the operation of a target company's business relies heavily on fixed assets, a prospective buyer may conduct an asset valuation when attempting to determine a price for the business. The justification for an asset valuation in this case is that the buyer should pay no more for the target company than he would pay to obtain or build a comparable set of assets on the open market. Within these guidelines, the buyer can choose how to value these substitute assets using (1) the "cost of reproduction" or (2) the "cost of replacement" method. The cost of reproduction takes into account the cost to construct a substitute asset using the same materials as the original at current prices, while the cost of replacement utilizes the cost to replace the original asset at current prices adhering to current standards. In either case, it is also necessary to consider the time that would be required to assemble the assets and initiate normal operations.

When using the asset valuation method, all assets of the target company, both tangible and intangible, must be considered. Tangible assets, as the name implies, refers to actual physical things like machinery and equipment, real estate, vehicles, office furniture and fixtures, land, and inventory. Markets exist where these assets are actively traded, and therefore their value is fairly easy to determine. Intangible assets include patents, trade secrets, brands, customer lists, supplier relationships, and other similar items that do not trade actively in an established market. These intangibles are often referred to as the company's *goodwill* and defined as the difference in value between the company's hard assets and the true value of the company. While intangibles do have legitimate value, it is often difficult to convince a buyer of the exact value that an intangible asset provides. Generally, it is in the seller's best interest to supply an acquirer with as much information about the company's intangibles as possible. The greater the value of goodwill that can be attributed to specific, well-defined intangibles, the higher the price at which the company is likely to be valued. For example, rather than lumping patents that a company holds under "intangible goodwill" or as a single line item, each patent should be listed separately and supporting documentation provided that details crucial facts such as patent scope, dates of expiration, and individual effects on the company's operations.

Discounted Cash Flow (DCF) Valuation Method. Perhaps the most commonly used method for determining the price of a company is the DCF valuation method. In a DCF valuation, projections of the target company's future free cash flow are discounted to the present and summed to determine the current value. The implication of a DCF valuation is that when ownership of the target company changes hands, the buyer will own the cash flows created by the continued operations of the target. Key elements of the DCF model are financial projections, the concept of free cash flow, and the cost of capital used to calculate an appropriate discount rate.

The first step in a DCF valuation is developing projections of the target company's financial statements. Intimate knowledge of the target company's operations and its historical financial results and numerous assumptions as to the implied future growth rate of the company and its industry are key elements of grounded financial projections. In addition, it is necessary to determine a reasonable forecast horizon, which, depending on the industry and the company stage, can range between five and ten years.

The next step in a DCF valuation is determining the target company's future free cash flows. The most basic definition of free cash flows is cash that is left over after all expenses (including cost of goods sold, operating and overhead expenses, interest and tax expenses, and capital expenditures) have been accounted for; it is capital generated by the business that is not needed for continued operations, and, accordingly, it is the capital available to return to shareholders without impairing the future performance of the business. Determining the free cash flows of a business is a function of understanding and utilizing the basic financial data provided in the target's projected financial statements. That being said, in determining a company's free cash flows, it is extremely important to have both general knowledge of financial statements and a thorough understanding of the target company's accounting practices, as projections are often heavily influenced by historical financial statement data.

After determining the free cash flows for the target over the designated forecast period (typically five years), a terminal value is assigned to all future cash flows (everything after five years), which should be consistent with both industry growth rates and inflation predications. (*Note:* During the Internet bubble, optimistic entrepreneurs often made the mistake of assuming that their company's growth rate would forever exceed that of the U.S. economy, yielding sizable yet unrealistic valuations.) Two primary methods are used for assigning a terminal value: (1) perpetual growth, which assumes that the target's free cash flow will grow indefinitely at a given rate, and (2) exit multiples implied by comparable company or transaction multiples described in previous sections.

Perhaps the most crucial concept of the discounted cash flow valuation method is that of a discount rate. As future free cash flows will occur in the future and the target business is being valued today, it is necessary to adjust future inflows of capital to today's dollars. This discount rate encapsulates the idea the money today is worth more than money in the future. If given the choice between $100 today and $100 two years from now, most people would choose the former, as they would have the opportunity to invest that money and would reasonably expect to receive more than $100 after two years has passed. This same concept, the time value of money, is used to apply an appropriate discount rate to the future free cash flows and the terminal value of a target business.

Finally, after discounting all future cash flows to today's dollar, the target company's cash flows can be summed to yield a final implied valuation. Unfortunately, like the other valuation methods described, the DCF valuation method has its flaws—the most prominent being that it is grounded in assumptions and financial projections that are prone to human error.

The Challenges of Valuing a Smaller Company

Smaller, closely held businesses have historically been more difficult to value because of the following informational challenges and risks, which in turn result in lower valuations. Smaller firms, in general, present certain "information risks" that make valuation more difficult because of:

- ▶ Lack of externally generated information, including analyst coverage, resulting in a lack of forecasts
- ▶ Lack of adequate press coverage and other avenues to disseminate company-generated information
- ▶ Lack of internal controls
- ▶ Possible lack of internal reporting

In addition, there are numerous firm-specific reasons why small firms are more difficult to analyze from a valuation perspective, such as:

- ▶ Inability to obtain any financing or reasonably priced financing
- ▶ Lack of product, industry, and geographic diversification
- ▶ Inability to expand into new markets
- ▶ Lack of management expertise
- ▶ Higher sensitivity to macro- and microeconomic movements
- ▶ Lack of dividend history
- ▶ More sensitivity to business risks, supply squeezes, and demand lulls
- ▶ Inability to control or influence regulatory activity and union activity
- ▶ Lack of economies of scale or cost disadvantages
- ▶ Lack of access to distribution channels
- ▶ Lack of relationships with suppliers and customers
- ▶ Lack of product differentiation or brand name recognition
- ▶ Lack of the deep pockets necessary for staying power

Because investors in private companies assume a higher degree of risk, they expect higher rates of return than they would from investments in public-company securities. As a result, private-company valuations tend to be lower. This discount, known aptly as the *private-company discount*, can range from 20 percent to 50 percent and depends on the type of business and the numerous factors outlined previously. While the selling company can estimate what the discount will be based on assumptions of the acquirer's perceived risk, the actual discount cannot be determined until a transaction is consummated.

While the detailed methods of valuation described in this chapter can provide a decent starting point for estimating the price at which a transaction will occur, unfortunately, that is often all that they provide.

The final negotiated price can vary widely and is dependent on diverse factors, including market conditions, the timing of the negotiations and the valuation date, the internal motivation and goals of both the buyer and the seller, the operating synergies that will result from the transaction, the structure of the transaction, and other factors that may not even be defined explicitly. When all is said and done, only a consummated transaction will provide a 100 percent accurate valuation.

10.

Financing the Acquisition

Let's assume that the buyer's team has followed all of the steps in the process thus far: It has identified its strategic objectives, prepared the acquisition plan, identified the qualified candidates, narrowed the field, negotiated and signed the letter of intent, conducted the valuation and negotiated the purchase price, completed due diligence, and instructed counsel to start working on the definitive documents.

The team breathes a sigh of relief until it realizes: *How will we finance this transaction? How much of the purchase price will we pay for from our own cash reserves and how much will we raise from third-party sources of debt and equity? And the answer is not always obvious and often complex. For example, in 2017, when Amazon bought Whole Foods, it had more than adequate cash reserves to finance the acquisition directly, but instead chose to issue low-interest bearing corporate bonds in the amount of $16 billion to help finance the deal. It chose to borrow at these rates over periods as long as forty years, rather than dig into its cash board of nearly $25 billion. In fact, 2017 was a very popular year for Fortune 500 companies to issue low-interest bonds to finance both M&A and organic growth, including issuances by AT&T ($22.5 billion),*

Microsoft ($17 billion), Broadcom ($13.5 billion), and Apple ($10 billion); however, in many cases, the cash raised was still sitting in reserves and not yet allocated as of the end of 2017.

There are a wide range of options for financing a transaction, from a simple equity financing to a layered transaction with multiple levels of debt and equity. Since each transaction is unique, the structures will vary and the leverage ratios and strategic reasons for building the "cap stack" in a certain way will change based on deal terms and capital market conditions. Each deal presents its own challenges, its own set of seller's needs, its own financial-market conditions, and so forth. And each source of acquisition financing will have its own unique set of evaluation criteria, transactional focus, cost of capital, expectations, deal terms, and covenants. Overall, the key factors that affect the structure are the size and complexity of the transaction, the buyer's cash position, the market for the buyer's securities, the terms of the purchase price, and the macro financial-market conditions.

A key to the type and availability of funding is the structure of the company that is being acquired. A company with little debt, significant assets, and strong cash flow is a good candidate for an acquisition with a significant portion of long-term debt financing. On the other hand, your options will be severely limited if the company has poor cash flow, existing debt, and encumbered assets. As the capital markets shifted and credit markets tightened in 2008 and 2009, the debt-to-equity ratios for financing a typical acquisition changed dramatically for both financial and strategic buyers. The leverage and financial returns that a buyer could enjoy when it put only 15 to 30 percent of its own cash down were quite significant, but the returns available evaporated quickly when lenders began to demand much higher coverage ratios for each transaction, assuming that they continued to lend at all. As the economic conditions improved in 2010 to 2014, ratios began to improve. By 2015 to 2017, some would say that the aggressive lending conditions that led to the 2008 meltdown had returned. Only time will tell whether another bubble burst is coming.

Three primary issues to address as you plan your acquisition financing are finding the ideal amount of debt that should be raised, determining a capital structure with the future success of the company in mind, and the cost of the funds.

This chapter looks at some common sources of debt and equity financing used by buyers in connection with acquisition financing. The various possibilities are shown in Figure 10-1.

Figure 10-1. The Stunning Value of Digital Companies

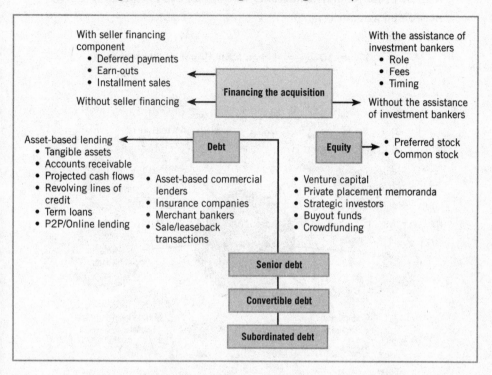

AN OVERVIEW OF FINANCING SOURCES

The Seller as a Source of Financing

For small- and middle-market transactions, seller financing or "take-back" paper is a common practice, and is often a critical component in getting many smaller- and middle-market deals closed. The basic mechanics of seller financing are detailed here, and the many buckets of capital are displayed in Figure 10-2. The simplest way to provide seller financing is to have the buyer make a down payment, with the seller carrying a note for the rest of the purchase price. The business itself and the significant business assets provide the primary collateral for the note. A lien on the property is filed with the secretary of state's office to further document the transaction. If the buyer defaults on the note, the seller is first in line to step back in and take over the business. In this situation, the buyer is agreeing to pay the seller according to the terms of the promissory note. The terms of the promissory note (interest rate, length, principal payments, and so on) can vary depending on the negotiated agreement.

Figure 10-2. Develop an M&A Financing Strategy

For the seller, taking back a note for part or all of the purchase price may be the only way to sell the business, since banks have fairly strict lending criteria for acquisition loans. For the buyer, seller financing can be important because of the less rigorous qualification standards and more lenient terms than a bank would have.

In many of these transactions, a buyer will typically use a bank for primary financing but may need a seller note in order to bridge a purchase price gap. In this case, the seller note is subordinated and second in line to the commercial bank if the buyer defaults on the primary loan.

Additional security for the seller note, above and beyond the business itself, is sometimes requested. Types of security can include a personal residence as additional collateral, commercial real estate, investments, or even a personal guarantee.

The buyer may use seller financing either to keep the seller motivated to contribute to the company's future success or to force the seller to prove that the business truly has the upside potential that has been represented. In other words, this form of financing requires the seller to absorb some of the risk.

The previous discussion has covered seller financing that is *fixed*, such as a simple installment sale or unsecured promissory note. Other types of seller financing are *equity*, such as taking some of the buyer's common or preferred stock (or convertible debt) as payment; *contingent*, such as warrants (options to purchase the shares at a fixed price at a later point in time); or other types of conditional payments, such as earn-outs. With an earn-out, the seller receives additional payments only if the acquired business performs above a specified level in the future, or in the event that a specific post-closing condition is met, or if a certain event occurs (or does not occur), such as FDA approval or the issuance of a patent. Sellers that agree to accept a portion of their consideration in this manner must recognize the economic risks. If the buyer defaults on its obligations, the seller could ultimately end up owning the business again.

Debt-Financing Alternatives

Asset-Based Lending. Although the many types and sources of debt financing should be considered, a traditional commercial bank loan is the most common source of acquisition capital for small and growing buyers. Asset-based lending is a key driver for financing acquisitions. The bank will loan money based on the amount of collateral available (inventory, accounts receivable, and fixed assets). Banks will often lend up to 80 percent of the eligible collateral. The buyer/borrower is responsible for obtaining the balance of the purchase price. The buyer/borrower is also responsible for ensuring that there is sufficient working capital after making loan payments to continue operations and execute the business plan.

Cash Flow Financing. Another type of financing that is available for acquisitions is cash flow lending. This is an option for firms with predictable cash flows. The bank will want proof that the cash flows are sustainable in the future based on the historical financials. The financial institution will determine the loan structure based on the ability of the cash flows to meet the debt obligation.

Subordinated Mezzanine Debt. Subordinated debt financing can include both debt and equity. Compared to traditional debt and equity, there are dramatically fewer sources of subordinated debt. This type of debt is much riskier than senior debt and, thus, more expensive. To secure this type of financing, one should expect to pay a higher interest rate and give equity, typically in the form of warrants.

Equity Financing

Equity financing has the greatest risk, as it is lowest in the pecking order in the event of a bankruptcy. To compensate for the risk, equity investors demand higher returns than the other financing sources. In many small- and middle-market transactions, the buyer provides the equity. If additional equity is needed, however, there are numerous sources, including private equity firms, venture capitalists, and angel investors.

UNDERSTANDING THE LENDER'S PERSPECTIVE

In recent years, commercial banks have changed the way in which they make loans for merger and acquisition deals. The local approval of loans is a steadily fading practice, and the loan-approval process has come to resemble the due diligence review of a securities offering. Lenders now behave like investors, conducting competitive analyses, determining market share trends, and so forth. These stricter loan standards mean that buyers must have more equity than before. In most instances, sellers' take-back notes must be entirely subordinated to the institutional financing. The classic leveraged buyout of the 1980s is a rarity for banks today, primarily because collateral alone is no longer sufficient; cash flow and balance sheet strength have become equally important.

These stricter loan standards mean that fewer debt-driven deals are getting done, but the deals that are being done are at lower interest rates and have generally lower default rates. In addition, virtually all institutional lenders have taken a harder line on collateralized financing. Inventories, once a building block of many merger and acquisition loans, are becoming extremely difficult to finance. Rapidly changing technology can make high-tech goods obsolete almost overnight, while the steady increase in retail chain store failures threatens the worth of the surviving stores' merchandise.

The real estate component may also be difficult to finance. Money is available, but underwriting requirements are increasingly onerous. Whereas once the loan-to-market-value ratio was 60 or 65 percent, now lenders will advance only 50 or 60 percent of the appraised value. For loans to manufacturers and distributors, lenders usually restrict their loans to high-ceiling, general-purpose buildings—a criterion that can sink many potential LBOs. All would-be borrowers are subject to often daunting scrutiny regarding soil contamination and other environmental hazards. Finally, real estate lenders, like institutional lenders in general, now place great emphasis on cash flow, both historical and projected.

FINANCING DEALS IN TIMES OF TURMOIL

A U.S. economic contraction rooted in the housing and financial sectors spread worldwide, and interconnected global commerce and financial markets sank in unison. Losses spread from subprime mortgages to other widely held financial instruments, of which banks and investment funds had used leverage to purchase large quantities. In the most extreme cases, several of the nation's largest financial institutions collapsed as their ability to borrow short-term to fund their long-term investments vanished. The failure of the Fed's monetary easing and the Treasury's financial support to immediately facilitate lending and bail out ailing financial institutions led to a frenzied panic that resulted in this striking credit crisis and the ensuing recession being insurmountable. Lack of confidence in investment banks' abilities to continue funding operations in the short-term debt markets uprooted their business model and led to their extinction. Uncertainty about the extent and location of losses caused banks to tighten lending standards, increasing the cost of financing for corporate America and exacerbating an economic slowdown that was already under way. A move toward stringent lending conditions and more conservative investment criteria triggered a wave of de-leveraging worldwide that continued well into 2010.

The IPO Market

The year 2008, plagued by widespread uncertainty and a global recession, saw a meager 24 IPOs, raising $23.1 billion in proceeds (which is deceptive because it included Visa's $19.7 billion IPO), compared to the 197 offerings in 2007, which raised more than $43.2 billion. While new issuance was low at the beginning of the year and throughout the summer, the second half of 2008 experienced the longest IPO drought since the recessionary period of the 1970s. Investors proved unwilling to take on the risk of newly public companies and were not lured by the desire for growth. In 2009, a select few companies gained access to the public capital markets via IPOs, such as Open Table.com, an online restaurant reservation system; Rosetta Stone, a language-training company; Rail America, a transportation-services company; and Vitamin Shoppe, a health products retailer, reflecting the limited scope of industry sectors perceived as having enough growth to support post-IPO valuations. The IPO markets slowly improved by 2015–2017, with successful to relatively successful IPOs by Acacia, Novan, and Twilio. The total IPOs in 2016 were *less* in the aggregate than the single biggest IPO of 2014, which was by Alibaba for $21.8 billion.

The Private Investment in Public Equity (PIPE) Market

With the public new issue markets severely hampered by the economic downturn, issuers of all market capitalizations and sectors turned to the PIPE market to raise capital. Despite a smaller number of offerings, with just over 1,000 transactions closing in 2008 (compared to 1,556 in 2007), the PIPE marketplace recorded its highest grossing year, with $103 billion in proceeds, demonstrating the continued mainstream nature and proliferation of the product. However, more recently, from 2015 to 2017, the PIPE market has slowed down. PIPE issuance by growth companies has decreased, as multibillion-dollar transactions in traditional sectors (e.g., energy and financial), such as Rio Tinto, Barclays, Citigroup, and National City Corporation, accounted for a significant portion of the year's proceeds. The most notable PIPE transactions in the traditional sectors included Warren Buffett's capital injections into Goldman Sachs and General Electric, including $8 billion in preferred stock and significant warrant coverage.

The Private Equity Market

Private companies seeking financing in 2008 encountered a difficult and competitive environment, as the number of completed financings fell 15 percent but by 2016 had rebounded to a whopping 3,985 global transactions with an aggregate value of $319 billion according to reports by Pitchbook and Bain. As the IPO and M&A markets were weaker and still recovering, a lack of exit opportunities constrained venture capital investing activities. As a result, investors embraced a conservative approach to financial projections, putting downward pressure on valuations and focusing on private companies with lower risk and recurring revenues. As Grant Thornton observes, private equity firms are returning to the days where they spend substantially more time looking for high-quality companies to invest in, and they are performing more thorough due diligence rather than jumping into an investment headfirst. Also, private equity firms have adapted to the changing market by opting to do cross-border deals. Middle-market investment banking firms, like Harris Williams & Co., for example, say that they expect to spend more time on globalization and emerging markets. But even in challenging times where funds had a tough time raising fresh capital, it was estimated that in the fall of 2009, there was over $440 billion in capital still "sitting on the sidelines" in the coffers of U.S. private equity funds, ready to be deployed, down from an estimated peak of $800 billion in 2006 and 2007, but still a significant amount of inert capital that had climbed back up to nearly $1 trillion by 2017

The Convertible Securities Market

The convertible securities market was the worst hit by this global recession. New issue activity has slowed dramatically in recent years; convertible arbitrage returns plummeted 50 percent and investors still remain on the sidelines as of 2017 in part due to low interest rates. A wave of massive financial-sector offerings early in the year contributed to gross proceeds just 3 percent below the trailing four-year average. Growth-sector issuers accessed the convertible market to raise $13 billion through forty-six transactions, outpacing proceeds in the growth IPO and follow-on markets combined. Depressed convertible prices have led to a surge in issuer buybacks and restructurings.

Before attempting to understand the types of loans available from commercial banks, it is important to understand the perspective of the average commercial bank when it analyzes the buyer's loan proposal. Banks are in the business of selling money, and capital is the principal product in their inventory. However, bankers are both statutorily and personally averse to risk. The bank's shareholders and board of directors expect that loan officers will take all necessary steps to minimize the risk to the institution in each transaction and obtain the maximum protection in the event of default. Therefore, the types of loans available to the buyer/borrower, the terms and conditions of loan agreements, and the steps taken by the bank to protect its interests all have a direct relationship to the level of risk that is perceived by the lending officer and the loan committee. The management team that has been assigned to obtain the acquisition financing from a commercial bank must be in a position to show how the typical risks in an acquisition will be mitigated in preparation for the negotiation of the loan documentation. While the steps in the loan process still remain the same, macroeconomic conditions have tightened the oversight adopted by the bank at each such step.

STEPS IN THE LOAN PROCESS

There are two key steps in obtaining acquisition financing from typical commercial lenders: preparation and learning where to look.

Step 1: Preparing the Loan Proposal

The loan proposal should focus on the history of the buyer, the performance of the seller, and the reasons why the proposed deal makes sense. The proposal should also contain a copy of the signed letter of intent and the financial statements of both parties. From the buyer/borrower's perspective, this will mean a loan proposal package that demonstrates the presence of a strong management team; an accounts receivable management program; the ability of the combined entity to service the debt, shown in financial statements and projections; the stability of the company through its long-standing and synergistic relationships with suppliers, distributors, and employees; and an understanding of the trends in the marketplace. The loan proposal should also explain the structure of the proposed transaction and give the underlying rationale for selecting this structure. All of these factors will be assessed by a loan officer in determining the merits of the proposed deal and the relative risk to the bank in making a loan in connection with the proposed acquisition.

Although the exact elements of a buyer/borrower's loan proposal will vary depending on the size of the company, its industry, and the terms of the proposed transaction, most lenders want the following fundamental questions answered:

Who is the borrower?

How much capital is needed and when?

How will the capital be allocated, and for what specific purposes?

Why does the proposed transaction make sense from a financial, strategic, and operational perspective?

What additional market share, cost savings, or other efficiencies will be achieved as a result of this transaction?

How will the combined entity service its debt obligations (e.g., application and processing fees, interest, principal, or balloon payments)?

What protection (e.g., tangible and intangible assets to serve as collateral) can the borrower provide the bank in the event that the company is unable to meet its obligations?

Although the answers to these questions are all designed to assist the banker in an assessment of the risk factors in the proposed transaction, they are also intended to provide the commercial loan officer with the information necessary to persuade the loan committee to approve the transaction. You must understand that once the loan officer is convinced of the merits of the deal, he will then serve as an advocate on behalf of the buyer/borrower in presenting the loan proposal to the bank's loan committee. The loan documentation, terms, rates, and covenants that the loan committee will specify as a condition for making the loan will be directly related to the ways in which the buyer/borrower is able to demonstrate its ability to mitigate and manage the risk to the lender in connection with financing the proposed transaction.

The loan proposal should include the following categories of information, many of which can be borrowed or modified from the acquisition plan:

- **Summary of the request.** This gives an overview of the history of the buyer and the seller, the amount of capital needed, the proposed repayment terms, the intended use of the capital, and the collateral available to secure the loan.

- **History of the borrower.** This provides a brief background of the buyer and/or the seller; its capital structure; the key founders; the stage of development and plans for growth; a list of key customers, suppliers, and service providers; management structure and philosophy; plant and facilities; the key products and services offered; and an overview of any intellectual property owned or developed.

- **Market data.** This section gives an overview of trends in the industry; the size of the market; the buyer's and/or seller's market share; an assessment of the competition (direct and indirect); proprietary advantages; marketing, public relations, and advertising strategies; market research studies; and future industry prospects.

- **Financial information.** Pro forma post-acquisition balance sheets and projected income statements, federal and state tax returns, appraisals of key assets or company valuations, current balance sheet, credit references, and a two-year income statement are included here. The role of the capital requested (with respect to the buyer's and/or seller's plans for growth), an allocation of the loan proceeds, and the buyer's and/or seller's ability to repay must be carefully explained, and a discussion of its ability to service the debt must be supported by a three-year projected cash flow statement on a monthly basis.

- **Schedules and exhibits.** A schedule of supporting documents (such as a letter of intent between buyer and seller) and background information on the seller's performance are provided. Résumés of the buyer's principals, recent articles about the buyer or seller, a schedule of patents and trademarks, a picture of the seller's products or site, and an organization chart of the proposed management structure for the post-closing business should also be appended as exhibits to the loan proposal.

Step 2: Understanding the Types of Commercial Bank Loans

During the process of planning the capital structure and in preparing the loan proposal, it is important for the buyer/borrower to understand the various types of loans that are available from a commercial bank (one or more of which could be tailored to meet specific requirements) in the context of a proposed acquisition. Loans are usually categorized by the term of the loan, the expected use of the proceeds, and the amount of money to be borrowed. The availability of these loans depends on both the nature of the industry and the bank's assessment of the company's creditworthiness.

The following are typical loan categories:

- *Short-term loans.* These are ordinarily used for a specified purpose, with the lender's expectation being that the loan will be repaid at the end of the project. For example, a seasonal business may borrow capital in order to build up its inventory in preparation for the peak season. When the season comes to a close, the lender expects to be repaid immediately. Similarly, a short-term loan could be used to cover a period when the company's customers or clients are in arrears; when the accounts receivable are collected, the loan is repaid. Short-term loans are usually made in the form of a promissory note (see the discussion of loan documentation later in this chapter) payable on demand, and they may either be secured by the inventory or accounts receivable that the loan is designed to cover or be unsecured, in which case no collateral will be required. Unless the company is a start-up or operates in a highly volatile industry (thereby increasing the risk in the eyes of the lender), most short-term loans will be unsecured, thereby keeping the loan documentation and the bank's processing time and costs to a minimum. Lenders generally view short-term loans as self-liquidating in that they can be repaid by foreclosing on the current assets that the loan has financed. The fact that the bank's transactional costs are low, along with the perception of the lower risk during this short period of time, makes short-term borrowing somewhat easier for a growing business to obtain and serves as an excellent means for establishing a relationship with a bank and demonstrating creditworthiness.

■ *Operating lines of credit.* These consist of a specific amount of capital that is made available to the company on an "as-needed" basis over a specified period of time. A line of credit may be short term (60 to 120 days) or intermediate term (one to three years), renewable or non-renewable, and at a fixed or fluctuating rate of interest. Borrowers should be especially careful to negotiate ceilings on interest rates; to avoid excessive commitment, processing, application, and related up-front fees; and to ensure that repayment schedules will not be an undue strain for the company. The company should also ensure that its obligations to make payments against the line of credit are consistent with its own anticipated cash flow projections.

■ *Intermediate-term loans.* These are usually provided over a three- to five-year period for the purposes of acquiring equipment, fixtures, furniture, and supplies; expanding existing facilities; acquiring another business; or providing working capital. These loans are almost always secured not only by the assets being purchased with the loan proceeds, but also by the other assets of the company, such as inventory, accounts receivable, equipment, and real estate. Such a loan usually calls for a loan agreement, which typically includes restrictive covenants that govern the operation and management of the company during the term of the loan. The restrictive covenants are designed to protect the interests of the lender and ensure that all payments are made on a timely basis, before any dividends, employee bonuses, or noncritical expenses are paid.

EQUITY FINANCING

Equity financing involves the offering and sale of the buyer's securities for the purpose of raising the capital to pay the seller and to provide working capital for the new combined company. Securities are sold via private placements, through negotiations with buyout or venture funds, and to strategic investors. There are a wide variety of resources available to identify sources of equity capital, including:

National Investment Banking Association (NIBA)
P.O. Box 6625
Athens, GA 30604
(706) 208-9620

http://www.nibanet.org/
Emily Foshee, executive director

Pratt's Guide to Private Equity & Venture Capital Sources
Published by Thomson Reuters and available in hard copy or as an online
service. This is a combination of two previous publications: *Pratt's Guide to
Venture Capital Firms* and *Directory of Buyout Financing Sources*.
(646) 223-6787

National Venture Capital Association (NVCA)
1655 Fort Myer Drive
Suite 850
Arlington, VA 22209
(703) 524-2549
http://www.nvca.org/

National Association of Small Business Investment Companies (NASBIC)
1100 G Street, NW
Suite 750
Washington, DC 20005
(202) 628-5055
http://www.nasbic.org/

Private Equity Council
950 F Street, NW
Suite 550
Washington, DC 20004
(202) 465-7700
http://www.privateequitycouncil.org

Figure 10-3. Tips for Managing Tripartite Transactions

The buyer/borrower faces the challenge of trying to keep its transactions for raising debt or equity capital on track along with its
deal with the seller. These tripartite transactions can be difficult to
manage, but the following tips should keep everything in harmony for
a synchronized closing.

➡ Timing is everything. Like an orchestra leader, the buyer must
   ensure that the lender is in the loop at all appropriate times on
   due diligence, deal negotiations, pre-closing conditions, and the
   coordination of closing. It is incumbent on the buyer to make sure

that the financing transaction closes prior to the closing of the acquisition itself.

➡ The lender will be doing due diligence on the buyer as well as its own independent due diligence on the seller. The lender's due diligence will be not only on the two companies, but also on the viability of the post-closing integration plan and the documentation of the transaction. The lender will want to see the executed confidentiality agreements, executed letters of intent, responses to due diligence requests, and all other documents that may directly or indirectly affect its rights as a lender.

➡ The lender will want to review the buyer's acquisition plan, with a particular focus on the value of the collateral securing the loans (where applicable), the historical earnings and cash flows of the seller, the track record and experience of the buyer, trends within the seller's industry, and the pro forma financial projections for a post-closing consolidated company.

➡ The buyer must pay careful attention to *cost-of-capital* issues and debt-to-equity ratios, which will vary from transaction to transaction. The sources of capital and their expected return on investment will also vary. For example, a senior lender, who will insist on a preferred position over other creditors, such as the subordinated lender, will often lend up to 70 percent of the purchase price, depending on the amount of assets available for collateral and the strength of the projected (as well as the historical) cash flows. If the senior lenders are properly secured, then they may not be as difficult in the negotiation of loan covenants and minimum interest rates. The subordinated lenders, on the other hand, are typically willing to provide 10 to 30 percent of the purchase price, but will generally demand a 15 to 30 percent annual return over a five- to ten-year investment horizon. Both the senior lender and the subordinated lender will usually look to the buyer to provide between 15 and 30 percent of the total capital required for the transaction. The general rule is, the larger the lender's portion of the acquisition financing puzzle, the higher its expected return on investment. If the buyer turns to the equity markets, it should be aware that most buyout funds, venture capitalists, and private investors will be looking for 20 to 30 percent returns on their investments.

In addition to consulting these directories, buyers should consider contacting national underwriters and even insurance companies that have participated in the equity financing of larger acquisitions.

Before turning to a few of these strategies in more detail, let's take a look at the types of equity securities that may be offered and sold by the buyer/offeror to acquisition financing sources. The various forms of equity securities include common stock, preferred stock, and warrants and options. Each type of equity security carries with it a different set of rights, preferences, and potential rates of return in exchange for the capital contributed to the company. For example, the typical growing company (whose value to an investor is usually greatly dependent on intangible assets such as patents, trade secrets or goodwill, and projected earnings) will tend to issue equity securities before incurring additional debt, because its balance sheet lacks the assets necessary to secure the debt and additional debt is likely to increase the risk of company failure to unacceptably dangerous levels.

The three types of equity securities are:

1. **Common stock.** An offering of common stock and the related dilution of interest is often a traumatic experience for owners of growing companies who currently operate closely held corporations. The need for growth capital beyond what is available through personal savings or corporate retained earnings results in a realignment of the capital structure and a redistribution of ownership and control. Although the offering of additional common stock is generally costly and will entail a surrender of some ownership and control, it does offer the company an increased equity base and a more secure foundation upon which to build a company, while the likelihood of obtaining future debt financing is greatly increased.

2. **Preferred stock.** In exchange for their capital, purchasers of preferred stock receive dividends at a fixed or adjustable rate of return (similar to a debt instrument), with priority over dividends distributed to the holders of the common stock and a preference in the distribution of assets in the event of liquidation. The preferred stock may or may not have certain rights with respect to voting, convertibility into common stock, anti-dilution rights, or redemption privileges that may be exercised either by the company or by the holder.

Although the fixed dividend payments are not tax deductible and ownership of the company is again diluted, the balance between risk and reward is still achieved because the principal that is invested need not be returned (unless there are provisions for redemption). In addition, the preferred stockholders' return on investment is limited to a fixed rate of return (unless there are provisions for conversion of the preferred stock into the common), and the claims of the preferred stockholders are subordinated to the claims of creditors and bondholders in the event of a failure to pay dividends or upon the liquidation of the company. The use of convertible preferred stock is especially popular with venture capitalists.

3. **Convertible securities.** Convertible securities provide the holder with an option to convert the underlying security, such as a note or preferred stock (based on specified terms and conditions), into common stock. The incentive for conversion is usually the same as that for the exercise of a warrant, namely, that the price of the common stock is higher than the current rate of return provided by the convertible security. Convertible securities offer several distinct advantages to a company, such as:

- An opportunity to obtain growth capital at lower interest rates and with less restrictive covenants, in exchange for giving investors a chance to participate in the company's success if it meets its projections and objectives.
- A means of generating proceeds 10 to 30 percent greater than the sale price of common stock at the time the convertible security is issued. This provides greater earnings per share because the company can obtain the same capital by selling fewer shares of convertible securities than by selling common stock.
- A general broadening of the market of prospective purchasers for the securities, since certain buyers may wish to avoid a direct purchase of common stock but would consider an investment in convertible securities.

Private Placement Offerings

A *private placement offering* is any type of offering of securities by a small or growing company that does *not* need to be registered with the SEC. In order to determine whether a private placement is a sensible strategy for raising acquisition capital, it is imperative that the buyer/offeror have a fundamental understanding of federal and state securities laws affecting private placements (an overview of which is provided here), be familiar with the preparation requirements, and have a team of qualified legal and accounting professionals to assist with the preparation of the offering documents or private placement memorandum (PPM).

The private placement generally offers reduced transactional and ongoing costs for the offeror because of its exemption from many of the extensive registration and reporting requirements imposed by federal and state securities laws. The private placement alternative usually also offers the ability to structure a more complex and confidential transaction, since the offerees will typically consist of a small number of sophisticated investors. In addition, a private placement permits a more rapid penetration into the capital markets than would a public offering.

Federal Securities Law. As a general rule, the Securities Act of 1933 requires the filing of a registration statement with the SEC prior to the offer to sell any security in interstate commerce unless an exemption is available, of which private placement is the most commonly recognized. The penalties for failing to register or for disclosing inaccurate or misleading information are quite stringent. Registration is also an expensive and time-consuming process, and a network of underwriters and broker/dealers must be assembled to make a market for the security. In addition, a registrant is also subject to strict periodic reporting requirements.

To qualify for a private placement, the buyer/offeror must work with legal counsel to structure the transaction within the various categories of exemptions available. These include Section 4(2), the broad "private offering" exemption designed for "transaction(s) not involving any public offering"; Section 3(a)(11), an intrastate exemption; and the mostcommon, Regulation D, which encompasses three specific transactional exemptions from Sections 3(b) and 4(2).

Section 4(2) allows an exemption from registration for transaction(s) by an issuer not involving a public offering. The vague language of the

Figure 10-4. Some of the Buyer's Options to Raise Acquisition Capital, from Simplest to Most Complex

Simplest					Most Complex
1	2	3	4	5	6
Buyer uses its own cash or securities* to pay seller	Buyer uses cash/securities, and seller provides some financing through notes and loan-outs	Buyer provides equity for 25 percent to 50 percent of purchase price, and balance is provided by senior lender—a revolver for the deal and post-closing working capital	Buyer provides equity for 25 percent of purchase price, with 50 percent from senior lender and 25 percent from subordinated lender	Buyer provides equity for 30 percent of purchase price (which must be raised through a securities offering or negotiations with a buyout fund) and 50 percent from a senior lender and 20 percent from a subordinated lender	The total purchase price is a combination of: • cash from buyer (equity) • notes taken back by seller • securities of the buyer • cash from senior lender • cash from subordinated lender • cash from equity source, such as buyout fund, PPM, or venture capitalist

*Although paying the seller with your own stock appears to be the simplest option, be sure to work with counsel to ensure that these shares are properly issued and authorized, and that the impact on valuation and dilution is considered carefully.

act has been a source of much controversy and confusion in the legal and financial communities. Over the years, court cases have established that to qualify for this exemption, targeted investors in a 4(2) offering must have access to the same kind of information that would be available if the issuer were required to register. However, terms like *access to* and *same kind* generally leave discretion concerning the exact method of presenting the necessary information to the company and its attorney. In relying on an exemption under Section 4(2), the offering should be structured in accordance with the five following guidelines:

1. The offering should be made directly to prospective investors, without the use of any general advertising or solicitation.
2. The number of offerees should be limited.
3. The offering should be limited to either insiders (such as officers of the company or family members) or sophisticated investors who have a preexisting relationship with you or with the company.
4. The prospective investor should be provided (at a minimum) with recent financial statements, a list of critical risk factors (which influence the investment), and an open invitation to inspect the company's facilities and records.
5. If you are in doubt as to whether Section 4(2) applies to a particular offering, *do not rely on it*; instead, attempt to structure the transaction within one of the Regulation D exemptions.

Section 3(a)(11) allows for an exemption for "any security which is part of an issue offered and sold only to persons resident within a single state by an issuer which is a resident and doing business within such state." The key issue in relying on this exemption is ensuring that the offering is truly an intrastate offering. This test is deceptive; however, the SEC has adopted Rule 147 to assist in determining whether the requirements of Section 3(a)(11) have been met. Precautionary steps must be taken to ensure that all offerees are residents of the particular state, because even one nonresidential offeree will jeopardize the availability of the exemption.

Rule 504 under Regulation D permits offerings and sales of not more than $1 million during any twelve-month period by any issuer that is not subject to the reporting requirements of the Securities Exchange Act of 1934 and that is not an investment company. Rule 504 places virtually no limit on the number or the nature of the investors that participate in the offering. The SEC also requires that its Form D be filed for all offerings under Regulation D within fifteen days of the first sale. *But even if accreditation is not required, it is strongly recommended that certain baseline criteria be developed and disclosed in order to avoid unqualified or unsophisticated investors.*

Even though no formal disclosure document or prospectus needs to be registered and delivered to offerees under Rule 504, there are many procedures that still must be understood and followed, and a disclosure document is nevertheless strongly recommended. An offering under Rule 504 is still subject to the general antifraud provisions of the Securities Exchange Act; thus, every document or other information that is actually provided to the prospective investor must be accurate and not misleading by virtue of its content or its omissions. Finally, a buyer/offeror seeking to raise capital under Rule 504 should examine applicable state laws very carefully because, although many states have adopted overall securities laws similar to Regulation D, many of these laws do not include an exemption similar to Rule 504, and as a result a formal memorandum (which is discussed later in this chapter) may need to be prepared.

Rule 505 under Regulation D is often selected over Rule 504 (by many companies) because its requirements are consistent with many state securities laws. Rule 505 allows for the sale of up to $5 million of the issuer's securities in a twelve-month period to an unlimited number of "accredited investors" and up to thirty-five non-accredited investors (regardless of their net worth, income, or sophistication). An accredited investor is any person in at least one of the eight categories set out in Rule 501(a) of Regulation D. Included in these categories are officers and directors of the company who have policymaking functions and outside investors who meet certain income or net worth criteria. Rule 505 has many of the same filing requirements and restrictions imposed by Rule 504 (such as the need to file a Form D), in addition to an absolute prohibition on advertising and general solicitation for offerings and restrictions on which companies may be issuers. Any company that is subject to the "bad boy" provisions of Regulation A is disqualified from being a Rule 505 offeror, and this applies to persons who have been subject to certain disciplinary, administrative, civil, or criminal proceedings, or sanctions that involve the company or its predecessors.

Rule 506 is similar to Rule 505; however, the issuer may sell its securities to an unlimited number of accredited investors and up to thirty-five non-accredited investors. The key distinction under Rule 506 is that any non-accredited investor must be "sophisticated." A "sophisticated investor" is one who does not fall into any of the eight categories specified by Rule 501(a), but is believed by the issuer to "have knowledge and experience in financial and business matters that render him capable of evaluating the merits and understanding the risks posed by the transaction (either acting alone or in conjunction with his 'purchaser representative')." The best way to remove any uncertainty over the sophistication or accreditation of a prospective investor is to request that the investor complete a comprehensive confidential offeree questionnaire before the securities are sold. Rule 506 does eliminate the need to prepare and deliver disclosure documents in any specified format, as long as only accredited investors participate in the transaction. As with Rule 505, there is an absolute prohibition on advertising and general solicitation. For buyer/borrowers needing more than $5 million to complete the proposed acquisition, this exemption is the most attractive because it has no maximum dollar limitation.

State Securities Laws. Regulation D was designed to provide a foundation for uniformity between federal and state securities laws. This objective has been met in some states, but it still has a long way to go on a national level. Full compliance with the federal securities laws is only one level of regulation that must be taken into account when developing plans and strategies to raise capital through an offering of securities. Whether or not the offering is exempt under federal laws, registration may still be required in the states where the securities are to be sold under "blue sky" laws.

The level of review varies widely among the states, ranging from very tough "merit" reviews designed to ensure that all offerings of securities are fair and equitable to very lenient "notice only" filings designed to promote full disclosure. The securities laws and requirements of each state where an offer or sale will be made should be checked very carefully prior to the distribution of the offering documents. Every state in the nation does, in fact, have some type of statute governing securities transactions and securities dealers. When drafting the offering, these laws should be reviewed to determine:

- ► Whether the particular limited offering exemption selected under federal law will also apply in the state
- ► Which pre-sale or post-sale registration with the applicable states or mandatory state legends is required
- ► The remedies available to an investor who has purchased securities from a company that has failed to comply with applicable state laws
- ► Who may offer securities for sale on behalf of the company

Small Corporate Offering Registration. Most states have now adopted the Small Corporate Offering Registration (SCOR), which simplifies Regulation D as a source of acquisition financing for small businesses. SCOR allows for a question-and-answer format disclosure document, called the U-7, which you can fill in with the assistance of your accountant or attorney. This new format significantly reduces the cost of compliance without sacrificing the quality of the information available to prospective investors to reach an informed decision. There are restrictions on the structure of offerings that can be made under the U-7, the details of which should be discussed carefully with your attorney.

Preparing the Private Placement Memorandum. The offeror should work with legal counsel to prepare the document and exhibits that will constitute the private placement memorandum (known as the PPM). The PPM describes the background of the company, the details of the proposed transaction, the historical performance of the seller, the risks to the investor, and the terms of the securities being sold. In determining the exact degree of disclosure that should be included in the document, there are several factors that affect the type of information that must be provided and the format in which the data are to be presented, such as the:

- ► Minimum level of disclosure that must be made under federal securities laws (which depends, in part, on the exemption from registration being relied upon).
- ► Minimum level of disclosure that must be made under an applicable state's securities laws (which naturally depends on the state or states in which an offering or sale of the securities is to be made).

▶ Expectations of the targeted investors. Some investors will expect a certain amount of information presented in a specified format, regardless of what the law may require.

▶ Complexity or the nature of the company and the terms of the offering.

Many offerors should prepare detailed disclosure documents regardless of whether or not they are required to do so in order to avoid liability for misstatements, fraud, or confusion, especially if the nature of the company and/or the terms of its offering are very complex.

Each transaction or proposed offering of securities must be carefully reviewed by legal counsel to first determine the minimum level of disclosure that must be provided to prospective investors under applicable federal and state laws. Once this is established, the costs of preparing a more detailed document than may be required should be weighed against the benefits of the additional protection provided to the company by a more comprehensive prospectus. The key question will always be: "What is the most cost-effective vehicle for providing the targeted investors with the information that they require and that both applicable law and prudence dictate that they must have?" There are no easy answers.

The specific disclosure items to be included in the PPM under federal securities laws and any applicable state laws will vary depending on the size of the offering and the nature of the investors. The text should be descriptive, not persuasive, and should allow the reader to reach her own conclusions as to the merits of the securities being offered by the company. At a minimum, every effective PPM must include the following material:

■ *Introductory materials.* These introduce the prospective investor to the basic terms of the offering. A cover page should include a brief statement about the buyer and the seller, the core business of each company, the terms of the offering (often in table form), and all required "legends" required by federal and state laws. The cover page should be followed by a summary of the offering, which serves as an integral part of the introductory materials and a cross-reference point for the reader. The third and final part of the introductory materials is usually a statement of the investor suitability standards, which includes a discussion of the federal and state securities laws applicable to the offering and the definitions of an accredited investor as applied to the offering.

■ *Description of the company.* This is obviously a statement of the buyer's and seller's history and should include a discussion of each company's history, principal officers and directors, products and services, management and operating policies, performance history and goals, competition, trends in the industry, advertising and marketing strategy, suppliers and distributors, intellectual property rights, key real and personal property, customer demographics, and any other material information that would be relevant to the investor.

■ *Risk factors.* This is usually the most difficult section to write, yet it is viewed by many people as clearly being one of the most important to the prospective investor. Its purpose is to outline all the factors that make the offering or the projected acquisition plans risky or speculative. Naturally, the exact risks to the investors posed by the offering will depend on the nature of the company and the trends within that industry.

■ *Capitalization of the issuer.* This discussion should cover the capital structure of the buyer/offeror both before and after the offering and before and after the proposed acquisition. For the purposes of this section of the PPM, all authorized and outstanding securities must be disclosed (including all long-term debt).

■ *Management of the company.* This section should include the name, age, special skills or characteristics, and biographical information on each officer, director, or key consultant; compensation and stock option arrangements; bonus plans; special contracts or arrangements; and any transactions between the company and individual officers and directors (including loans, self-dealing, and related types of transactions). The role and identity of the buyer/offeror's legal and accounting firms should also be disclosed, along with those of any other "expert" retained in connection with the offering.

■ *Terms of the offering.* This should describe the terms and conditions, the number of shares, and the price. If the securities are to be offered through underwriters, brokers, or dealers, then the name of each distributor, the terms of the relationship, the commissions to be paid, the obligations of the distributor (e.g., guaranteed or best-efforts offering), and any special rights, such as the right of a particular underwriter to serve on the board of directors, any indemnification provisions, or other material terms of the offering, must be included.

- *Allocation of proceeds.* This section must state the principal purposes for which the net proceeds will be used and the approximate amount intended to be used for each purpose. You should give careful thought to this section because any deviation from the use of funds as described in the PPM could trigger liability.

- *Dilution.* This should include a discussion of the number of shares outstanding prior to the offering, the price paid, the net book value, the effect of the proposed offering on existing shareholders, and the dilutive effects on new purchasers at the completion of the offering. Often the founding shareholders (and sometimes their key advisors or the people who will help promote the PPM) will have acquired their securities at prices substantially below those in the prospective offering.

- *Description of securities.* This should explain the rights, restrictions, and special features of the securities being offered. It should also explain provisions of the articles of incorporation or bylaws that affect capitalization (such as preemptive rights, total authorized stock, different classes of shares, or restrictions on the declaration and distribution of dividends).

- *Financial statements.* The financial statements to be provided by the issuer will vary depending on the amount of money to be raised, the applicable federal and state regulations, and the company's nature and stage of growth. Provide a discussion and explanation of these financial statements and an analysis of the company's current and projected financial condition.

- *Exhibits.* Such things as the articles of incorporation and bylaws, key contracts or leases, brochures, news articles, marketing reports, and résumés of the principals may be appended as exhibits to the PPM.

Subscription Materials. Once the prospective investors and their advisors have made a decision to provide capital to the buyer/offeror in accordance with the terms of the PPM, there is a series of documents that must be signed to evidence the investors' desire to subscribe to purchase the securities offered by the PPM. The various subscription materials that should accompany the PPM serve several purposes, such as to protect the company against a claim of noncompliance and to screen out potentially difficult investors. The two key documents are the:

- **Subscriber questionnaire.** This is developed in order to obtain certain information from prospective offerees and then serves as evidence that they have the sophistication level and the ability to fend for themselves that are required by a PPM. You should obtain information regarding the prospective purchasers' background, citizenship, education, employment, and investment and/or business experience.

- **Subscription agreement.** This is the contract between the purchaser (investor) and the issuer of the securities. It should contain acknowledgment of:

  1. The receipt and review of the PPM by the subscriber
  2. The restricted nature of the securities to be acquired and knowledge of the fact that the securities were acquired under an exemption from registration
  3. Any particularly significant suitability requirements (such as amount of investment or passive income, tax bracket, and so forth) that the issuer feels may be crucial to the purchaser's ability to obtain the benefits of the proposed investment
  4. An awareness of specific risks disclosed in the information furnished
  5. The existence of the purchaser representative (if one is used)

The subscription agreement should also require a signature to confirm the accuracy and completeness of the information contained in the offeree or purchaser questionnaire, the number and price of the securities to be purchased, and the manner of payment.

The subscription agreement often contains an agreement on the part of the purchaser to indemnify the issuer against losses or liabilities resulting from any misrepresentations on the part of the prospective purchaser that would void or destroy the exemption from registration that the issuer is attempting to invoke. The subscription agreement should also contain representations on the part of the subscriber with respect to its authority to execute the agreement.

Venture Capital Funds

A buyer/offeror whose transaction does not qualify for debt financing from a commercial bank and for which a private placement is not appropriate might consider an institutional venture capital or buyout firm as a source of acquisition financing. The term *venture capital* has been defined in many ways, but it refers generally to relatively high-risk, early-stage financing of young emerging growth companies. The professional venture capitalist is usually a highly trained finance professional who manages a pool of venture funds for investment in growing companies on behalf of a group of passive investors. Another major source of venture capital available to buyer/offerors who meet certain minimum size requirements is a Small Business Investment Company (SBIC). An SBIC is a privately organized investment firm that is specially licensed under the Small Business Investment Act of 1958 to borrow funds through the Small Business Administration for subsequent investment in the small-business community. Finally, some private corporations and state governments also manage venture capital funds that may have equity capital available for acquisition financing.

The Investment Decision. Regardless of the buyer/offeror's particular stage of development or the specific details of the proposed acquisition transaction, there are several key variables that all venture capital firms will consider in analyzing the acquisition plan that is presented. These variables generally fall into four categories: (1) the management team, (2) products and services offered, (3) the markets in which the target company and the buyer/offeror compete, and (4) the anticipated return on investment. In determining whether the growing company would qualify for venture capital, its management team must be prepared to answer the following questions:

Management Team

► What are the background, knowledge, skills, and abilities of each member?
► How is this experience relevant to the specific industry in which the buyer/offeror competes?
► How are the risks and problems that are often inherent to the buyer/offeror's industry handled by the members of the management team?

Products and Services

- ▶ At what stage of development are the buyer/offeror's products and services?
- ▶ What is the specific market opportunity that has been identified by the proposed transaction?
- ▶ How long will this "window of opportunity" remain open?
- ▶ What steps are necessary for the company to exploit this opportunity?
- ▶ To what extent are the company's products and services unique, innovative, and proprietary?

The Growing Company's Targeted Markets

- ▶ What is the stage in the life cycle of the industry in which the buyer/offeror plans to operate on a post-closing consolidated basis?
- ▶ What are the size and projected growth rate of the company's targeted market?
- ▶ What methods of marketing, sales, and distribution will be utilized in attracting and keeping customers?
- ▶ What are the strengths and weaknesses of each competitor (whether it be direct, indirect, or anticipated) in the targeted market?

Return on Investment

- ▶ What are the buyer/offeror's current and projected valuation and performance in terms of sales, earnings, and dividends?
- ▶ To what extent have these budgets and projections been substantiated?
- ▶ Has the company overestimated or underestimated the amount of capital that will be required for the growth and development of its acquisition plan?
- ▶ How much money and time have the owners and managers already invested?

Negotiating and Structuring the Investment. The negotiation and structuring of most venture capital transactions revolve around the need to strike a balance between the concerns of the buyer's management team (such as dilution of ownership and loss of control) and the concerns of the venture capitalist (such as return on investment and mitigating the risk of company failure). The typical end result of these negotiations is a term sheet that specifies the key financial and legal terms of the transaction and then serves as a basis for the negotiation and preparation of the definitive legal documentation. The buyer/offeror should work with its legal counsel in order to understand the many traps and restrictions, such as contingent proxies and supermajority voting provisions, that are typically found in venture capital financing documents. The term sheet may also contain rights and obligations, including an obligation to maintain an agreed valuation of the company; the company's responsibility for certain costs and expenses in the event that the proposed transaction does not take place; or secure commitments for financing from additional sources prior to closing.

The initial negotiation of the term sheet and eventually the definitive documents will usually center on the types of securities to be used and the principal terms, conditions, and benefits offered by the securities. The type of securities ultimately selected will usually fall within one of the following categories:

- *Preferred stock* is the most typical form of security issued in connection with a venture capital financing because of the many advantages it offers to an investor, such as convertibility into common stock, dividend and liquidation preferences over the common stock, anti-dilution protection (allowing the venture capitalist to maintain its ownership position), mandatory or optional redemption schedules (allowing the company to repurchase the shares or the investors to "put" them back to the buyer), and special voting rights and preferences.

- *Convertible notes* are often preferred by a venture capitalist when higher-risk transactions are at issue because the venture capitalist is able to enjoy the senior position of a creditor over a shareholder until the risk of the company's failure has been mitigated.

- *Debt securities with warrants* are also preferred by venture capitalists because they protect the downside by providing interest payments and protect the upside by including warrants to purchase common stock at favorable prices and terms. The use of a warrant enables the investor to buy common stock without sacrificing its position as a creditor, as it would need to do if only convertible debt were used in the financing.

- **Common stock** is rarely chosen by venture capitalists (especially at early stages of development) because it does not offer the investor any special rights or preferences, a fixed return on investment, special ability to exercise control over management, or liquidity to protect against downside risks. One of the few times that a venture capitalist might select common stock might be when there are tax advantages to preserving the buyer's Subchapter S status under the Internal Revenue Code, which might be jeopardized if a class of preferred stock (with different economic terms) were to be authorized by an amendment of the buyer's corporate charter.

Once the type of security has been designated by the venture capitalist, steps must be taken to ensure that the authorization and issuance of the security are properly made under applicable state corporate laws. For example, if the company's charter does not provide for a class of preferred stock, then articles of amendment must be prepared, approved by the board of directors and shareholders, and filed with the appropriate state corporation authorities. The articles of amendment will include new provisions on voting rights, dividend rates and preferences, mandatory redemption provisions, anti-dilution protection (also called "ratchet clauses" because the price of the shares upon conversion is "ratcheted" down if the buyer's company issues shares below the conversion price), and related special rights and features. If debentures are selected, then negotiations will typically focus on the term, interest rate and payment schedule, conversion rights and rates, extent of subordination, remedies for default, acceleration and prepayment rights, and underlying security for the instrument as well as the terms and conditions of any warrants that are granted along with the debentures.

The legal documents involved in a venture capital financing must reflect the end result of the negotiation process and must contain all of the legal rights and obligations. These documents generally include the:

- ▶ Preferred stock or debenture purchase agreement (investment agreement)
- ▶ Stockholders' agreement
- ▶ Employment and confidentiality agreements

- ▶ Warrants (where applicable)
- ▶ Debentures or notes (where applicable)
- ▶ Preferred stock resolution (to amend the corporate charter, (where applicable)
- ▶ Contingent proxy
- ▶ Legal opinion of company counsel
- ▶ Registration rights agreement

The following is a brief overview of the nature and purposes of some of these documents:

- ■ *The investment agreement* describes all of the material terms and conditions of the financing. It also serves as a type of disclosure document because certain key historical and financial information is disclosed in the representations and warranties made to the investors. The representations and warranties (along with any exhibits) are designed to provide full disclosure to the investors, thus providing them with a basis for evaluating the risk of the investment and the structure of the transaction. The investment agreement will also provide for certain conditions that must be met by the company at (or prior to) closing as a condition for the investor's providing the venture capital financing. The conditions to closing are often used in negotiations to mitigate or eliminate certain risks identified by the investor (such as a class action suit by a group of disgruntled employees), but they usually are more of an administrative checklist of actions that must occur at closing, such as the execution of the stockholders', employment, and confidentiality agreements.

- ■ *The stockholders' agreement* will typically contain certain restrictions on the transfer of the company's securities, voting provisions, rights of first refusal, co-sale rights in the event of a sale of the founder's securities, anti-dilution rights, and optional redemption rights for the venture capital investors. Venture capitalists will often require the principal stockholders to become parties to the stockholders' agreement as a condition to closing on the investment. Any existing stockholders' or buy/sell agreements will also be carefully scrutinized and may need to be amended or terminated as a condition of the investment. For example, the investors may want to reserve a right to purchase additional shares of preferred stock (in order to preserve their respective equity ownership in the company in the event that another round of the preferred stock is subsequently issued). This is often accomplished through a contractual preemptive right (as opposed to such a right being contained in the corporate charter, which would make these rights available to all holders of the company's stock).

- *Employment and confidentiality agreements* will often be required of key members of the management team as a condition of the investment. These agreements define the obligations of each employee, the compensation package, the grounds for termination, the obligation to preserve and protect the company's intellectual property, and post-termination covenants (such as covenants not to compete or to disclose confidential information).

- *The contingent proxy* provides for a transfer of the voting rights attached to any securities held by a key principal to the venture capitalist upon the death or disability of such personnel. The proxy may also be used as a penalty for breach of a covenant or warranty included in the investment agreement.

- *The registration rights agreement* would require the venture capital investors to convert their preferred stock or debentures prior to the time that a registration statement is approved by the SEC; this is often required, since these registration rights are limited to the company's common stock. Many venture capitalists view the eventual public offering of the company's securities (pursuant to a registration statement filed with the SEC under the Securities Act) as the optimal method of achieving investment liquidity and maximum return on investment. As a result, the venture capitalist will protect his right to participate in the eventual offering with a registration rights agreement. The registration rights may be in the form of either "demand rights" (the investors' right to require the company to prepare, file, and maintain a registration statement) or "piggyback rights" (which allow the investors to have their investment securities included in a company-initiated registration). The number of each type of demand or piggyback rights, the percentage of investors necessary to exercise these rights, the allocation of the expenses of registration, the minimum size of the offering, the scope of indemnification, and the selection of underwriters and broker/dealers will all be areas of negotiation in the registration rights agreement.

A well-prepared acquisition plan, an understanding of the analysis conducted by the venture capitalist, and an understanding of the legal documents that are typically prepared in a venture capital financing will significantly increase your company's ability to gain access to this growing source of acquisition financing.

11.

The Purchase Agreement and Related Legal Documents

Once the due diligence has been completed, valuations and appraisals conducted, terms and price initially negotiated, and financing arranged, the acquisition team must work carefully with legal counsel to structure and begin the preparation of the definitive legal documentation that will memorialize the transaction. The drafting and negotiation of these documents will usually focus on the key terms of the transaction, the past history of the seller, the present condition of the business, and a description of the rules of the game for the future. They also describe the nature and scope of the seller's representations and warranties, the terms of the seller's indemnification of the buyer, the conditions precedent to closing of the transaction, the responsibilities of the parties during the time period between the execution of the purchase agreement and the actual closing (if not simultaneous), the terms and structure of payment, the scope of post-closing covenants regarding competition and related obligations, the deferred or contingent compensation components, and what will happen if things go awry post-closing, such as any predetermined remedies for breach of the contract. See Figure 11-1.

	SELLER'S COUNSEL	BUYER'S COUNSEL
	Figure 11-1. Roles of Counsel: Mergers and Acquisitions Transactions.	
Early Stage	• Legal Audit/preparing for the due diligence process • Review of Offering Memorandum and presentation materials	• Assist the development of the Acquisition Plan and screening process • Preliminary due diligence on wide range of targets
LOI/Due Diligence	• Prepare document/data room for due diligence • Review and negotiate Letter of Intent	• Legal and strategic diligence on target • Review and negotiate the Letter of Intent
Acquisition Documents	• Review and negotiate the definitive documents • Narrow the R&Ws and Covenants and shift Allocation of Risk	• Review and negotiate the definitive documents • Widen the scope of the R&Ws and covenants and shift Allocation of Risk
Post-closing	• Enforce any post-closing compensation terms and pro-seller covenants • Work with seller on asset/estate protections and post-closing projects • Work on post-closing balance sheet adjustments	• Enforce post-closing obligations of the seller • Work on post-closing integration issues • Work with buyer on asset transaction

REGULATORY COUNSEL	THIRD-PARTY COUNSEL
• Works to obtain regulatory approvals to allow for the closing of the transactions	• Represents lenders, venture investors, vendors, customers, landlords, etc. that may be required to approve the proposed deal
• Advises on post-closing regulatory issues	• Investment bankers and other advisors may also have their own counsel
• Represents the debt and equity sources of capital that may be required to finance the transaction	

The key terms of the purchase agreement will often be dictated by four major variables:

1. The relative drafting and negotiating skill of each party's legal counsel
2. The special risks and unique structural challenges of the transaction (typically a reflection of problems identified during due diligence)
3. The relative bargaining strength of the parties
4. Market conditions at the time the transaction is consummated

On this fourth point, it is critical to understand that there is a wide variety of terms and conditions in the purchase agreement that may vary depending on the state of the overall economy. What terms may be "fair and reasonable" or "market" will be driven both by the specifics of the transaction and by whether the marketplace at the time of the deal is viewed as being more heavily weighted in favor of sellers, such as in 2006 and 2007, or in favor of qualified and cash-flush buyers, such as in 2008 and 2009. As we saw in Chapter 9, market conditions can also dictate the prevailing EBITDA multiples, but here they are also driving specific purchase agreement terms, such as the scope of the indemnification, the amount to be withheld in escrow for unknown liabilities (the holdback), limitations on specific types of post-closing liabilities (the basket), limitations on the amount of damages suffered by the buyer that can be recovered by making claims against the seller (the cap), the amount of equity to be retained by the seller or its team (the rollover), the extent of the conditional or contingent consideration (the earn-out), and a variety of other provisions.

In a buyer's market, the terms that allocate risk will be much more heavily weighted in favor of the buyer, translating into larger holdbacks, more earn-outs, lower or "dollar-one" baskets, longer indemnity survival periods, and higher caps relative to the overall purchase price. In a seller's market, it is typical to experience the converse of these terms unless there are significant risks uncovered during due diligence and/or a significant disparity in the bargaining power of the parties.

By way of illustration only, Figure 11-2 gives some typical terms depending on market conditions.

Figure 11-2. Typical Terms		
KEY TERMS	**BUYER'S MARKET**	**SELLER'S MARKET**
Indemnity survival period	24 to 36 months	9 to 18 months
Deductible basket (as a percentage of sale price)	Dollar one to 0.75 percent	2.5 percent to 8 percent
Damages cap (as a percentage of purchase price)	Unlimited to 30 percent	25 percent to 40 percent
Escrow (as a percentage of overall purchase price—risk agnostic)	15 percent to 25 percent	5 percent to 10 percent
Term of escrow	24 to 36 months	6 to 12 months

CASE STUDY: GCC ACQUIRES TCI

For the balance of this chapter, assume that Growth Co. Corp. (GCC) has identified Target Co., Inc. (TCI), a closely held manufacturer, as an acquisition candidate, but is concerned about unknown or contingent liabilities stemming from some prior product liability claims against TCI that may resurface. A memorandum of understanding is negotiated so that GCC will acquire substantially all of the assets of TCI for $10 million. The financing arranged by GCC will come from the four following sources:[1]

1. $2,000,000 in cash from the internal capital reserves and retained earnings of GCC
2. $3,000,000 in debt financing provided by Business Bank Corp. (BBC), which will be secured by the assets of TCI
3. $4,500,000 in seller's take-back financing by TCI and in the securities of GCC, payable as follows:
   a. $2,000,000 subordinated five-year promissory note
   b. $1,000,000 in the common stock of Growth Co. Subsidiary, Inc. (GCS), a new subsidiary established by GCC to manage and operate the assets being acquired
   c. $1,300,000 (as a target it could be more, it could be less) in the form of a contingent earn-out based upon the financial performance (such as a percentage of sales or net profits) of GCS over the next three years
   d. $200,000 in the form of a two-year consulting agreement at $100,000 per annum for the founding shareholders of TCI[2]
4. $500,000 of TCI debt that will be assumed by GCC

In structuring this deal, notice that GCC has created a new subsidiary to receive, manage, and operate the assets being acquired from

---

1. This financing structure may be more complex than the typical asset acquisition at this level; however, it is designed to provide the reader with some different approaches to structuring such an acquisition.

2. Note that when part of the overall consideration to the seller will be a consulting agreement, there are often certain fiduciary issues that must be addressed in terms of a majority shareholder being favored over the minority shareholders. There are also certain tax advantages to the buyer when the deal is structured in this fashion.

TCI. This is a risk management tactic that will help to insulate GCC assets in the event of a subsequent dispute and make the accounting for the earn-out component easier to calculate. GCC has also managed to shift the allocation of risk back to the seller by negotiating roughly 40 percent of the purchase price as being either contingent or deferred. From a liquidity and timing perspective, this deal is also favorable to GCC, since it must provide only 20 percent of the acquisition cost from its own funds and has several years to repay the lion's share of its obligations to BBC and TCI. Notably, if GCC was paying the full or even majority of the purchase price in cash, it would have greater leverage in the negotiations. The officers of GCC have also managed to convince the shareholders of TCI to buy into the future business plan of GCS, since they have agreed to take 25 percent of their consideration in stock, in a consulting agreement, and in the form of a contingent earn-out. Notwithstanding these attractive features to GCC/GCS, the TCI shareholders are not exactly in terrible shape either—they receive 50 percent of their selling price in cash at closing, get $500,000 of their accounts payable assumed by GCS/GCC, and are second in line (behind BBC) with a security interest in the assets sold.

The transaction discussed here involves a wide variety of legal documents that must be prepared and negotiated in order to consummate the transaction, such as:

- ▶ Asset purchase agreement (among GCC, GCS, and TCI).
- ▶ List of schedules and exhibits to the asset purchase agreement (to be compiled and prepared by TCI and its counsel).
- ▶ Intercreditor agreement (between BBC and TCI).
- ▶ Loan agreement (among BBC, GCC, and GCS).
- ▶ Promissory note, security agreement, and financing statements (for BBC loan).
- ▶ Promissory note, security agreement, and financing statements (for TCI take-back financing).
- ▶ Noncompetition and nondisclosure agreements (for TCI management team to GCC and GCS).
- ▶ Consulting agreements (which serve as part of the deferred compensation to certain TCI shareholders).
- ▶ Employment agreements (to the extent that any of TCI's employees will be hired).

▶ Assignment of key contracts and third-party consent agreements (e.g., leases, loan agreements, and so on) from TCI to GCS.

▶ Board of directors and shareholders resolutions of TCI approving the transaction.

▶ Board of directors resolutions of GCC and GCS approving the transaction.

▶ Certificates for the GCS common stock (for TCI shareholders).

▶ Assumption of liabilities agreement (also known as a liabilities undertaking by GCS to TCI, subject to the consent of the TCI creditors). In addition, TCI may want to obtain estoppel certificates or novation agreements from creditors covered by this agreement.

▶ Bill of sale (for TCI assets sold to GCC and GCS).

▶ Bulk sales affidavits (if applicable under Article 6 of the state commercial code) from TCI to its creditors.

▶ Disclosure documents to TCI shareholders for issuance of GCS warrants (if required by federal or state securities laws).

▶ Opinion of TCI counsel (to GCC and GCS).

▶ Lien search reports on TCI assets.

▶ Certificates of compliance with representations, warranties, and conditions precedent by TCI president and secretary.

▶ Earn-out agreement (may be included in the main body of the asset purchase agreement or be separate).

▶ Indemnification agreement (may be included in the main body of the asset purchase agreement or be separate).

▶ Escrow agreement (if negotiated); proceeds of sale price to be placed in escrow until certain post-closing conditions are met and post-closing adjustments are made by TCI, or as a contingency reserve fund in the event that representations and warranties are subsequently found to be untrue.

▶ Resignation and release agreements (from TCI employees who will not be retained after the transaction).

▶ Personal guarantees (by key shareholders of GCC if demanded by BBC or TCI to secure the promissory notes).

▶ License agreements (if any, to the extent that intellectual property rights are being retained by TCI and exclusively licensed by GCS).

▶ Allocation certificates for federal, state, and local tax filings (as well as UCC filings where applicable).

Note: Had the transaction been structured as a stock purchase rather than an asset transaction, then TCI shareholders would also have to produce duly endorsed stock certificates, current corporate financial statements, certified copies of the corporate financial statements, certified copies of the corporate articles and bylaws, certificates of good standing, officer and director releases, termination and resignation agreements, termination of personnel and retirement plans (where applicable), and all other material corporate documentation at the closing. The structure is dictated by a combination of tax implications, the nature of the business, and the goals of the buyer.

Now, let's take a look at a few of these agreements in more detail.

The Asset Purchase (or Acquisition) Agreement

This document includes a statement of the parties to the transaction, identification of the specific tangible and intangible assets that are being sold and liabilities that are being assumed/assigned, the manner in which the assets and liabilities will be sold, the terms and conditions of the transaction, the amount and terms of payment of the consideration to be paid by the purchaser, the assurances of the seller as to the status and performance of the assets being sold, the rights of each party if another party fails to perform as contemplated by the agreement or otherwise breaches its representations and warranties, and the timetable for the closing of the transaction. The purchase agreement can be more easily understood by looking at its key components based on the three critical categories of issues to be addressed as set forth in Figure 11-3.

The asset purchase agreement should be balanced to protect the interests of both parties. From the buyer's perspective, the asset purchase agreement should provide as much detail as possible concerning the status and performance of the business to be acquired; shift risk to the seller by establishing grounds for the buyer to terminate the transaction if the representations and warranties prove untrue and a basis for renegotiation if facts develop indicating that the transaction, as structured, is not what the buyer had bargained for; and provide a basis after closing for the buyer to seek monetary damages from the seller should the representations, warranties, and covenants of the agreement prove untrue.

The asset purchase agreement should provide a means for updating the information delivered to the purchaser by the seller and, if the

Figure 11-3. Understanding Key Components of the Asset Purchase Agreement: Consideration, Mechanics, and Risk Allocation.		
CONSIDERATION	**MECHANICS**	**ALLOCATION OF RISK**
Structure	Conditions to closing	Representations and warranties (R&Ws) two-way street (due diligence driven)
Scope of purchase	Timetable	Indemnification
Price	Covenants (including covenants not to compete)	Holdbacks and baskets
How/when paid	Third-party and regulatory approvals	Escrows
Deferred consideration/security	Schedules (exceptions/ substantiation)	If seller is taking buyer's stock or notes, then R&Ws are a two-way street
Earn-outs and contingent payments	Opinions	Collars
Other ongoing financial relationships between buyer and seller	Dispute resolution	R&W insurance
Employment/consultant agreements	Post-closing conditions	Methods for dealing with surprises
Post-closing adjustments		

transfer of the business is to occur on a date subsequent to the date on which the asset purchase agreement is signed, the asset purchase agreement should include covenants of the seller regarding its conduct of the business from the date of the asset purchase agreement through the closing or termination of the asset purchase agreement.

The initial draft of the asset purchase agreement is prepared by GCC's counsel, as it is the purchaser who is responsible for ensuring that the purchaser acquires the assets and liabilities bargained for without assuming responsibility for any undisclosed obligations of the business or the seller.

An outline of the GCC/TCI asset purchase agreement is as follows:

▶ Recitals identifying TCI and GCC, stating their relative roles, and identifying the assets being sold

► Clauses that provide for the transfer of the assets being sold, the price to be paid and the manner in which the price will be paid (in the event that securities are being issued in payment of the purchase price, methods of valuing those securities might be appropriate in this section), and, in connection with the transfer of assets, provision for the buyer's assumption of liabilities

► Representations and warranties of TCI

► Representations and warranties of GCC

► A statement of the manner in which TCI will conduct the business (including restrictions on certain types of operations or merger purchases) prior to the closing

► Those conditions that are to precede the obligations of GCC to be performed at the closing

► Those conditions that are to precede the obligations of TCI to be performed at the closing

► A summary of the closing itself, the mechanics thereof, and the documents to be delivered at the closing

► Agreements and commitments relating to the relationship of the parties and the activities of the business sold after the closing

► Agreements relating to the survival of the representations and warranties of the parties and, importantly, the indemnification provisions to be provided by TCI and GCC

► For an asset transfer, provisions relating to bulk sales laws

► For a stock transfer, provisions relating to the securities laws and rights to resell securities issued pursuant to registration statements or otherwise

► A provision relating to brokers

► Provisions related to employee benefits

► Miscellaneous provisions, including notices, the completeness of the agreement, the law governing the interpretation of the agreement, whether or not the provisions of the agreement will be severable, and other general provisions desired by the parties

Legal counsel to GCC should also specify all conditions precedent to the obligations of the parties to close the transaction in the asset purchase agreement. Conditions are generally factors that are beyond either party's control, such as regulatory approval or consents, the existence or nonexistence of which will excuse one or both parties from their obligation to close the transaction. The asset purchase agreement should include remedies for losses, liabilities, damages, or expenses arising out of a party's breach either before or after the acquisition.

There is a wide variety of issues in the asset purchase agreement that will be hotly negotiated between TCI and GCC, which are discussed here. Common mistakes in preparing an asset purchase agreement are given in Figure 11-4.

Figure 11-4. Common Mistakes in Preparing and Negotiating the Purchase Agreement

1. *Lack of attention on customization of the R&Ws.* The R&Ws are a key component of the Purchase Agreement that drive rush allocation issues. Yet, sellers often ignore the details and do not give careful thought to what they consider to be boilerplate and legal jargon. A post-closing dispute is *not* a great time for sellers to be reading these clauses for the first time. Similarly, lazy buyers will often plug in standard R&W clauses, failing to customize their specific concerns that they have about the seller's business and/ or specific issues and problems that were identified in the due diligence process.

2. *The inadvertent assumption of liabilities.* Smart buyers use the definitive purchase agreement provisions to hold sellers accountable for certain types of liabilities, but the failure to do so can result in the buyer stepping into the shoes of the seller inadvertently or unwittingly. A buyer inheriting liability that rightfully should have been retained by the seller can have a detrimental impact on the overall economics of the transaction. Be on the lookout for employment discrimination claims, pre-closing tax liabilities, product liability claims, and related issues that are often easily overlooked.

3. *Right deal, wrong structure.* Just as the parties often overfocus on price and underfocus on terms, so, too, can be the case with deal structure. Mistakes can be made when the "deal looks good on paper" but the structure selected is creating a material (and avoidable) adverse liability on one or more of the parties.

Experienced tax advisors should weigh in on the proposed structure *before* the "cement" has dried.

4. ***Sloppy indemnification clauses and procedures.*** From the buyer's perspective, the indemnified language in the purchase agreement should be custom-tailored to the nature of the seller's business and to the specific risks and concerns identified in due diligence. The interplay between time and dollar limits must be carefully considered. Certain types of businesses may be better served by larger time periods even if with smaller dollar sizes, and vice versa for other types of businesses. The clauses should also consider *how* the buyer will collect on a specific indemnification claim once it has been triggered. The consideration may be spread among one hundred or more shareholders—ask *who* will be accountable and push for a larger holdback, which will serve as protection until the indemnification period has expired.

Indemnification. One of the most contested areas is the indemnification provisions, usually because GCC/GCS will want to be reimbursed for any transaction or occurrence that took place before closing that subsequently gives rise to some claim or liability. TCI shareholders, on the other hand, will want to make a "clean break" from any liability attached to the assets being conveyed, including any responsibility for events that arose even before closing.

As discussed earlier in this book, one of the key aspects of an acquisition is the *negotiation and allocation of the risks* to each party, both before and after closing. The goal is to allocate risk in a balanced and economically appropriate manner. The buyer is concerned with both *core risks*, such as those raised by a misrepresentation or breach of covenant by the seller, and *collateral risks*, such as those raised by facts and circumstances that were not necessarily anticipated by the parties at the time of the negotiation. Buyers and their counsel will often seek a full indemnity from the seller against any specific liabilities that have not been assumed by the buyer as part of the transaction and any damages or loss (including costs and expenses) that were incurred as a result of inaccuracy in representations, warranties, or agreements. The party claiming indemnity is required to provide specific written notice of those claims to the other party and permit the other party to contest the claim. The indemnity provisions should provide for mutual access to all personnel and material that may be relevant to the claim and that no claim will be settled without the written consent of the injured party.

Indemnity provisions, along with opinions of counsel, are usually among the most contested negotiated items in a purchase agreement. The key variables to be negotiated, as set forth here, include time (the period of indemnity for post-closing obligations), the deductibles/baskets, the "caps" or ceilings on liability, one measure of damages, and the possible offsets to the seller's obligation to indemnify. The seller will usually be unwilling to provide a comprehensive set of indemnity provisions.

Counsel for the seller may also try to negotiate a "basket" or a "trigger" as part of the trade-off for cash adjustments and no personal liability for the buyer's stockholders. In our example, if the aggregate claims for which GCC demanded to be indemnified did not exceed $250,000, and a basket of $250,000 had been agreed to, no indemnity could be sought and GCC would be entitled to indemnification only for amounts in excess of $250,000. If TCI's counsel suggests that a trigger of $250,000 rather than a basket should be built into the indemnity, then the trigger would provide that GCC could not seek indemnity unless the aggregate amount for which it was to be indemnified exceeded the triggering amount, in this case $250,000. However, once the amount for which the indemnity was sought did exceed $250,000, GCC/GCS would have the right under the indemnity provision to recover from TCI all monies from the first dollar involved. In such a case, the indemnity section could be drafted to state that any remedies available to either party were cumulative, so that they could be exercised one on top of another, and that they could be exercised at any time.

TCI and its advisors will seek a wide variety of additional limitations on the indemnification provisions. In addition to the basket negotiations, TCI could seek to establish a ceiling on overall liability, a limitation on the types of claims for which the seller can be held liable, a limitation on claims to only those for which the seller had actual knowledge (which makes the buyer's burden of proof much higher in the event of a subsequent dispute), a limitation on the types of assets that would be available to repay GCC in the event of a claim, an exclusion of certain parties who will be held liable for certain types of claims, and a limitation on the time after closing (survival), after which GCC/GCS may no longer proceed against the seller for a breach or misrepresentation. It is not uncommon for the seller, in this case TCI, to attempt to negotiate some staged step-down in the amount of the overall indemnification ceilings over time following the closing. Sellers should also be aware of "double-dipping," which occurs when a breach triggers both a purchase price adjustment and a claim for indemnification and is an over-enrichment of the buyer.

A sample negotiated indemnification provision (with a trigger) might look like Figure 11-5.

Note: The indemnification provision would then go on to address the procedures for making an indemnification claim.

M&A Centric Insurance Policies. The seller may also want to investigate obtaining insurance from a third-party provider for inadvertent or negligent violations of the covenants leading to an indemnification claim. Insurance policies of this type have become relatively commonplace, but they typically will not cover fraud, grossly negligent violations of the representations and warranties, or fraudulent breaches of the covenants. As insurance policies have gained credibility over the years, buyers have also begun to recognize the value of insurance policies as a tool to mitigate risk and provide protection against the unknowns. This type of insurance policy is known as Representation and Warranty (R&W). Other types of insurance policies such as Tax Indemnity Insurance and Contingent Liability Insurance protect against known risks that are discovered during the diligence process. Tax Indemnity Insurance is commonly used to insure a tax opinion or backstop, and typically in the case of tax-free reorganizations, liquidating trust status, cancellation of indebtedness, or the treatments of capital gains vs. ordinary income. The cost is generally 4 to 8 percent of the policy limit, though it varies based on the specifics of the transaction, and often no deductible is required. Covered items include additional tax liability, fines and penalties, interest, legal costs, and tax gross-up. Contingent Liability Insurance covers exposure for successor liability, specific indemnities, fraudulent conveyance, or legislative/regulatory risks. It is often tied to a specific issue identified in the diligence process as having a high risk of exposure. However, in order to insure the risk, it must be quantifiable, may not involve moral hazard, and there must be an analysis of the probability. The cost varies depending on the type of risk.

The type of insurance required will depend on various factors including the type of industry, the size of the deal, and the risks identified during the diligence process. As the insurance market continues to grow, companies can customize their policies more creatively with respect to the scope of coverage, liability limits, premium rates, and deductible levels based on their specific needs. The cost is approximately 3 to 4 percent of the policy limit and is often split between the buyer and seller—though this depends on the respective negotiating power of each party.

The terms of the Purchase Agreement will also significantly drive the scope of coverage and terms of the policy. Given that a seller has limited exposure, buyers will seek more comprehensive representations and warranties. However, the parties will need to address the concerns of the insurer as well, who will want to ensure all necessary steps are taken by the buyer and seller to minimize its risk, including reviewing (i) the buyer's diligence review process and findings, (ii) seller's disclosure schedules, and (iii) any other related agreements that implicate the insurer. The insurer will want to be sure the buyer has adequately vetted the seller and understands what risks are involved—though the parties and their attorneys should be mindful that sharing legal due diligence reports with an insurance provider waives privilege. Nevertheless, the insurer will want to understand what level of disclosure is required by the seller (e.g., a monetary threshold set forth in the agreement), and may require the buyer to diligence risks and obligations at a lower threshold. Additionally, disclosures made in the schedules will generally be excluded from coverage.

Other key terms in R&W policies that track the terms of the Purchase Agreement include the definitions of knowledge and losses and materiality scrapes. In insurance policies, knowledge is generally limited to actual knowledge of key members of the buyer's deal team who were involved in the due diligence process. Consequential damages will generally be excluded from insurance policies—unless they are explicitly provided for in the Purchase Agreement, in which case the insurer will strive to keep both the Purchase Agreement and policy consistent. Additionally, terms that are limited by materiality in the Purchase Agreement will be limited in the policy as well. The insurer will also conform the terms of the insurance agreement with respect to the indemnity terms and survival periods, which dictate the period during which the seller is on the hook for claims relating to certain representations and warranties.

Claims relating to certain specific industries may be excluded from coverage, or may require a separate, more specific insurance policy, such as claims related to environmental risks, health-care reimbursements, cyber security, and FCPA. Recently, insurance companies have been seeking every opportunity to minimize their payout obligations and even rescind an entire policy for reasons such as untimely filing of a claim or even a technical error in the insurance application. This increases the risk for buyers, as the process of recovering from an insurance company can be complex—particularly if a seller has enough leverage to eliminate indemnity provisions altogether and require the buyer to rely solely on R&W insurance. The buyer should evaluate the amount of protection it needs when considering such an option.

The most common types of insurance breaches involve provisions relating to financial statements (primarily breach of accounting rules and misstatements of accounts receivable/payable), compliance with laws, intellectual property, and tax. A recent study identified a correlation between deal size and the frequency of claims made. One explanation for this correlation is that the larger the deal size the more difficult and complex the diligence process is, and often there is greater pressure to complete the transaction quickly. Thus there is a greater likelihood that something will be overlooked because parties will focus on what they believe are the high-risk areas in order to efficiently complete the diligence review. Policies typically survive for three to six years, but a majority of claims arise in the first six months, and the second most claims in the first year.

Representations and Warranties. TCI will be expected to make a wide range of written and binding representations and warranties (R&Ws) to GCS. These provisions are designed to broadly articulate information about the transactions as well as to create recourse against TCI in the event of inaccurate disclosures. The R&Ws will include that the sale is not in breach of any other agreement or obligation of TCI, that the assets are free and clear of all clouds on title to the assets, that the assets are in good operating condition, that all material facts have been disclosed, and so forth. Naturally, GCC/GCS will want the scope of the R&Ws to be as broad and comprehensive as possible, primarily because these clauses serve as a form of insurance policy for GCS. GCS will also want to have as many parties as possible be *making* the R&Ws (e.g., not just TCI, but also key shareholders). GCS will also want protection if it turns out that any representation or warranty has been breached, especially in an asset deal, where the selling entity is likely to be an empty shell on a post-closing basis (this is another reason that GCS may insist on key TCI shareholders being parties to the representations and warranties). It will be incumbent on TCI and its counsel to negotiate limitations on the scope of these provisions, where necessary.

Figure 11-5

Indemnification by the Seller. The Seller, TCI, and its shareholders, jointly and severally, covenants and agrees to indemnify, defend, protect, and hold harmless GCC and GCS and their respective officers, directors, employees, stockholders, assigns, successors, and affiliates (individually, an "Indemnified Party" and collectively, "Indemnified Parties") from, against, and in respect of:

(a) all liabilities, losses, claims, damages, punitive damages, causes of action, lawsuits, administrative proceedings (including formal proceedings), investigations, audits, demands, assessments, adjustments, judgments, settlement payments, deficiencies, penalties, fines, interest (including interest from the date of such damages) and costs and expenses (including without limitation reasonable attorneys' fees and disbursements of every kind, nature, and description) (collectively, "Damages") suffered, sustained, incurred, or paid by the GCC Indemnified Parties in connection with, resulting from, or arising directly or indirectly out of:

  (i) any misrepresentation or breach of any warranty of the Sellers, set forth in this Agreement or in any schedule or certificate delivered by or on behalf of the Seller in connection herewith; or

  (ii) any nonfulfillment of any covenant or agreement on the part of any of the Sellers set forth in this Agreement; or

  (iii) the business, operations, or assets of the Sellers prior to the Closing Date or the actions or omissions of the Sellers' directors, officers, shareholders, employees, or agents prior to the Closing Date (except as to the Assumed Liabilities); or

  (iv) failure to comply with country of origin marking requirements imposed by the Federal Trade Commission or by the U.S. Customs and Border Protection, including without limitation damages arising out of breaches of any contract relating to failure to deliver product as required under any contract, or ▼

delivery of nonconforming goods pursuant to any contract, fines, or other penalties for violations of such requirements; or

(v) the Excluded Liabilities.

(b) any and all damages incident to any of the foregoing or to the enforcement of this section.

Limitation and Expiration. Notwithstanding the above:

(a) there shall be no liability for indemnification under Section 7.1 unless, and solely to the extent that, the aggregate amount of damages exceeds $250,000 (the "Indemnification Threshold"); provided, however, that the Indemnification Threshold shall not apply to (i) adjustments to the Purchase Price; (ii) damages arising out of any breaches of the covenants of the Seller set forth in this Agreement or representations made in Sections 3.13 (environmental matters), 3.16 (inventory), 3.19 (employee benefit plans), 3.20 (conformity with law; litigation), 3.21 (taxes), or 3.26 (intellectual property); or (iii) the Excluded Liabilities;

(b) the indemnification obligations under this Section 7 or in any certificate or writing furnished in connection herewith shall terminate on the later of clause (i) or (ii) of this Section 7.2(b):

    (i) (1) third anniversary of the Closing Date, or (2) with respect to representations and warranties contained in Sections 3.14 (real and personal property), 3.19 (employee benefit plans), 3.21 (taxes), and the Excluded Liabilities, on (A) the date that is six (6) months after the expiration of the longest applicable federal or state statute of limitation (including extensions thereof), or (B) if there is no applicable statute of limitation, (x) ten (10) years after the Closing Date; or

    (ii) the final resolution of a claim or demand (a "Claim") pending as of the relevant dates described in clause (i) of this Section 7.2(b) (such claim referred to as a "Pending Claim");

(c) for purposes of the indemnity in this Section 7, all representations contained in Section 3 are made without any limitations as to materiality; and

(d)   for purposes of the Indemnification Threshold, all damages in-
      curred by GCC or any of its affiliates under any of the related
      Acquisition Agreements shall be included within the Indemnifi-
      cation Threshold under this Agreement.

The scope of the representations and warranties contained in the definitive purchase agreement is one of the most difficult aspects of closing a transaction. This is the section in which the TCI shareholders must "represent and warrant" everything about the company that has been told or implied to GCC/GCS. Representations and warranties set forth the financial responsibility for problems that may arise in the future, but that may not exist or be known to the parties at closing. The buyer typically views post-closing events that reduce assets or increase liabilities as being the responsibility of the seller. These provisions set forth the financial responsibility of each party if certain unknown or unforeseen problems arise in the future as a result of an existing sit-uation. In many of the representations and warranties, GCC may be willing to accept the phrase "to the best of the seller's knowledge" as a qualifier to certain provisions. In addition, some matters lend them-selves to outside testing or evaluation by experts. Relying on the reports of outside experts may significantly reduce or even eliminate the need for certain areas to be addressed. In other cases, a time and/or dollar limit on a particular representation or warranty will be sufficient to allow the seller to provide assurances in situations in which it would otherwise be unwilling to do so. For example, a dollar limit is often attached to environmental and product liability representations and warranties. Liability matters. Sellers should make certain that their advisors are familiar with the types of representations and warranties they are likely to face and that the advisors are skilled in finding mutu-ally acceptable positions. During actual negotiations, sellers should make a sincere attempt to understand the buyer's underlying motiva-tion in requesting each warranty and representation and point out any facts or circumstances that may be inconsistent with a given request. In our example, TCI and its counsel should expect that GCC will insist on the following types of representations and warranties:

■ The transaction is not in breach of any license or other agreement or in violation of any order or decree of any court or other government body.

- TCI's business entity is properly organized under state corporate law, is in good standing, and is qualified to do the business it is doing in the states in which it is doing business.

- TCI has clear title to all assets that have been made part of the sale, these assets are not subject to any undisclosed restrictions or claims, and they are in good operating condition.

- TCI has no knowledge or reason to know that its business relationship has changed with any customer or group of customers whose purchases constitute more than a stated percentage (usually 5 percent) of the business's sales for the previous year.

- TCI represents that all required tax returns have been filed and that all required payments have been made.

- Licenses, zoning, and other permissions necessary to conduct TCI's business as it is being conducted have been obtained, and benefits may be transferred to GCC/GCS.

- TCI will need to represent and warrant the following facts regarding the accuracy of its financial statements (as presented to GCC):

  1. The statements fairly present the financial condition of the business as of the date of the statements.
  2. TCI is not subject to any material liability, including contingent liability, that is not reflected or noted in the financial statements.
  3. The statements have been prepared in accordance with generally accepted accounting principles.
  4. Since the date of the statements, TCI has not transferred any assets to or on behalf of any owner or employee other than in payment of customary salaries.

- TCI is not in default on any material contract or loan nor is it aware of any claims pending or threatened against it.

- TCI owns specified patents, trademarks, trade names, and copyrights, and has no knowledge of any claims of infringement pending or threatened.

- TCI is in compliance with all applicable local, state, and federal laws, and has had no notice of any claimed violations.

■ TCI has not engaged or authorized anyone to act as broker or finder in connection with the sale.

Conditions Precedent to Closing. This section is essentially a checklist of events that must occur as a condition to closing the transaction. Both GCS and TCI will have their share of items that must be accomplished and documents or consents that must be signed. The nature and scope of these conditions must be carefully considered, since failure to satisfy them will give the opposing party the right to walk away from the transaction.

Material Adverse Effect/Change (MAE/MAC) Clauses. As a result of the recent credit market turmoil and general adverse economic conditions, there has lately been a significant increase in buyers attempting to renege on previously announced merger and acquisition deals. Although such buyers are advancing a variety of claims and legal theories to support their positions, many of these arguments are based, in whole or in part, on an assertion that the target business has suffered a material adverse effect (MAE), also referred to as a material adverse change (MAC). Such clauses typically provide that if, between the signing and the closing of the transaction, the business being sold suffers a material adverse effect (the definition of which is typically highly negotiated), the buyer is not obligated to close the transaction. Some of these deals have resulted in a reduced purchase price after renegotiations (e.g., the 2009 acquisition of Home Depot Inc.'s supply unit by an investor group led by Bain Capital LLC, the 2008 acquisition of Accredited Home Lenders Inc. by Lone Star Funds, and the two hundred transactions between Exxon Mobil and XTO Energy for $29 billion where the MAE clauses protected the buyer in the event of a change in regulations and ultimately the anticipated changes in the law did happen), some have been terminated by the parties upon mutual agreement (e.g., the merger between MGIC Investment Corp. and Radian Group Inc.), and some have ended up in court (e.g., the acquisition of Genesco Inc. by Finish Line Inc., which resulted in a hotly debated court decision). Both GCS and TCI would ideally want to use the MAE clause, in particular in current times, as a mechanism to allocate the risk of adverse changes to the business being sold between signing and closing. Typically, GCS will try to carve out the narrowest possible exceptions to the MAE clause and seek to include a whole list of events that trigger a right to renege on the deal.

As a procedural matter, case law has established that the party that is seeking to terminate an agreement on account of the fact that the other party has suffered an MAE has the burden of proving that the MAE has occurred. Case law has also shown that, typically, the bar for establishing an MAE is high, and buyers should be cautious about relying on an MAE clause to get out of a deal. However, even though based on case law precedents it may ultimately be difficult for a buyer to establish that a target business suffered an MAE in a fully litigated case, in many instances the mere claim by a buyer that an MAE has occurred may provide the buyer with sufficient leverage and instill in the seller sufficient uncertainty that the parties come to a negotiated resolution long before a court has a chance to rule on the matter. Indeed, the Finish Line decision also proves how important it is to avoid drafting ambiguities, miscommunications, and defeated expectations by sufficiently defining the exceptions to the MAE clause. Another alternative is to make certain events conditions precedent rather than including them in the MAE clause, thus avoiding hotly argued legal issues like "reasonable foreseeability" or "sufficient duration."

Conduct of Business Prior to Closing. TCI must have a contractual obligation to preserve the goodwill of the business and the condition of the assets during the time period between the execution of the purchase agreement and the closing of the transaction. The parties should negotiate all affirmative and negative covenants that will be imposed on the conduct of TCI during this time period, as well as the penalties for noncompliance (e.g., reduction in the purchase price or the ability of GCC to walk away from the deal).

Other Key Agreements in an Asset Purchase

Intercreditor Agreement. An intercreditor agreement is a contract among multiple lenders (in this case TCI and BBC) to a particular borrower (GCC and GCS). The document governs the priority rights of the various lenders in the collateral (the assets acquired by GCC and GCS), otherwise known as subordination. Subordination and standby provisions govern "who gets what proceeds when" in the event of a default by the borrower. In the GCC/TCI transaction, it is likely that BBC and its counsel will prepare this agreement and demand that BBC receive the senior priority rights.

Noncompetition Agreements. Covenants against competition and disclosure of confidential information are commonly a key part of any business acquisition. This is especially true in situations like the GCC/TCI transaction, where the members of the target's management team may be left out of the transaction and are therefore likely candidates to be future competitors. Counsel for GCS will naturally want to include covenants that are broad in terms of the scope of subject matter, duration, and geographic territory. Although these agreements will be carefully scrutinized by the courts as potential restraints of trade, agreements prohibiting sellers from competing against buyers are given considerably more latitude in a business purchase transaction than in other areas, such as employment or consulting agreements.

Earn-Out Agreements. When earn-out agreements are negotiated as part of the purchase price in an acquisition, part of the consideration payable to TCI essentially becomes contingent on the ability of GCS to meet its financial and growth projections. In the GCC/TCI transaction, TCI shareholders are betting on the ability of the GCS management team to manage and operate the assets being acquired in an efficient and profitable manner. If any of the TCI shareholders will become members of the GCS management team, then the earn-out provides an incentive for performance from which both GCC and TCI can gain. The key terms of the earn-out agreement to be negotiated are the formula to be used (e.g., tied to gross sales, earnings, or some other measure); the duration of the earn-out; the floor and ceiling on the payout to be provided to TCI shareholders; the controls that TCI shareholders will have, if any, over the budgets and expenditures made by GCS or GCC; the effect of the business distress or bankruptcy of GCS on the earn-out; and the tax implications of the transaction.

The typical earn-out provides *additional* consideration to the seller if certain financial and/or performance targets are met. But buyers may also want to consider *reverse earn-outs* as an additional *penalty* if performance targets are *not* met. For example, if the seller accepts a combination of cash and promissory notes, the principal of the note or the interest rate could be reduced if minimal performance criteria are not met, representations or warranties are breached, or sales fall below a given level.

Earn-outs can be used as incentives, as equalizers, or as risk-mitigators. As an incentive, the earn-out may be used as a sweetener to motivate the founding entrepreneur (as seller) to stay on board to help build the business after closing or to ensure that a technical or engineering team remains in place after closing. The parties may even make a portion of the earn-out contingent on certain key management or personnel staying with the company for a certain period of time. As an equalizer, it can be used to resolve differing views concerning the valuation of the seller's business, particularly when the seller feels that its stock or assets are being undervalued. As a risk-mitigator, the earn-out can be used to hold a seller's feet to the fire regarding its representations of the future value of the company and to help ensure against overpayment if a buyer is unsure or unclear about the future value of the business.

The key issues to be addressed in the negotiation and structuring of the earn-out provisions include:

- ► The financial formula to be used to determine the contingent payments to be made to the seller (e.g., specified minimum sales levels, net income before taxes, and so on).
- ► The audit and inspection rights to be granted by the seller to ensure against underpayment by the buyer.
- ► The business plan and financial benchmarks that are fair and reasonable over the course of the earn-out period. These performance-driven milestones may be better measuring sticks for the payment of the earn-out than a strict financial formula, especially for high-tech businesses.
- ► The term of the earn-out period, the method and frequency of payment, and the form of consideration itself, such as cash, stock, notes, or warrants.
- ► The relationship of the earn-out to the other liability and risk allocation sections of the acquisition agreement.

SAMPLE SCHEDULE OF DOCUMENTS TO BE EXCHANGED AT A TYPICAL CLOSING

- ► Deeds, bills of sale, and any other documents and instruments that the buyer deems sufficient to transfer title to the seller's assets
- ► Certificate by shareholders that the representations are true as of the closing date and that the shareholders have met their obligations under the agreement

▶ Certificate by officers of the acquired corporation that the representations and warranties are true as of the closing date and that the corporation has met its obligations under the agreement

▶ Duly endorsed stock certificates

▶ Written opinion of the seller's attorney to the effect that, to the best of the attorney's knowledge, all representations are true, the agreement has been duly executed and constitutes a valid obligation of the seller, and the noncompetition agreement is valid and enforceable

▶ Employment agreements

▶ Shareholder incentive agreements

▶ A certified copy of duly adopted resolutions by the board of directors and the shareholders authorizing the sale

▶ A certified copy of the articles of incorporation and bylaws

▶ Incumbency certificate for each person executing documents relating to the sale

▶ Title insurance covering real estate

▶ Releases of any claims that officers or directors may have against the seller or the buyer

▶ Written resignations of certain officers and directors

▶ Letter from accountant certifying the financial statements and certifying that, following inquiries, the accountant has no knowledge of any material adverse change in the business's financial position between the date of the financial statements and closing

▶ Certificate of good standing from each state in which the corporation to be acquired has been doing business

▶ Estoppel certificates from creditors whose debts have been assumed by the buyer

▶ Copy of bulk sales notice (for asset acquisitions)

Scope of the Assets

The typical buyer will want to specify a virtual laundry list of categories of assets to be purchased, but the classic seller will want to modify the list by using words like *exclusively* or *primarily*. The seller may want to exclude all or most of the cash on hand from the schedule of assets to be transferred. In some cases, the seller may want to license some of the technology rights in lieu of selling them outright, or, at the very least, license back what has been sold.

Security for the Seller's Take-Back Note

When the seller is taking back a note from the buyer for all or part of the consideration, the issue of security for the note is always a problem. Naturally, the seller will want noncontingent personal and corporate guarantees from the buyer and from anyone else that it can manage to get. The buyer will be reluctant to offer such broad security. Several "creative" compromises have been reached between the parties, including partial or limited guarantees, the acceleration of the note based on post-closing performance, the right to repurchase the assets in the event of a default, the issuance of warrants or preferred stock in the event of default, commercial lender–like covenants to prevent the buyer from getting into a position where it is unable to pay the note (such as dividend restrictions, limitations on excessive salaries, limitations on excessive or risky investments, and so on), or contingent consulting agreements in the event of a default.

Who's on the Hook for the Financial Statements?

The financial statements provided by the seller to the buyer in connection with the due diligence and prior to closing are often a hotly contested item. The timing and scope of the financial statements and the standard to which they will be held are at issue. The buyer and its team may prefer a "hot-off-the-press" and recently completed audited set of financials from a Big 4 or major regional accounting firm, and the seller will want to serve up a "best efforts" unaudited and uncertified guesstimate. Somewhere in between is where most deals wind up, with verbiage such as "of a nature customarily reflected," "prepared in substantial accordance with GAAP," and "fairly present the financial condition" being bantered around. The scope of the liabilities included on the statements and who will bear responsibility for unknown or undisclosed liabilities will also be negotiated in the context of the overall discussion of the financial statements.

Playing with the Buzzwords

Any veteran transactional lawyer knows that there are certain key "buzzwords" that can be inserted into sections of the purchase agreement that will detract or enhance or even shift liability by and among the buyer and seller. Depending on which side of the fence you are on, look out for words or phrases like the following as tools for negotiation and as phrases:

- ▶ "materially"
- ▶ "to the best of our knowledge"
- ▶ "could possibly"
- ▶ "without any independent investigation"
- ▶ "except for . . ."
- ▶ "subject to . . ."
- ▶ "reasonably believes . . ."
- ▶ "ordinary course of business"
- ▶ "to which we are aware"
- ▶ "would not have a material adverse effect on . . ."
- ▶ "primarily relating to . . ."
- ▶ "substantially all"
- ▶ "solely"
- ▶ "might" (instead of "would")
- ▶ "exclusively"
- ▶ "other than claims that may be less than $"
- ▶ "have received no written notice of . . ."
- ▶ "have used our best efforts (or commercially reasonable efforts) to . . ."
- ▶ "endeavor to . . ."

The Existence and Scope of the Non-compete

It is only natural for the buyer to expect that the seller will agree to stay out of the business being sold for some reasonable amount of time. Depending on the seller's stage of life and post-closing plans, which may include actual retirement, the parties are likely to argue over the scope, duration, and geographic focus of the covenant against noncompetition. The more difficult issues often arise when a conglomerate is spinning off a particular division or line of business and the remaining divisions will continue to operate in industries similar or parallel to the business being sold to the buyer. The allocation of the purchase price to a non-compete covenant raises certain tax issues that must be analyzed, and these covenants may have only limited enforceability under applicable state laws if their scope or duration is deemed to be unreasonable or excessive.

Allocation of Risk

As discussed earlier in this chapter, the heart and soul of the purchase agreement is, in many ways, merely a tool for *allocating risk*. The buyer will want to hold the seller accountable for any post-closing claim or liability that arises relating to a set of facts that occurred while the seller owned the company or that has occurred as a result of a misrepresentation or material omission by the seller. The seller, on the other hand, wants to bring as much finality to the transaction as possible to allow some degree of sleep at night. Like a children's game of "hot potato," risks are shifted back and forth in the negotiations until settled at closing. When both parties are represented by skilled negotiators, a middle ground is reached, both in general and on specific issues of actual or potential liability. The buyer's counsel will want to draft changes, covenants, representations, and warranties that are strong and absolute, and the seller's counsel will seek to insert phrases like "except insignificant defaults or losses that have not, or are not likely to, at any time before or after the closing, result in a material loss or liability to or against the buyer," leaving some wiggle room for insignificant or nonmaterial claims. The battleground will be the indemnification provisions and any exceptions, carve-outs, or baskets that are created to dilute these provisions. The weapons will be the buzzwords referred to earlier.

As a reference point, an abbreviated version of the asset purchase agreement for use in the GCC/TCI transaction is provided as Figure 11-6. This sample agreement is included to give the reader a feel for what the starting point or first draft of the agreement will look like before the negotiation process begins.

Figure 11-6. GCC/TCI Asset Purchase Agreement

THIS ASSET PURCHASE AGREEMENT ("Agreement") is made and entered into this _____ day of _____ , 20__ , by and among Growth Co. Corp., a Maryland corporation (the "Buyer") and Target Co., Inc., a New York corporation (the "Seller"), and Jane C. Doe and John F. Doe individually (each a "Shareholder" and collectively, the "Shareholders").

W I T N E S S E T H :

WHEREAS, the Seller is engaged in the equipment manufacturing business and activities related thereto (herein referred to as the "Business"); and

WHEREAS, Seller and the Shareholders (constituting all of the beneficial shareholders of the Seller), desire to sell, convey, transfer, assign and deliver to Buyer the Business and substantially all of the assets, properties and operations used in the Business, and Buyer desires to purchase the Business and such assets, properties and operations, on the terms and subject to conditions contained in this Agreement, and other agreements related hereto.

NOW, THEREFORE, in consideration of the mutual benefits to be derived from this Agreement, the receipt and sufficiency of which are hereby acknowledged, the parties hereto hereby agree as follows:

1. SALE AND PURCHASE OF ASSETS.

1.1 *Sale of Assets to Buyer.* Upon the terms and subject to the conditions herein set forth, at the Closing referred to in Section 3, Seller shall sell, transfer, assign, convey and deliver to Buyer, and Buyer shall purchase and acquire from Seller, all of the properties, assets and goodwill that are used in the Business, of whatever kind and nature, real or personal, tangible or intangible (including all rights of the Seller arising from its operation of the Business) and excluding only those assets referred to in Section 1.2 of this Agreement (collectively, the "Assets"), as those Assets exist on the Closing Date (as defined in Section 3). The Assets include, but are not limited to, the following:

(a) all of Seller's machinery, equipment, equipment leases, chemicals, supplies, vehicles, furniture, fixtures, tools, computers and all other personal property, wherever located, which are used in the Business, including, but not limited to, the items listed on *Schedule 1.1(a)*;

(b) all interests of Seller in real property, including leases, options, rights of way, zoning and development rights and easements described in *Schedule 1.1(b)*;

(c) all inventory of Seller used in the Business, wherever located, including, without limitation, the parts, chemicals and materials listed on *Schedule 1.1(c)*;

(d) all of Seller's computer software used in the Business, and all rights, title and interest of Seller in, to and under all trademarks, trademark rights, trademark applications, patents, patent rights, patent applications, trade secrets, inventions, training and equipment manuals, technology, methods, manufacturing, engineering, technical and any other know-how, processes, projects in development, trade names, service marks, other intellectual property rights, and other proprietary information of the Seller used in or relating to the Business. All material intellectual property, including all trade names and patents used or held by Seller, are listed on *Schedule 1.1(d)*;

(e) all of Seller's rights under any written or oral contracts, unfilled service and/or purchase orders, agreements, leases, instruments, registrations, licenses, certificates, distribution agreements or other documents, commitments, arrangements or authorizations relating to the Business, including, but not limited to, the agreements and other instruments identified on *Schedule 1.1(e)* (the "Contracts"); *provided*, that nothing contained in this Agreement shall be construed as an attempt to agree to assign any contract which is by itself non-assignable without the consent of the other party or parties thereto, unless such consent shall be given;

(f) all rights in connection with all permits, certificates, licenses, approvals, registrations and authorizations of Seller which may be necessary or desirable in order to conduct the Business (the "Permits");

(g) all of Seller's rights under manufacturers' and vendors' warranties relating to those items included in the Assets and all of Seller's similar rights against third parties relating to items included in the Assets;

(h) all of Seller's accounts receivable, notes and other receivables, unbilled costs and fees, all prepaid items, amounts on deposit of Seller, and other current assets existing on the Closing Date, including, but not limited to, the receivables and other assets set forth on *Schedule 1.1(h)*, but excluding cash and cash equivalents;

(i) all goodwill, customer and vendor lists, telephone numbers, and other intangible property, and all of Seller's rights to commence or maintain future and existing actions relating to the operation of the Business or the ownership of the Assets, for events occurring after the Closing Date, and the right to settle those actions and retain the proceeds therefrom;

(j) all shares of stock and partnership interests owned by Seller, if any;

(k) all of Seller's rights under the insurance or similar policies in effect on or prior to the Closing Date set forth on *Schedule 1.1(k)*;

(l) all financial, operational, and any other files, logs, books and records and data of the Business of Seller, (collectively, "Books and Records") and including, without limitation, all correspondence, accounting records, personnel records, purchase orders and invoices, customer records, supplier records, advertising and promotional materials and files, and other business records which are owned by Seller relating to the Business.

1.2 *Excluded Assets.* The following assets (the "Excluded Assets") shall be retained by the Seller and shall not be sold or assigned to Buyer:

(a) all cash on hand and cash equivalents (excluding the prepaid proceeds from the Baxter Contract) and cash-value life and other split-life insurance policies of Seller;

(b) the corporate minute books and stock books of Seller; and

(c) any lease, commitment or other agreement listed on *Schedule 1.2(c)* with respect to which the Buyer does not desire to acquire concurrent with its purchase of the Assets under this Agreement, including any employee advance.

1.3 *Method of Conveyance.* The sale, transfer, conveyance, and assignment by the Seller of the Assets to the Buyer in accordance with Section 1.1 hereof shall be effected on the Closing Date by the Seller's execution and delivery to the Buyer of a general assignment and bill of sale, in substantially the form attached hereto as *Exhibit A* (the "General Assignment and Bill of Sale"). At the Closing, all of the Assets shall be transferred by the Seller to the Buyer free and clear of any and all liens, encumbrances, mortgages, security interests, pledges, claims, equities, and other restrictions or charges of any kind or nature whatsoever (collectively, "Liens") except for a lessor's interest in any leased assets or as otherwise listed in *Schedule 4.5(a)*.

2. PURCHASE PRICE. The purchase price to be paid by the Buyer for the Assets to be sold, transferred, and conveyed by the Seller pursuant to this Agreement shall be:

(a) cash in the amount of Three Million Dollars ($3,000,000), paid by cashier's check or wire transfer, subject to adjustment as described in Section 2.2; and

(b) two promissory notes, one for the principal amount of Five Hundred Thousand Dollars ($500,000) (the "Short-Term Note"); and the second for the principal amount of Eight Hundred Thousand Dollars ($800,000) (the "Long-Term Note" and, together with the Short-Term Note (the "Notes"), each Note subject to adjustment as described in Sections 2.3(a) and 2.3(b), in the forms attached hereto as *Exhibits B-1 and B-2*, with the Short-Term Note secured by a pledge of marketable securities pursuant to a Pledge Agreement and a Stock Power in the forms attached hereto as *Exhibit C* and *Exhibit D*.

3. CLOSING.

3.1 *Date of Closing.* Subject to the terms and conditions set forth herein, the closing of the transactions contemplated hereby (the "Closing") shall be held at 10:00 a.m. at the offices of counsel for the Seller on or before _____, 20__, provided that all conditions to the Closing have been satisfied, or at such other time, date, and place as shall be fixed by agreement among the parties hereto. The date on which the Closing shall occur is referred to herein as the "Closing Date." At the Closing, the parties shall execute and deliver the documents referred to in Section 3.2.

3.2   *Items to be Delivered at Closing.* At the Closing and subject to the terms and conditions herein contained:

(a)   Seller shall deliver or cause to be delivered to Buyer the following:

(i)   one or more Bills of Sale and such other good and sufficient instruments and documents of conveyance and transfer executed by Seller, in a form reasonably satisfactory to Buyer and its counsel, as shall be necessary and effective to transfer and assign to and vest in Buyer all of Seller's right, title, and interest in and to the Assets, including without limitation, (A) good and valid title in and to all of the Assets owned by Seller, (B) good and valid leasehold interests in and to all of the Assets leased by Seller as lessee, and (C) all of the Seller's rights under all agreements, contracts, instruments and other documents included in the Assets to which Seller is a party or by which it has rights on the Closing Date;

(ii)   all third-party consents required to be delivered as a condition to Closing as set forth in Section 8.2(d), which may be necessary or desirable in connection with the transfer of the Assets, including the Contracts and the Permits;

(iii) all of the agreements, contracts, commitments, leases, plans, computer programs and software, data bases whether in the form of computer tapes or otherwise, manuals and guidebooks, customer lists, supplier lists, and other documents, books, records, papers, files, office supplies, and data belonging to the Seller which are part of the Assets;

(iv) one or more Assignment and Assumption Agreements executed by Seller;

(v)   executed lease for the Seller's home offices (the "Darien Property"), attached hereto as *Exhibit M* and assignment of lease for the Seller's Wisconsin warehouse and office (the "Wisconsin Property"), transferring the leasehold and subleasehold interests in said properties to Buyer;

(vi) a written opinion of Joseph P. Doe, Esq., counsel for Seller, dated the Closing Date, in the form of *Exhibit F* hereto;

(vii) a certificate, signed by a duly authorized officer of the Seller and dated the Closing Date, representing that the conditions contained in Section 8.2(b) of this Agreement have been satisfied;

(viii) certified copies of resolutions of the Seller's Board of Directors and its Shareholders with respect to the approval of this Agreement and the transactions contemplated hereby (*Exhibit O*);

(ix) Employment Agreements, executed by Jane C. Doe and John F. Doe, respectively (*Exhibit G* and *Exhibit H*, respectively); and

(x)   any other opinions, certificates, or other documents and instruments required herein to be delivered by the Seller or the Shareholders.

(b) Buyer shall deliver or cause to be delivered to the Seller the following:

(i)   the Purchase Price pursuant to Section 2 hereof;

(ii) a certificate, signed by a duly authorized officer of the Buyer and dated the Closing Date, representing that the conditions contained in Section 8.1(a) of this Agreement have been satisfied;

(iii) certified copies of resolutions of the Manager of the Buyer with respect to the approval of this Agreement and the transactions contemplated hereby;

(iv) executed counterparts of the lease amendments with respect to the Darien and Wisconsin Properties;

(v)   the executed Promissory Notes;

(vi)   the Operating Agreement of the Buyer, providing for the Equity Interest in the Buyer to be issued to Seller, in accordance with Section 2.1(c) hereof;

(vii)   the Pledge Agreement and the Pledged Collateral Account Agreement executed by the Pledgor in accordance with Section 8.1(f) hereof;

(viii) executed Employment Agreements as provided in Section 8.2(f); and

(ix)   any other certificates or other documents and instruments required herein to be delivered by Buyer.

4. REPRESENTATIONS AND WARRANTIES OF THE SELLER. In order to induce the Buyer to enter into this Agreement and to consummate the transactions contemplated hereby, the Seller and each of the Shareholders, jointly and severally, hereby represent and warrant to the Buyer as follows:

4.1 *Organization and Authority.* Seller is a corporation duly organized, validly existing, and in good standing under the laws of the State of Illinois. Seller has the full power and authority to enter into and perform this Agreement, to own, operate, and lease its properties and assets, to carry on its business as it is now being conducted, and to execute, deliver, and perform its obligations under this Agreement and consummate the transactions contemplated hereby. Each Shareholder has the full power and authority to enter into and perform this Agreement. Seller has delivered to the Buyer complete and correct copies of its Articles of Incorporation and Bylaws, each as amended to date. Seller is duly qualified to do business as a foreign corporation and in good standing in Anytown.

4.2 *Authorization of Agreement.* The execution, delivery, and performance by the Seller of this Agreement and of each and every document and instrument contemplated hereby and the consummation of the transactions contemplated hereby and thereby have been duly and validly authorized and approved by all necessary corporate action of the Seller. This Agreement has been duly executed and delivered by the Seller and by each of the Shareholders and constitutes (and, when executed and delivered, each such other document and instrument will constitute) a valid and binding obligation of the Seller and each of the Shareholders, enforceable against the Seller and each of the Shareholders in accordance with its terms.

4.3 *Capitalization and Share Ownership of Seller.* The Seller's authorized capital stock consists of one thousand (1,000) shares of common stock, no par value. There are 1,000 shares of the Seller's common stock presently outstanding, all of which shares are owned by the Shareholders, free and clear of all Liens. All of the Shareholders' shares have been duly authorized and validly issued, are fully paid and nonassessable. No equity securities (or debt securities convertible into equity securities) of the Seller, other than the Shareholders' shares, are issued and outstanding. There are no existing contracts, subscriptions, options, warrants, calls, commitments, or other rights of any character to purchase or otherwise acquire any common stock or other securities of the Seller.

4.4 *Non-Contravention; Consents and Approvals.*

(a) Neither the execution and delivery by the Seller of this Agreement nor the consummation by the Seller or the Shareholders of the transactions contemplated hereby, nor compliance by the Seller or the Shareholders with any of the provisions hereof, will (i) conflict with or result in a breach of any provision of the Articles of Incorporation or Bylaws of the Seller, (ii) result in the breach of, or conflict with, any of the terms and conditions of, or constitute a default (with or without the giving of notice or the lapse of time or both) with respect to, or result in the cancellation or termination of, or the acceleration of the performance of any obligations or of any indebtedness under, any contract, agreement, lease, commitment, indenture, mortgage, note, bond, license, or other instrument or obligation to which the Seller or any Shareholder is a party or by which the Seller, the Shareholders, or any of the Assets may be bound or affected, (other than such breaches, conflicts, and defaults set forth in *Schedule 4.4(a)* hereto, which shall have been waived at or prior to the Closing), (iii) result in the creation of any Lien upon any of the Assets, or (iv) violate any law or any

rule or regulation of any administrative agency or governmental body, or any order, writ, injunction, or decree of any
court, administrative agency, or governmental body to which
the Seller, the Shareholders, or any of the Assets may be
subject.

(b) Except as set forth in *Schedule 4.4(b)* hereto, no approval,
authorization, consent, or other order or action of, or filing
with, or notice to any court, administrative agency, or other
governmental authority or any other person is required for
the execution and delivery by Seller or the Shareholders of
this Agreement or the consummation by the Seller and the
Shareholders of the transactions contemplated hereby.

(c) A description of all Permits held by Seller and necessary
or desirable for the operation of the Business are set forth
in *Schedule 4.4(c)* hereto. All Permits listed in *Schedule
4.4(c)* are valid, and neither Seller nor any Shareholder has
received any notice that any government authority intends to
modify, cancel, terminate, or deny renewal of any Permit. No
current or former stockholder, officer, director, or employee
of Seller or any affiliate of Seller owns or has any proprietary, financial, or other interest in any Permit which Seller
owns or uses. Seller has conducted the Business in compliance with the requirements, standards, criteria, and conditions set forth in the Permits and other applicable orders,
approvals, variances, rules, and regulations and is not in
violation of any of the foregoing. The transactions contemplated by this Agreement will not result in a default under
or a breach of or violation of or adversely affect the rights
and benefits afforded to the Seller by any Permits. Except
as set forth in *Schedule 4.4(c)* hereto, no approval by a governmental authority is required for transfer to Buyer of such
Permits.

4.5 *Ownership of Assets*

(a) the Seller has and will have at the Closing good, valid, and
marketable title to each and every item of the tangible and
intangible personal property and assets included in the
Assets, and valid leasehold interests in all leases of tangible

personal and real property included in the Assets, free and clear of any Liens except as set forth in *Schedule 4.5(a)*. At the Closing, the Seller will transfer to Buyer good, valid, and marketable title to the Assets, free and clear of any and all Liens, except as set forth in *Schedule 4.5(a)*.

(b) No affiliate of the Seller has, or has indirectly acquired, any right, title, or interest in or to any of the Assets.

(c) The Seller has not sold, transferred, assigned, or conveyed any of its right, title, and interest, or granted or entered into any option to purchase or acquire any of its right, title, or interest, in and to any of the Assets or the Business. No third party has any option or right to acquire the Business or any of the Assets.

4.6 *Balance Sheet; Existing Condition; Ordinary Course.* Attached hereto as *Schedule 4.6* are (i) the Seller's unaudited balance sheet (the "2016 Balance Sheet") as of December 31, 2006 (the "Balance Sheet Date"), together with the related unaudited statements of income, shareholders equity, and cash flows for the year then ended, and (ii) the Seller's unaudited balance sheets as of December 2015 and 2014, together with the related unaudited statements of income, shareholders equity, and cash flows for the years ended December 31, 2015, and 2014 (such unaudited financial statements for 2014, 2015, and 2016 being referred to herein collectively as the "Financial Statements"). The Financial Statements (i) are true, complete, and correct, (ii) are in accordance with the books and records of the Seller, (iii) fairly, completely, and accurately present the financial position of the Seller as of the respective dates thereof and the results of the Seller's operations for the periods presented, and (iv) were prepared in conformity with generally accepted accounting principles consistently applied throughout the periods covered thereby. Since the Balance Sheet Date, except as set forth in *Schedule 4.6* hereto, there has not been with respect to the Seller:

(a) any material adverse change in the Assets or the Business of the Seller from their condition as set forth on the 2016 Balance Sheet;

(b) any damage, destruction, or loss, whether covered by insurance or not, materially and adversely affecting the Business or Assets of the Seller or any sale, transfer, or other disposition of the Assets other than in the ordinary course of business;

(c) any declaration, setting aside, or payment of any dividend, or any distribution with respect to the capital stock of the Seller, or any direct or indirect redemption, purchase, or other acquisition by the Seller of shares of its capital stock, or any payment to any affiliate of any intercompany payable or any transfer of Assets to any affiliate; or

(d) except as set forth on *Schedule 4.6(d)*, any increase in the compensation payable by the Seller to any Shareholder or any of the Seller's officers, employees, or agents, or in the payment of any bonus, or in any insurance, payment, or arrangement made to, for, or with any such officers, employees, or agents.

Since the Balance Sheet Date, Seller has conducted its Business in the ordinary course and has made no material change to its marketing, purchasing, collections, or accounting procedures.

4.7 *Litigation.* There is no litigation, suit, proceeding, action, claim, or investigation, at law or in equity, pending or, to the best knowledge of the Seller or any Shareholder, threatened against, or affecting in any way the Assets, the Seller, or any Shareholder's ability to own or operate the Business, or which questions the validity of this Agreement or challenges any of the transactions contemplated hereby or the use of the Assets after the Closing by the Buyer. Neither the Seller, nor any of the Shareholders, nor any of the Assets is subject to any judgment, order, writ, injunction, or decree of any court or any federal, state, municipal, or other governmental authority, department, commission, board, bureau, agency, or other instrumentality.

4.8 *Compliance with Laws.* Except as set forth in *Schedule 4.8*, the Seller's Business has at all times been conducted in compliance with all applicable laws, regulations, ordinances, and other requirements of governmental authorities (including applicable federal, state, and local laws, rules, and regulations respecting occupational safety and health standards). Except as set forth in *Schedule 4.8*, neither the Seller nor any Shareholder has received any notice, advice, claim, or complaint from any employee or governmental authority that the Seller has not conducted, or is not presently conducting, its business and operations in accordance with all applicable laws and other requirements of governmental authorities.

4.9 *Permits and Licenses.* The Seller has all permits, certificates, licenses, approvals, registrations, and authorizations required in connection with the conduct of the Business. The Seller is not in violation of, and has not violated, any applicable provisions of any such permits, certificates, licenses, approvals, registrations, or authorizations. Except as set forth on *Schedule 4.9*, all permits, certificates, licenses, approvals, registrations, and authorizations of the Seller which are necessary for the operation of the Seller's Business are freely transferable.

4.10 *Contracts.*

(a) *Schedule 4.10(a)* contains a true and complete list of all material contracts and agreements related to or involving the Business or the Assets or by which any of the Assets is subject or bound in any material respect, including, without limiting the generality of the foregoing, any and all: contracts and agreements for the purchase, sale, or lease of inventory, goods, materials, equipment, hardware, supplies, or other personal property; contracts for the purchase, sale, or lease of real property; contracts and agreements for the performance or furnishing of services; joint venture, partnership or other contracts, agreements, or arrangements involving the sharing of profits; employment agreements; and agreements containing any covenant or covenants which purport to limit the ability or right of the Seller or any other person or entity to engage in any aspects of the business related to the Assets or compete in any aspect of such business with any person or entity (collectively, the "Scheduled Contracts"). As used herein, the terms "contract" and "agreement" mean and include every material contract, agreement, commitment, arrangement, understanding, and promise whether written or oral. A complete and accurate copy of each written Scheduled Contract has been delivered or made available to the Buyer or, if oral, a complete and accurate summary thereof has been delivered to the Buyer. Except as set forth on *Schedule 4.10(a)*, the Scheduled Contracts are valid, binding, and enforceable in accordance with their respective terms, are in full force and effect, and were entered into in the ordinary course of business on an "arms-length" basis and consistent with past practices. The Seller is not in breach or default of any of the Scheduled Contracts and, except as set forth on *Schedule 4.10(a)*, no occurrence or circumstance exists which constitutes (with or without the giving of notice or the lapse of time or both) a breach or default by the other party thereto. Neither the Seller nor any Shareholder has been notified or advised by any party to a Scheduled Contract of such party's intention or desire to terminate or modify any such contract or agreement. Neither the Seller nor any Shareholder has granted any Lien on any Scheduled Contract included in the Assets.

(b) Except as set forth on *Schedule 4.10(b)* and this Agreement, neither the Seller nor any Shareholder is a party to, and neither the Seller nor any Shareholder nor any of the Assets is subject or bound in any respect by any written or oral contract and agreement related to or involving the Business which will affect in any manner the Buyer's ownership, use, or operation of the Assets, including, without limitation, any contracts or agreements (i) for the purchase, sale or lease of inventory, goods, or equipment or for the performance or furnishing of services; (ii) for the furnishing of services for which the Seller has received payment in advance of furnishing such services and has not yet furnished such services; and (iii) containing any covenant or covenants which purport to limit the ability or right of the Seller or any other person or entity to engage in any aspects of the business related to the Assets or compete in any aspect of such business with any person or entity.

(c) Except as set forth on *Schedule 4.10(c)*, all Scheduled Contracts included in the Assets will be fully and validly assigned to the Buyer as of the Closing.

(d) Except as set forth in *Schedule 4.10(d)*, there is no Scheduled Contract or any other Contract included in the Assets which cannot be terminated without any further obligation, payment, or penalty upon thirty (30) days' notice or more to the other party or parties to such Contract.

4.11 *Condition of Purchased Assets.* Each and every one of the tangible Assets to be purchased by Buyer pursuant to this Agreement is in good operating condition and repair, ordinary wear and tear excepted, and is fit and suitable for the purposes for which they are currently used by Seller. The Assets include all of the properties and assets of Seller required, necessary, or desirable to enable Buyer to conduct the operation of the Business in the same manner in which the Business has been conducted prior to the date hereof by Seller.

4.12 *Customers.* Seller has delivered to Buyer a complete and accurate list of all customers which has been included in *Schedule 4.12*. Except as set forth in *Schedule 4.12*, no current customer (i) has cancelled, suspended, or otherwise terminated its relationship with the Seller or (ii) has advised the Seller or any of the Shareholders of its intent to cancel, suspend, or otherwise terminate such relationship, or to materially decrease its usage of the services provided by Seller.

4.13 *Employee Benefit Plans.* Except as set forth in *Schedule 4.13*, there are not currently, nor have there ever been, any Benefit Plans (defined below) in place or established by Seller. "Benefit Plan" means any bonus, incentive compensation, deferred compensation, pension, profit sharing, retirement, stock purchase, stock option, stock ownership, stock appreciation rights, phantom stock, leave of absence, layoff, vacation, day or dependent care, legal services, cafeteria, life, health, accident, disability, workmen's compensation, or other insurance, severance, separation, or other employee benefit plan, practice, policy, or arrangement of any kind, whether written or oral, including, but not limited to, any "employee benefit plan" within the meaning of Section 3(3) of ERISA. All group health plans of the Seller have been operated in compliance with all applicable federal and state laws and regulations.

4.14 *Warranties. Schedule 4.14* sets forth a complete and correct copy of all of the Seller's standard warranties (collectively, the "Warranties" or individually a "Warranty") currently extended by the Seller to the customers of the Seller. There are no warranty claims outstanding against the Seller.

4.15 *Trademarks, Patents, Etc.* Except as set forth in *Schedule 4.15*, the Seller does not own or have any rights to any patents, trademarks, trade names, brand names, service marks, service names, copyrights, inventions, or licenses and rights and applications with respect to the foregoing (collectively, the "Marks and Patents"). All the Marks and Patents are valid and have not been abandoned, and there are no prior claims, controversies, lawsuits, or judgments which affect the validity of the Seller's rights to the Marks and Patents nor are there any legal proceedings, claims, or controversies instituted, pending, or, to the best knowledge of the Seller or the Shareholders, threatened with respect to any of the Marks and Patents, or which challenge the Seller's rights, title, or interest in respect thereto. Except as set forth on *Schedule 4.15*, none of the Marks and Patents are the subject of any outstanding assignments, grants, licenses, liens, obligations, or agreements, whether written, oral, or implied. All required renewal fees, maintenance fees, amendments, and/or other filings or payments which are necessary to preserve and maintain the Marks and Patents have been filed and/or made. The Seller owns or has the right to use all Marks and Patents and the like necessary to conduct its Business as presently conducted and without conflict with any patent, trade name, trademark, or the like of any other person or entity.

4.16 *Insurance.* Set forth in *Schedule 4.16* is a complete and accurate list of all insurance policies which the Seller maintains with respect to its Business or the Assets. Such policies are in full force and effect. Such policies, with respect to their amounts and types of coverage, are adequate to insure fully against risks to which the Seller, the Business, or the Assets are normally exposed in the operation of the Business. There has not been any material adverse change in the Seller's relationship with its insurers or in the premiums payable pursuant to such policies. The insurance coverage provided by the Seller's insurance policies shall not be affected by, and shall not lapse or otherwise be terminated by, reason of the execution of this Agreement. Neither the Seller nor either Shareholder has received any notice respecting the cancellation of such insurance policies.

4.17 *Environmental Matters.*

   (a) Except as set forth on *Schedule 4.17(a)* attached hereto, Seller has obtained all permits, licenses, and other authorizations (collectively, the "Licenses") which are required in connection with the conduct of the Business under all applicable Environmental Laws (as defined below) and regulations relating to pollution or protection of the environment, including Environmental Laws and regulations relating to emissions, discharges, releases, or threatened releases of pollutants, contaminants, chemicals, or industrial, toxic, or hazardous substances or wastes into the environment (including without limitation, ambient air, surface water, groundwater, or land) or otherwise relating to the manufacture, processing, distribution, use, treatment, storage, disposal, transport, or handling of pollutants, contaminants, chemicals, or industrial, toxic, or hazardous substances or wastes.

   (b) Except as set forth in *Schedule 4.17(b)*, Seller is in substantial compliance in the conduct of the Business with all terms and conditions of the Licenses and is in substantial compliance with all other limitations, restrictions, conditions, standards, prohibitions, requirements, obligations, schedules, and timetables contained in the Environmental Laws or contained in any regulation, code, plan, order, decree, judgment, injunction, notice (written or verbal), or demand letter issued, entered, promulgated, or approved thereunder.

   (c) Except as set forth on *Schedule 4.17(c)*, neither Seller nor any Shareholder is aware of, nor has Seller received any written or verbal notice of, any past, present, or future events, conditions, circumstances, activities, practices, incidents, actions, or plans which may interfere with or prevent compliance or continued compliance with any Environmental Laws or any regulations, code, order, decree, judgment, injunction, notice (written or verbal), or demand

letter issued, entered, promulgated, or approved thereunder, or which may give rise to any common law or legal
liability, or otherwise form the basis of any claim, action,
demand, suit, proceeding, hearing, study, or investigation
based on or related to the Seller's, processing, storage, distribution, use, treatment, disposal, transport, or handling,
or the emission, discharge, release, or threatened release
into the environment, of any pollutant, contaminant, chemical, or industrial, toxic, or hazardous substance or waste.

(d) There is no civil, criminal, or administrative action, suit,
demand, claim, hearing, notice, or demand letter, notice of
violation, investigation, or proceeding pending or threatened
against Seller or the Shareholders in connection with the
conduct of the Business relating in any way to any Environmental Laws or regulation, injunction, notice, or demand
letter issued, entered, promulgated, or approved thereunder.

(e) For purposes of this Agreement, "Environmental Laws"
means collectively, all federal, state, and local environmental
laws, common law, statutes, rules, and regulations including,
without limitation, the Comprehensive Environmental Response, Compensation and Liability Act (42 U.S.C. Sec.
9061 et seq.), as amended, the Hazardous Materials Transportation Act (49 U.S.C. Sec. 1801 et seq.), as amended,
the Resource Conservation and Recovery Act (42 U.S.C.
Sec. 6901 et seq.), as amended, the Federal Water Pollution
Control Act (33 U.S.C. Sec. 1251 et seq.), as amended, the
Safe Drinking Water Act (42 U.S.C. Sec. 300f et seq.), as
amended, the Clean Air Act (42 U.S.C. Sec. 7401 et seq.),
as amended, the Toxic Substances Control Act (15 U.S.C.
Sec. 2601 et seq.), as amended, the Federal Emergency
Planning and Community Right-to-Know Act (42 U.S.C. Sec.
11001 et seq.), as amended, any so-called "superfund" or
"super-lien" law and such statutes and ordinances as may
be enacted by state and local governments with jurisdiction
over any real property now owned or leased by the Seller
or any real property upon which the Seller now conducts
its Business and any permits, licenses, authorizations, variances, consents, approvals, directives, or requirements of,
and any agreements with, any governments, departments,

commissions, boards, courts, authorities, agencies, officials, and officers applicable to such real property or the
use thereof and regulating, relating to, or imposing liability
or standards of conduct concerning any pollutant, contaminant, chemical, or industrial, toxic, or hazardous substance
or waste.

4.18 *Notes, Accounts, or Other Receivables.* Set forth on *Schedule
1.1(h)* is a complete list of Seller's notes, accounts, or other
receivables included in the Assets as existing on the Closing
Date and included in the Estimated Accounts Receivable valuation pursuant to Section 2.2. All of the Seller's notes, accounts,
or other receivables included on *Schedule 1.1(h)* are properly
reflected on the books and records of the Seller, and are in their
entirety valid accounts receivable arising from bona fide transactions in the ordinary course of business.

4.19 *Real Estate.*

(a) The Seller does not own any real property.
(b) The Seller has valid leasehold interests in all of the real
property which it leases or purports to lease, free and
clear of any Liens, other than the interests of the lessors,
including the Darien Property and the Anytown Property.
(c) The Seller enjoys peaceful and undisturbed possession
under all of the leases pursuant to which Seller leases real
property (the "Real Property Leases"). All of the Real Property Leases are valid, subsisting and in full force and effect,
and there are no existing defaults, or events which with the
passage of time or the giving of notice, or both, would constitute defaults by the Seller or by any other party thereto.
(d) Neither Seller nor any Shareholder received notice of any
pending condemnation, expropriation, eminent domain, or
similar proceedings affecting all or any portion of any real
property leased by the Seller and no such proceedings are
contemplated.
(e) The Shareholders enjoy peaceful and undisturbed possession of the Darien Property and have the right to lease
and collect all rents on the Darien Property and clear of
any Liens.

4.20 *No Guarantees.* The Seller has not guaranteed or pledged any Assets with respect to any obligation or indebtedness of any person or entity and no person or entity has guaranteed any obligation or indebtedness of the Seller.

4.21 *Taxes.*

    (a) The Seller has timely filed or will timely file all requisite federal, state, and other Tax (defined below) returns, reports, and forms ("Returns") for all periods ended on or before the Closing Date, and all such Tax Returns are true, correct, and complete in all respects. Neither the Seller nor any Shareholder has any knowledge of any basis for the assertion of any claim relating or attributable to Taxes which, if adversely determined, would result in any Lien on the assets of such Seller or any Shareholder or otherwise have an adverse effect on the Seller, the Assets, or the Business.

    (b) For purposes of this Agreement, the term "Tax" shall include any tax or similar governmental charge, impost, or levy (including, without limitation, income taxes, franchise taxes, transfer taxes or fees, sales taxes, use taxes, gross receipts taxes, value added taxes, employment taxes, excise taxes, ad valorem taxes, property taxes, withholding taxes, payroll taxes, minimum taxes, or windfall profits taxes) together with any related penalties, fines, additions to tax or interest imposed by the United States or any state, county, local, or foreign government or subdivision or agency thereof.

4.22 *Labor Matters. Schedule 4.22* sets forth a true and complete list of all employees of Seller together with a brief summary of their titles, duties, terms of employment and compensation arrangements, including the salary and any bonus, commission, or other compensation paid to each employee during the twelve (12) month period prior to the date hereof and the current employment and compensation arrangements with respect to each such employee. Further, with respect to employees of and service provided to Seller:

    (a) Seller is not a party to any collective bargaining or similar labor agreements, no such agreement determines the terms and conditions of employment of any employee of Seller, no collective bargaining or other labor agent has been certified as a representative of any of the employees of the Seller, and no representation campaign or election is now in progress with respect to any of the employees of the Seller;

(b) Seller is and has been in compliance in all material respects with all applicable laws respecting employment and employment practices, terms and conditions of employment and wages and hours, including without limitation, any such laws respecting employment discrimination and harassment, workers' compensation, family and medical leave, the Immigration Reform and Control Act, and occupational safety and health requirements, and has not and is not engaged in any unfair labor practice;

(c) there is not now, nor within the past three years has there been, any unfair labor practice complaint against Seller, pending or to Seller's best knowledge, threatened before the National Labor Relations Board or any other comparable authority; nor any labor strike, slowdown, or stoppage actually ending or, to Seller's best knowledge, threatened against or directly affecting Seller; there exist no other labor disputes with regard to Seller's employees or relative to Seller's Employee Technician Manual ("Manual"), including, without limitation, any reports of harassment, substance abuse, disciplinary, safety, or punctuality problems in contravention of Seller's Manual, or other acts or omissions filed or recorded by or against any employee of Seller. Seller's cessation of operations will not violate any laws, rules, regulations, or employment policies applicable to its employees.

(d) As of the Closing Date, each employee of the Seller has received any pay owed him or her with respect to vacation, compensatory or sick time, and any other employee benefits due, except as otherwise set forth in *Schedule 4.22(d)*.

4.23 *Absence of Undisclosed Liabilities.* Neither the Seller nor any Shareholder has any material liabilities or obligations with respect to the Business, either direct or indirect, matured or unmatured or absolute, contingent or otherwise, other than (a) those reflected in the 2006 Balance Sheet and (b) those liabilities or obligations incurred, consistently with past business practice, in or as a result of the normal and ordinary course of business since the Balance Sheet Date.

4.24 *Liabilities.* The liabilities to be assumed by Buyer pursuant to this Agreement consist solely of liabilities of Seller under Contracts included in the Assets which relate solely to the operation of the Business and the Assumed Liabilities in *Schedule 1.2.*

4.25 *Accuracy of Documents and Information.* The information provided to the Buyer by the Seller and the Shareholders with respect to the Seller, the Assets, and the Business, including the representations and warranties made in this Agreement and in the Schedules attached hereto, and all other information provided to the Buyer in connection with their investigation of the Seller, does not (and will not at the Closing Date) contain any untrue statement of a material fact and does not omit (and will not omit at the Closing Date) to state any material fact necessary to make the statements or facts contained herein or therein not misleading.

4.26 *Brokers and Agents.* Neither Seller nor any Shareholder has employed or dealt with any business broker, agent, or finder in respect of the transactions contemplated hereby.

5. NON-COMPETITION. Each of the Shareholders agrees that for a period of six (6) years from the date of this Agreement, he or she shall not, directly or indirectly: (a) engage in competition with the Buyer in any manner or capacity (e.g., as an advisor, consultant, independent contractor, principal, agent, partner, officer, director, stockholder, employee, member of any association, or otherwise) or in any phase of the business conducted by the Buyer during the term of this Agreement in any area where the Buyer is conducting or initiating operations during the period described above; provided, however, that ownership by a Shareholder as a passive investment, of less than one percent (1%) of the outstanding shares of capital stock of any corporation listed on a national securities exchange or publicly traded in the over-the-counter market shall not constitute a breach of this provision; (b) hire or engage or attempt to hire or employ any individual who shall have been an employee of the Buyer at any time during within one (1) year prior to such action taken by a Shareholder, whether for or on behalf of such Shareholder or for any entity in which such Shareholder shall have a direct or indirect interest (or any subsidiary or affiliate of any such entity), whether as a proprietor, partner, coventurer, financier, investor or stockholder, director, officer, employer, employee, agent, representative, or otherwise; or (c) assist or encourage any other person in carrying out, directly or indirectly, any activity that would be prohibited by the above provisions of this Section if such activity were carried out by Shareholder, either directly or indirectly; and in particular each Shareholder agrees that he or she will not, directly or indirectly, induce any employee of the Buyer to carry out, directly or indirectly, any such activity. In the event of any conflict between this provision and the terms of an Employment Agreement in full force and effect, the Employment Agreement will govern.

6. REPRESENTATIONS AND WARRANTIES OF THE BUYER. In order to induce the Seller to enter into this Agreement and to consummate the transactions contemplated hereby, each of the Buyer, jointly and severally, hereby represents and warrants to the Seller as follows:

6.1 *Buyer's Organization.* The Buyer is a limited liability company duly organized, validly existing, and in good standing under the laws of the State of Maryland. The Buyer has all requisite power and authority to own and operate and lease its properties and assets, to carry on its business as it is now being conducted, and to execute, deliver, and perform its obligations under this Agreement and consummate the transactions contemplated hereby.

6.2 *Authorization of Agreement.* The execution, delivery, and performance by the Buyer of this Agreement and of each and every agreement and document contemplated hereby and the consummation of the transactions contemplated hereby and thereby have been duly authorized by all necessary corporate action of the Buyer. This Agreement has been duly and validly executed and delivered by Buyer and constitutes (and, when executed and delivered, each such other agreement and document will constitute) a valid and binding obligation of the Buyer, enforceable against the Buyer in accordance with its terms.

6.3   *Non-Contravention; Consents.* Neither the execution and delivery by the Buyer of this Agreement nor the consummation by the Buyer of the transactions contemplated hereby, nor compliance by the Buyer with any of the provisions hereof, will (i) conflict with or result in a breach of any provision of the Articles of Organization or Operating Agreement of the Buyer, (ii) result in the breach of, or conflict with, any of the terms and conditions of, or constitute a default (with or without the giving of notice or the lapse of time or both) with respect to, or result in the cancellation or termination of, or the acceleration of the performance of any obligations or of any indebtedness under any contract, agreement, commitment, indenture, mortgage, note, bond, license, or other instrument or obligation to which the Buyer is now a party or by which the Buyer or its respective properties or assets may be bound or affected (other than such breaches, conflicts, and defaults as shall have been waived at or prior to the Closing), or (iii) violate any law or any rule or regulation of any administrative agency or governmental body, or any order, writ, injunction, or decree of any court, administrative agency, or governmental body to which the Buyer may be subject. No approval, authorization, consent, or other order or action of, or filing with or notice to any court, administrative agency, or other governmental authority or any other person is required for the execution and delivery by the Buyer of this Agreement or consummation by the Buyer of the transactions contemplated hereby (other than such consents as shall have been obtained at or prior to the Closing).

6.4   *Litigation.* There is no litigation, suit, proceeding, action, claim, or investigation, at law or in equity, pending, or to the best knowledge of the Buyer, threatened against, or affecting in any way, the Buyer's ability to perform its obligations as contemplated by this Agreement.

6.5   *The Equity Interest.* The Equity Interest has been duly authorized and issued in accordance with the terms hereof and the Operating Agreement.

6.6 *Accuracy of Financial Statements*. The Financial Statement for (personal balance sheet of buyer) set forth in *Schedule 6.6*, is true and correct in all material respects.

7. FURTHER AGREEMENTS OF THE PARTIES.

7.1 *Operation of the Business.* From and after the Balance Sheet Date until the Closing Date, except to the extent contemplated by this Agreement or otherwise consented to in writing by the Buyer, the Seller shall have continued to operate its Business in substantially the same manner as presently conducted and only in the ordinary and usual course and substantially consistent with past practice and in substantial compliance with (i) all laws and (ii) all leases, contracts, commitments, and other agreements, and all licenses, permits, and other instruments, relating to the operation of the Business, and will use reasonable efforts to preserve intact its present business organization and to keep available the services of all employees, representatives, and agents. The Seller and each of the Shareholders shall have continued to use all reasonable efforts, consistent with past practices, to promote the Business and to maintain the goodwill and reputation associated with the Business, and shall not take or omit to take any action which causes, or which is likely to cause, any material deterioration of the Business or the Seller's relationships with material suppliers or customers. Without limiting the generality of the foregoing, (a) the Seller will have maintained all of its equipment in substantially the same condition and repair as such equipment was maintained prior to the Balance Sheet Date, ordinary wear and tear excepted; (b) the Seller shall not have sold, transferred, pledged, leased, or otherwise disposed of any of the Assets, other than in the ordinary course of business; (c) the Seller shall not have amended, terminated, or waived any material right in respect of the Assets or the Business, or do any act, or omit to do any act, which will cause a breach of any material contract, agreement, commitment, or obligation by it; (d) the Seller shall have maintained its books, accounts, and records in accordance with good business practice and generally accepted accounting principles consistently applied; (e) the Seller shall not have engaged in any activities or transactions outside the ordinary course of business; (f) the Seller shall not have declared or paid any dividend or make any other distribution or payment of any kind in cash or property to the Shareholder or other affiliates; and (g) the Seller shall not have increased any existing employee benefits, established any new employee benefits plan, or amended or modified any existing Employee Plans, or otherwise incurred any obligation or liability under any employee plan materially different in nature or amount from obligations or liabilities incurred in connection with the Employee Plans.

7.2 *Consents; Assignment of Agreements.* Seller shall obtain, at the earliest practicable date, all consents and approvals of third parties (whether or not listed on *Schedule 4.4*) which are necessary or desirable for the consummation of the transactions contemplated hereby (including, without limitation, the valid and binding transfer of the Assets to Buyer) (the "Consents"). The Consents shall be written instruments whose form and substance are reasonably satisfactory to Buyer. The Consents shall not, without Buyer's express consent, impose any obligations on Buyer or create any conditions adverse to Buyer, other than the conditions or obligations specified in this Agreement.

7.3 *No Discussions.* The Seller shall not enter into any substantive negotiations or discussions with any third party with respect to the sale or lease of the Assets or the Business, or the sale of any capital stock of the Seller, or any other merger, acquisition, partnership, joint venture, or other business combination until the earlier to occur of (a) the Closing Date or (b) the termination of this Agreement.

7.4 *Employee Matters.* The Seller shall permit the Buyer to contact and make arrangements with the Seller's employees for the purpose of assuring their employment by the Buyer after the Closing and for the purpose of ensuring the continuity of the Business, and the Seller agrees not to discourage any such employees from being employed by or consulting with the Buyer. Nothing herein shall obligate the Buyer to employ or otherwise be responsible for any of the Seller's employees (other than the persons with whom the Buyer has entered or will enter into an employee agreement in accordance with Section 8.2 hereof) or to pay any employee any compensation or confer any benefit earned or accrued prior to the Closing Date, except as set forth in *Schedule 4.22(d)*.

7.5 *Notice Regarding Changes.* The Seller shall promptly notify the Buyer in writing of any change in facts and circumstances that could render any of the representations and warranties made herein by the Seller materially inaccurate or misleading.

7.6 *Furnishing of Information.* The Seller will allow Buyer to make a complete examination and analysis of the Business, Assets, and records, financial or otherwise, of the Seller. In connection with the foregoing review, Seller agrees that it shall furnish to the Buyer and Buyer's representatives all such information concerning the Seller's Business, Assets, operations, properties, or affairs as may be reasonably requested.

7.7 *Notification to Customers.* At the Buyer's request and in a form approved by the Buyer, the Seller agrees to notify all customers of the Business identified by Buyer and all customers of the Business during the year preceding the Closing as identified by Buyer, either separately or jointly with the Buyer, of the Buyer's purchase of the Business and Assets hereunder and that all further communications or requests by such customers with respect to the Business and Assets shall be directed to the Buyer. Without limiting the foregoing, promptly following the Closing, the Seller shall send a letter, in a form approved by the Buyer, to each debtor with respect to the notes, accounts, or other receivables included in the Assets directing that all payments on account of such receivables made after the Closing shall be made to the Buyer.

7.8 *Collection of Receivables.* The Seller agrees that it will reasonably cooperate with the Buyer in collecting the notes, accounts, and other receivables included in the Assets from any customers and will immediately deliver to the Buyer the amount paid on any and all receivables it collects after the Closing Date in connection with the Business, less out-of-pocket expenses incurred by Seller.

7.9 *Brokers and Agents.* Buyer, on the one hand, and the Seller, on the other hand, agree to indemnify and hold the other harmless from and against all fees, expenses, commissions, and costs due and owing to any other broker, agent, or finder on account of or in any way resulting from any contract or understanding existing between the indemnifying party and such person.

8. CONDITIONS PRECEDENT TO CLOSING.

8.1 *Conditions Precedent to the Obligations of Seller.* Seller's and Shareholders' obligations to consummate the transactions contemplated by this Agreement shall be subject to the fulfillment, at or prior to Closing, of each of the following conditions (any or all of which may be waived in writing, in whole or in part, by the Seller and the Shareholders):

(a) The Buyer shall have performed and complied in all material respects with each obligation and covenant required by this Agreement to be performed or complied with by them prior to or at the Closing.

(b) The representations and warranties of the Buyer contained herein shall be true and correct in all material respects at and as of the Closing Date as if made at and as of such time.

(c) Buyer shall have delivered to the Seller the items set forth in Section 3.2(b) of this Agreement.

(d) No action, suit, or proceeding by any person shall have been commenced and still be pending, no investigation by any governmental or regulatory authority shall have been commenced and still be pending, and no action, suit, or proceeding by any person shall have been threatened against the Buyer, the Seller, or the Shareholders (a) seeking to restrain, prevent, or change the transactions contemplated hereby or questioning the validity or legality of any such transactions or (b) which if resolved adversely to any party, would materially and adversely affect the business or condition, financial or otherwise, of the Buyer, or the Seller.

(e) All proceedings to be taken by the Buyer in connection with the transactions contemplated hereby and all documents incident thereto shall be reasonably satisfactory in form and substance to the Seller and its counsel, and the Seller and said counsel shall have received all such counterpart originals or certified copies or other copies of such documents as it or they may reasonably request.

(f) Buyer shall have delivered to the Seller the Pledge Agreement together with the marketable securities and other collateral securing the Note.

(g) Buyer shall have delivered to the Seller all such other certificates and documents as the Seller and its counsel shall have reasonably requested.

8.2 *Conditions Precedent to the Obligations of the Buyer.* The obligation of the Buyer to consummate the transactions contemplated by this Agreement shall be subject to the fulfillment, at or prior to Closing, of each of the following conditions precedent (any or all of which may be waived in writing, in whole or in part, by the Buyer):

(a) The Seller shall have performed and complied in all material respects with each obligation and covenant required by this Agreement to be performed or to be complied with by it on or prior to the Closing Date.

(b) The representations and warranties of the Seller and the Shareholders contained herein or in any Schedule attached hereto shall be true and correct in all material respects at and as of the Closing Date as if made at and as of such time.

(c) The Seller and the Shareholders shall have delivered or caused delivery of the items set forth in Section 3.2(a) hereof.

(d) Except as otherwise set forth in this Agreement, the Buyer shall have received written evidence, in form and substance satisfactory to it, that all material consents, waivers, authorizations, and approvals of, or filings with, or notices to, governmental entities and third parties required in order that the transactions contemplated hereby be consummated have been obtained or made.

(e) There shall not have occurred since the Balance Sheet Date any material damage or loss by theft, casualty, or otherwise, whether or not insured against by the Seller or the

Shareholders, of all or any material portion of the Assets, or any material adverse change in or interference with the Business or the properties, assets, condition (financial or otherwise), or prospects of the Seller.

(f) Buyer shall have entered into an employment agreement with Jane C. Doe and John F. Doe, in substantially the forms attached hereto as *Exhibit G* and *Exhibit H*, respectively.

(g) No action, suit, or proceeding by any person shall have been commenced and still be pending, no investigations by any governmental or regulatory authority shall have been commenced and still be pending, and no action, suit, or proceeding by any person shall have been threatened against the Buyer, the Seller, or the Shareholders, (a) seeking to restrain, prevent, or change the transactions contemplated hereby or questioning the validity or legality of any such transactions or (b) which if resolved adversely to any party, would materially and adversely affect the business or condition, financial or otherwise, of the Buyer, or the Seller.

(h) All proceedings to be taken by the Seller and the Shareholders in connection with the transactions contemplated hereby and all documents incident thereto shall be reasonably satisfactory in form and substance to the Buyer and its counsel, and the Buyer and said counsel shall have received all such counterpart originals or certified copies or other copies of such documents as it or they may reasonably request.

(i) Seller shall have delivered to the Buyer all such other certificates and documents as the Buyer or its counsel shall have reasonably requested.

9. INDEMNIFICATION; SURVIVAL OF REPRESENTATIONS AND WARRANTIES.

9.1 *Indemnification by Seller and Shareholders.* Each of the Sellers and the Shareholders, jointly and severally, covenants and agrees to indemnify, defend, protect, and hold harmless the Buyer and any of the Buyer's officers, directors, stockholders, representatives, affiliates, assigns, successors in interest, and current and former employees, each only in their respective capacities as such (collectively, the "Buyer Indemnified Parties"), from, against, and in respect of:

(a) any and all liabilities, claims, losses, damages, punitive damages, causes of action, lawsuits, administrative proceedings, demands, judgments, settlement payments, penalties, and costs and expenses (including, without limitation, reasonable attorneys' fees, travel expenses, expert witness fees, and disbursements of every kind, nature, and description) (collectively, "Damages"), suffered, sustained, incurred, or paid by Buyer or any other Buyer Indemnified Party in connection with, resulting from, or arising out of, either directly or indirectly:

   (i) any misrepresentation or breach of any warranty of the Seller or any Shareholder set forth in this Agreement or any Schedule or certificate delivered by or on behalf of the Seller or any Shareholder in connection herewith; or

   (ii) any nonfulfillment of any covenant or agreement on the part of the Seller or any Shareholder set forth in this Agreement; or

   (iii) the Business, operations, or Assets of the Seller prior to the Closing Date or the actions or omissions of the Seller's directors, officers, shareholders, employees, or agents prior to the Closing Date (except with respect to the Assumed Liabilities); or

   (iv) the Excluded Liabilities.

(b) any and all Damages incident to any of the foregoing or to the enforcement of this Section 9.1.

9.2 *Limitation and Expiration.* The indemnification obligations under this Section 10 or in any other certificate or writing furnished in connection with the transactions contemplated hereby shall terminate on the later of (a) the date that is six (6) months after the expiration of the longest applicable federal or state statute of limitation (including extensions thereof), or (b) if there is no applicable statute of limitation, four years after the Closing Date, or (c) the final resolution of a claim or demand (a "Claim") as of the relevant dates described above in this Section.

9.3 *Indemnification by Buyer.* The Buyer covenants and agrees to indemnify, defend, protect, and hold harmless the Shareholders, the Seller, and any of the Seller's officers, directors, stockholders, representatives, affiliates, assigns, successors in interest, and current and former employees, each only in their respective capacities as such (collectively, the "Seller Indemnified Parties"), from, against, and in respect of:

(a) any and all Damages sustained, incurred, or paid by Seller or any other Seller Indemnified Party in connection with, resulting from, or arising out of, either directly or indirectly:

　(i)　any breach of any warranty of the Buyer set forth in this Agreement or any Schedule or certificate delivered by or on behalf of the Buyer in connection herewith; or

　(ii)　any nonfulfillment of any covenant or agreement on the part of the Buyer set forth in this Agreement; or

　(iii)　the ownership of the purchased Assets or the operation of the Business by the Buyer following the Closing Date.

(b) any and all Damages incident to any of the foregoing or to the enforcement of this Section 9.3.

9.4 *Notice Procedures; Claims.* The obligations and liabilities of the parties under this Section with respect to, relating to, caused (in whole or in part) by or arising out of claims of third parties (individually, a "Third Party Claim" and collectively, "Third Party Claims") shall be subject to the following conditions:

(a) The party entitled to be indemnified hereunder (the "Indemnified Party") shall give the party obligated to provide the indemnity (the "Indemnifying Party") prompt notice of any Third Party Claim (the "Claim Notice"); provided that the failure to give such Claim Notice shall not affect the liability of the Indemnifying Party under this Agreement unless the failure materially and adversely affects the ability of the Indemnifying Party to defend the Third Party Claim. If the Indemnifying Party promptly acknowledges in writing its obligation to indemnify in accordance with the terms and subject to the limitations of such party's obligation to indemnify contained in this Agreement with respect to that claim, the Indemnifying Party shall have a reasonable time to assume the defense of the Third Party Claim at its expense and with counsel of its choosing, which counsel shall be reasonably satisfactory to the Indemnified Party. Any Claim Notice shall identify, to the extent known to the Indemnified Party, the basis for the Third Party Claim, the facts giving rise to the Third Party Claim, and the estimated amount of the Third Party Claim (which estimate shall not be conclusive of the final amount of such claim or demand). The Indemnified Party shall make available to the Indemnifying Party copies of all relevant documents and records in its possession.

(b) If the Indemnifying Party, within a reasonable time after receipt of such Claim Notice, fails to assume the defense of any Third Party Claim in accordance with Section 9.4(a), the Indemnified Party shall (upon further notice to the Indemnifying Party) have the right to undertake the defense, compromise, or settlement of the Third Party Claim, at the expense and for the account and risk of the Indemnifying Party.

(c) Anything in this Section 9.4 to the contrary notwithstanding, (i) the Indemnifying Party shall not, without the written consent of the Indemnified Party, settle or compromise any Third Party Claim or consent to the entry of judgment which does not include as an unconditional term thereof the giving by the claimant or the plaintiff to the Indemnified Party of an unconditional release from all liability in respect of the Third Party Claim; (ii) if such Third Party Claim involves an issue or matter which the Indemnified Party believes could have a materially adverse effect on the Indemnified Party's business, operations, assets, properties, or prospects of its business, the Indemnified Party shall have the right to control the defense or settlement of any such claim or demand, at the expense of the Indemnified Party without contribution from the Indemnifying Party; and (iii) the Indemnified Party shall have the right to employ its own counsel to defend any claim at the

Indemnifying Party's expense if (x) the employment of such counsel by the Indemnified Party has been authorized by the Indemnifying Party, or (y) counsel selected by the Indemnifying Party shall have reasonably concluded that there may be a conflict of interest between the Indemnifying Party and the Indemnified Party in the conduct of the defense of such action, or (z) the Indemnifying Party shall not have employed counsel to assume the defense of such claim in accordance with Section 9.4(a).

(d) In the event that the Indemnified Party should have a claim against the Indemnifying Party hereunder which does not involve a claim or demand being asserted against or sought to be collected from it by a third party, the Indemnified Party shall promptly send a Claim Notice with respect to such claim to the Indemnifying Party. If the Indemnifying Party does not notify the Indemnified Party within thirty (30) calendar days that it disputes such claim, the amount of such claim shall be conclusively deemed a liability of the Indemnifying Party hereunder.

(e) Nothing herein shall be deemed to prevent any Indemnified Party from making a claim hereunder for potential or contingent claims or demands, provided that (i) the Claim Notice sets forth (A) the specific basis for any such potential or contingent claim or demand and (B) the estimated amount thereof (to the extent then feasible) and (ii) the Indemnified Party has reasonable grounds to believe that such a claim or demand will be made.

9.5 *Survival of Representations, Warranties, and Covenants.* All representations, warranties, and covenants made by the Seller, the Shareholders, and the Buyer in or pursuant to this Agreement or in any document delivered pursuant hereto shall be deemed to have been made on the date of this Agreement (except as otherwise provided herein) and, if a Closing occurs, as of the Closing Date. The representations of the Seller and the Shareholders will survive and the Closing and remain in effect until, and will expire upon, the termination of the relevant indemnification obligation as provided in Section 9.2. The representations of Buyer will survive and remain in effect until and will expire upon, the later of the third anniversary of the Closing Date or the satisfaction in full of any payment obligation pursuant to the Promissory Note.

9.6 *Indemnification Trigger.* Notwithstanding the provisions of Section 9.1 or 9.3 above, neither Seller nor Buyer shall be liable to the other for any indemnification under this Section 9 unless and until the aggregate amount of Damages due to an Indemnified Party exceeds Two Hundred Thousand Dollars ($200,000) (the "Trigger Amount"). Once the Trigger Amount has been exceeded, the Indemnified Party shall be entitled to indemnification for all Damages, including the amount up to the Trigger Amount and any amount in excess thereof. The foregoing trigger provision shall not apply, however, with respect to any Damages suffered, sustained, incurred, or paid by an Indemnified Party related to Taxes or assessments by any governmental authority, or with respect to any claim of actual fraud or intentional misrepresentation relating to a breach of any representation or warranty in this Agreement.

9.7 *Remedies Cumulative.* The remedies set forth in this Section 9 are cumulative and shall not be construed to restrict or otherwise affect any other remedies that may be available to the Indemnified Parties under any other agreement or pursuant to statutory or common law.

10. POST-CLOSING MATTERS.

10.1 *Transition Services.* The Seller agrees to provide reasonable assistance to the Buyer in connection with the transition of the Business to the Buyer. The Shareholders will provide assistance to Buyer in accordance with their respective Employment Agreement.

10.2 *Further Assurances.* The Seller and each of the Shareholders hereby covenants and agrees to (a) make, execute, and deliver to the Buyer any and all powers of attorney and other authority which the Seller may lawfully make, execute, and deliver, in addition to any such powers and authorities as are contained herein, which may reasonably be or become necessary, proper, or convenient to enable the Buyer to reduce to possession, collect, enforce, own, or enjoy any and all rights and benefits in, to, with respect to, or in connection with, the Assets, or any part or portion thereof, and (b) upon the Buyer's request, to take, in the Seller's name, any and all steps and to do any and all things which may be or become lawful and reasonably necessary, proper, convenient, or desirable to enable the Buyer to reduce to possession, collect, enforce, own, and enjoy any and all rights and benefits in, to, with respect to, or in connection with, the Assets, and each and every part and portion thereof. The Seller and each of the Shareholders also covenants and agrees with the Buyer, its successors and assigns, that the Seller and each of the Shareholders will do, execute, acknowledge, and deliver, or cause to be done, executed, acknowledged, and delivered, any and all such further reasonable acts, instruments, papers and documents as may be necessary to carry out and effectuate the intent and purposes of this Agreement. From and after the Closing Date, Seller will promptly refer all inquiries with respect to ownership of the Assets or the Business to Buyer.

10.3 *Payment of Liabilities; Discharge of Liens.* The Seller shall satisfy and discharge, as the same shall become due, all of Seller's liabilities, obligations, debts, and commitments including but not limited to Tax liabilities, in accordance with this Agreement, other than the Assumed Liabilities.

10.4 *Transfer of Permits; Additional Consents.* Subsequent to the Closing, Seller shall use its commercially reasonable best efforts to effectively transfer to Buyer all Permits which were not so transferred at or prior to the Closing and to obtain all approvals, consents, and authorizations with respect to such transfers. In addition, subsequent to the Closing, to the extent requested by Buyer, Seller shall use its reasonable efforts to obtain any required consents of the other parties to the Scheduled Contracts included in the Assets to the assignment thereof to the Buyer which were not obtained at or prior to the Closing.

10.5 *Inspection of Documents, Books, and Records; Financial Reports.* Subsequent to the Closing, Buyer shall make available ▼

for inspection by Seller or its authorized representatives during regular business hours and upon reasonable notice, any original documents conveyed to Buyer under this Agreement. Upon reasonable notice to the Buyer, for five years from the Closing Date forward, Seller or its representatives shall be entitled, at Seller's expense, to audit, copy, review, and inspect the Buyer's books and records at the Buyer's offices during reasonable business hours. For so long as any payment obligation is outstanding under this Agreement, Buyer shall make available to Seller and its representatives, copies of Buyer's annual corporate tax returns and any quarterly financial statements or reports prepared or compiled by or for Buyer.

10.6 *Acceleration of Notes.* In the event that Buyer shall subsequently sell, convey, transfer, or assign assets of the Buyer to a nonaffiliated third party (other than as collateral under a lien or security arrangement), the value of which is greater than twenty-five percent (25%) of the total assets of the Buyer at the time of the transfer, all amounts of principal and interest then outstanding under both Notes shall become immediately due and payable.

11. RISK OF LOSS. Prior to the Closing, the risk of loss (including damage and/or destruction) of all of the Seller's property and assets, including, without limitation, the Assets, shall remain with the Seller, and the legal doctrine known as the "Doctrine of Equitable Conversion" shall not be applicable to this Agreement or to any of the transactions contemplated hereby.

12. MISCELLANEOUS.

12.1 *Entire Agreement.* This Agreement, and the Exhibits and Schedules to this Agreement, constitute the entire agreement between the parties hereto with respect to the subject matter hereof and supersede all prior negotiations, agreements, arrangements, and understandings, whether oral or written, among the parties hereto with respect to such subject matter (including, without limitation, the letter of intent dated _____, 20___, as amended, between the Seller and the Buyer).

12.2 *No Third Party Beneficiary.* Nothing expressed or implied in this Agreement is intended, or shall be construed, to confer upon or give any person, firm, corporation, partnership, association, or other entity, other than the parties hereto and their respective successors and assigns, any rights or remedies under or by reason of this Agreement.

12.3 *Amendment.* This Agreement may not be amended or modified in any respect, except by the mutual written agreement of the parties hereto.

12.4 *Waivers and Remedies.* The waiver by any of the parties hereto of any other party's prompt and complete performance, or breach, or violation of any provision of this Agreement, shall not operate nor be construed as a waiver of any subsequent breach or violation, and the failure by any of the parties hereto to exercise any right or remedy which it may possess hereunder shall not operate nor be construed as a bar to the exercise of such right or remedy by such party upon the occurrence of any subsequent breach or violation.

12.5 *Severability.* If any term, provision, covenant, or restriction of this Agreement (or the application thereof to any specific persons or circumstances) should be held by an administrative agency or court of competent jurisdiction to be invalid, void, or unenforceable, such term, provision, covenant, or restriction shall be modified to the minimum extent necessary in order to render it enforceable within such jurisdiction, consistent with the expressed objectives of the parties hereto. Further, the remainder of this Agreement (and the application of such term, provision, covenant, or restriction to any other persons or circumstances) shall not be affected thereby, but rather shall be enforced to the greatest extent permitted by law.

12.6 *Descriptive Headings.* Descriptive headings contained herein are for convenience only and shall not control or affect the meaning or construction of any provision of this Agreement.

12.7 *Counterparts.* This Agreement may be executed in any number of counterparts and by the separate parties hereto in separate counterparts, each of which shall be deemed to be one and the same instrument.

12.8   *Notices.* All notices, consents, requests, instructions, approvals, and other communications provided for herein and all legal process in regard hereto shall be in writing and shall be deemed to have been duly given (a) when delivered by hand, (b) when received by facsimile transmission, with printed confirmation of transmission and verbal (telephonic) confirmation of receipt, (c) one day after being sent by a nationally recognized overnight express service, or (d) five (5) days after being deposited in the United States mail, by registered or certified mail, return receipt requested, postage prepaid, as follows:

If to the Seller:	*If to Buyer:*
Target Co., Inc.	Growth Co. Corp.
16602 Side Avenue	12345 Main Street
Anytown, USA 01206	Anytown, USA 01234
Attn: President	Attn: Chief Executive Officer

or to such other address as any party hereto may from time to time designate in writing delivered in a like manner.

12.9   *Successors and Assigns.* This Agreement shall be binding upon and shall inure to the benefit of the parties hereto and their respective successors and assigns. None of the parties hereto shall assign any of its rights or obligations hereunder except with the express written consent of the other parties hereto.

12.10 *Applicable Law.* This Agreement shall be governed by, and shall be construed, interpreted, and enforced in accordance with, the internal laws of the State of Maryland.

12.11 *Expenses.* Each of the parties hereto agrees to pay all of the respective expenses incurred by it in connection with the negotiation, preparation, execution, delivery, and performance of this Agreement and the consummation of the transactions contemplated hereby.

12.12 *Confidentiality.* Except to the extent required for any party to obtain any approvals or consents required pursuant to the terms hereof, no party hereto shall divulge the existence of the terms of this Agreement or the transactions contemplated hereby without the prior written approval of all of the parties hereto, except and as to the extent (i) obligated by law or (ii) necessary for such party to defend or prosecute any litigation in connection with the transactions contemplated hereby.

12.13 *Attorneys' Fees.* In the event any suit or other legal proceeding is brought for the enforcement of any of the provisions of this Agreement, the parties hereto agree that the prevailing party or parties shall be entitled to recover from the other party or parties upon final judgment on the merits reasonable attorneys' fees and expenses, including attorneys' fees and expenses for any appeal, and costs incurred in bringing such suit or proceeding.

IN WITNESS WHEREOF, the parties have executed and delivered this Agreement on the date first above written.

GROWTH CO. CORP.

By:

_____, President

TARGET CO., INC.

By:

_____, Chief Executive Officer

12.

Keeping M&A Deals on Track: Managing the Deal Killers

Deal killers. We have all seen them and been forced to manage through them. They come in all shapes, sizes, and varieties, with different reasons, justifications, and rationalizations. They can emanate from the buyer, the seller, or any number of third parties, such as lenders, investors, key customers or suppliers, professional advisors—or all of the above. Some deal killers are legitimate for deals that deserve to die, and some are emotional, financial, or strategic in nature. They can be very costly to all parties to the transaction, especially when significant costs have already been incurred. And for certain advisors and investment bankers, they mean not getting paid. Clearly, deal killers inflict a lot of pain along their path of destruction of a transaction.

In troubled financial times, deal killers can come as a shock and can be based on something as simple as a stark difference in the mind-set of the parties or lenders or even investors about the markets. In strong and frothy economic times, deal killers will be rooted in greed and will often be based on disagreements over inflated valuations.

Following the high-profile failure of several buyouts in 2008–2010, sellers resisted provisions that permit a buyer, under certain conditions, to walk away simply by paying a fee. But buyers, who face their own challenges in securing commitments from banks to fund deals, began pushing back. Many transactions derailed in 2008 and 2009 because of factors such as deteriorating global financial market conditions, buyers developing cold feet in the middle of the deal, seller remorse, disappointment caused by record low valuations, or even an overall transactional fatigue resulting from a loss of momentum among parties that are running out of steam. In 2008 through 2010, over 2,000 "reported" transactions derailed due to market or other conditions, and countless smaller- and mid-market unreported transactions never made it to the closing table despite the time, effort, and good intentions at the outset. Protection and risk allocation terms that hold significance in deals are being more hotly contested. M&A players seem content to remain on the bench rather than be on the playing field, and a notable number of them have retired hurt. In some instances, an immediate surfacing of post-closing integration issues involving post-transactional shareholder value creation challenges kills what would have been a deal to die for two years ago. The volatility in stock markets, one of the major driving factors for M&A, has further increased the uncertainties arising in the middle of the deal. In 2010 through 2017, market conditions improved and then strengthened, which together with more robust valuations and project management tools helped keep more M&A transactions on track toward closing.

In M&A booms as well as in tight financial markets, most deal killers can be put into one of the following major categories:

- ▶ Price and valuation
- ▶ Terms and conditions
- ▶ Allocation of risk
- ▶ Third-party challenges
- ▶ Cold feet due to oscillating financial conditions

COMMUNICATION AND LEADERSHIP

The first step in keeping a transaction on track (and greatly increasing the chance of avoiding deal killers) is to have strong communication and leadership by and among all parties and key players to the transaction. As in football, each team (e.g., buyer, seller, source of capital, and so on) should appoint a quarterback who will be the point person for communication and coordination. Too many lines of communication will create confusion and misunderstanding—conditions that allow a deal killer to pollinate. The more the quarterbacks coordinate, communicate, and anticipate problems with the various members of their team and promptly discuss key issues with the quarterbacks of the other teams, the greater the chances that the transaction can and will close.

Some of the key tasks of the transactional quarterback and of each team to keep the transaction on track toward closing include:

- ▶ Putting a master strategic plan in place (with realistic expectations regarding financial and post-closing objectives)
- ▶ Building the right team
- ▶ Communication and teamwork
- ▶ Orchestration and leadership
- ▶ Momentum and timetable accord
- ▶ Avoiding emotion—the "don't call my baby ugly syndrome" (sellers) and falling in love with a given transaction (buyers)
- ▶ Early start on governmental and third-party appeals
- ▶ Creative problem solving
- ▶ Cooperation and support from financing sources
- ▶ Facilitating agreement on the key value drivers of the seller's business/intellectual capital issues

DIAGNOSING THE SOURCE OF THE PROBLEM

When a potential deal killer does arise, each quarterback should first diagnose the source of the problem. Where is the issue coming from and what can be done to fix it? A deal killer for one party may not be a deal killer for another party. Take a look at Figure 12-1. The old adage "where you stand often depends on where you sit" clearly applies here. For example, a lender to a buyer coming in at a higher lending rate than anticipated may significantly alter the attractiveness of the transaction from the buyer's perspective but may be viewed as a nonissue for the seller.

Figure 12.1. The Source of the Problem Will Dictate the Solution

Seller	**Stakeholders** ❑ Minority shareholders ❑ Key employees ❑ Venture capital investors ❑ Family members	**Third-Party Approaches** ❑ Regulatory ❑ Lenders ❑ Lessors ❑ Unions	A L L P A R T I E S
Buyer	**Sources of Capital** ❑ Debt ❑ Equity ❑ Mezzanine	**Professional Advisors** ❑ Lawyers ❑ CPAs ❑ Investment bankers ❑ Consultants	

UNDERSTANDING THE TYPES
OF DEAL KILLERS

Once the *source* of the deal killer has been analyzed, the respective quarterbacks should focus on the specific *type* of deal killer. Most deal killers can and should be resolved, through either creative restructuring, effective counseling, or precision document redrafting. Some deal killers *cannot* be resolved (they are just too big and hairy), and other deal killers *should not* be resolved (such as trying to squeeze a square peg into a round hole).

Deal killers come in a wide variety of flavors, and include the following:

- ▶ Egos clashing
- ▶ Misalignment of objectives
- ▶ Inexperienced players
- ▶ Internal and external politics (board level, executives, venture investors, and so on)
- ▶ Due diligence red flags/surprises
- ▶ Pricing and structural challenges (price versus terms)
- ▶ Valuation problems (tax/source of financing/in general)
- ▶ Third-party approval delays
- ▶ Seller's/buyer's/source of capital remorse

► Employee and customer issues
► Overdependence on the founder/key employee/key customer or relationship
► Loss of trust or integrity during the transaction process
► Nepotism
► Failure to develop a mutually agreeable post-closing integration plan
► Shareholder approvals
► Accounting/financial statement irregularities (post-WorldCom)
► Sarbanes-Oxley post-closing compliance concerns
► Breakdowns in leadership and coordination (too little or too many points of communication)
► Too little or too much "principal-to-principal" communication
► Crowded auctions
► Impatience to get to closing or loss of momentum (flow and timing issues)
► Incompatibility of cultures and/or business systems (e.g., IT infrastructure, costs and budgeting policies, compensation and reward programs, or accounting policies)
► Force-feeding deals that don't meet M&A objectives (square peg/round hole; bad deal avoidance/good deal capture— systems and filters)
► Who's driving the bus in this deal (mergers versus acquisitions)
► Changes in the seller's performance during the transaction process (upside surprises versus unexpected downside surprises)
► Loss of a key customer or strategic relationship during the transaction process
► Failure to agree on post-closing obligations, roles, and responsibilities
► Environmental problems (buyers being less willing to rely on indemnification and insurance protections)
► Unexpected changes in the buyer's strategy or operations during the transaction process (including a change in management or strategic direction)

CURING THE TRANSACTIONAL PATIENT

Although a detailed discussion of the tools available to "kill a deal killer" is beyond the scope of this chapter—and is probably as broad as the number of tools available to the Orkin man to kill the hundreds of different insects and rodents—some of the more common tools are listed here. The first step is for each quarterback to ensure that the transaction *can* and *should* be fixed. In some cases, it may be best for the stakeholders for all parties to just walk away, hopefully peacefully. But if the transaction *should* proceed, then these tools can be very valuable in mending a broken deal:

- ▶ Earn-outs or deferred and contingent post-closing consideration
- ▶ Representations, warranties, and indemnities (tools to adjust the allocation and assumption of risk, weighting of priorities issues)
- ▶ Adjusting the post-closing survival period of representations and warranties
- ▶ Holdbacks and security interests
- ▶ Closing-date audits
- ▶ Third-party performance guarantees/performance bonds/ escrows
- ▶ M&A insurance policies
- ▶ Restrictions on the sale by the seller of the buyer's securities issued as part of the overall consideration
- ▶ Recasting of financial projections and retooling post-closing business plans

MAINTAINING ORDER IN
THE M&A PROCESS: SIMPLE PRINCIPLES
FOR KEEPING DEALS ON TRACK

- ▶ Put a master strategic plan in place (with realistic financial and post-closing synergy expectations).
- ▶ Build the right team.

▶ Designate a quarterback for each team for orchestration and leadership.

▶ Ensure communication and teamwork.

▶ Maintain momentum and timetable accord.

▶ Avoid ego and emotion (sellers: "don't call my baby ugly" syndrome, and buyers: falling in love with a given transaction).

▶ Get an early start on government and third-party approvals.

▶ Have a clear understanding of conditions to closing.

▶ Engage in creative problem solving.

▶ Identify potential troublemakers and rabble-rousers.

▶ Ensure cooperation and support from financing sources (and *their* deal teams).

▶ Reach agreement on the key value drivers of the seller's business/intellectual capital issues.

▶ Focus, focus, focus.

The bottom line is: coordinate, communicate, and anticipate equals no surprises.

CONCLUSION

Bad deals deserve to die a peaceful death. Not all transactions are meant to be closed (1) at *this* time, (2) at *this* valuation, (3) between *these* parties, or (4) under *these* terms and conditions. But if a transaction can be saved, then it should be saved. The quarterback on each team must have the transactional experience, the business acumen, and the communication skills to diagnose the source and nature of the problem—and enough familiarity with all of the tools available to get the transaction back on track toward closing.

13.

Post-closing Challenges

The closing of a merger or acquisition usually leads to a great sigh of relief from the buyer, the seller, and their respective advisors. Everyone has worked hard to ensure that the process went smoothly and that all parties are happy with the end result. But the term *closing* can be misleading in that it suggests a sense of finality, when in truth, particularly for the buyer and the integration team, the hard work has just begun.

Often one of the greatest challenges for the buyer is the post-closing integration of the two companies. The integration of human resources, the corporate cultures, the operating and management information systems, the accounting methods and financial practices, and related matters is often the most difficult part of completing a merger or acquisition. It is a time of fear, stress, and frustration for most of the employees who were *not* on the deal team and who may have only limited amounts of information regarding their roles in the post-closing organization. The creation of sustainable value after the merger requires a tremendous amount of strategizing and care in a lot of vital areas.

It is estimated that as many as three out of every five M&A deals have an ineffective plan for the integration of the two companies. And even if there is a plan, well, plans don't always work out as anticipated. The consequences of a weak or ineffective transition plan are the buyer's inability to realize the transaction's true value because of either over-estimated post-merger synergies, wasted time and resources devoted to solving post-closing problems, a badly conducted due diligence, unsolvable cultural differences, underestimation of stakeholder resistance, or, in some cases, even litigation. In this post-Sarbox and post-Madoff age of shareholder value and transparency being placed at a premium, companies cannot afford to move forward with a transaction that lacks an effective post-closing game plan.

The focus of this chapter is on understanding and anticipating the nature and types of post-closing challenges faced by both buyer and seller *after* the deal is completed. The seller must facilitate a smooth transition of ownership and management to the buyer's team, without ego, emotion, or politics. The buyer must have procedures in place to prevent the seller from undermining these transitional efforts and to assume control of the company—also without ego, emotion, or politics. Post-closing challenges may arise in a wide variety of subject areas, some of which are addressed in this chapter: operations, finance, personnel, information systems, and many other areas, as set forth in the post-closing checklist in Figure 13-1. In order to achieve the desired synergies from a deal, effective and rigorous synergy management with a constant eye on milestones is required. As we will also see, a series of emotional and psychological factors must be considered, and strong leadership is needed to guide affected employees through the process. Let's drill down on a few of these issues.

Figure 13-1. Post-closing Checklist

Human Capital Issues

Cultural alignment

Integration of leadership team

Integration of staff

Termination plan due to efficiencies and overlap

Overseas workers

Union issues

Regulatory issues

Temporary workers and part-time employees

Independent contractors

Relationship Capital Issues

Integration of customer relationships

Integration of supplier relationships

Integration of channel partners

Integration of advisory teams and consultants

Integration of strategic alliance and joint venture partners

Subcontractors and teaming relationships

Infrastructure

Physical facilities

Warehousing and logistics

Information management and computer systems

Regulatory and Contractual Controls

Regulatory approvals

Post-closing assignments and consents

Branding and Marketing

Branding issues

Communications issues

Public relations strategy

Redefining the customer value proposition

Operational Issues

Store/office trade dress and alignment

Community relations

Amendments to real estate and operating leases

A TIME OF TRANSITION

Post-closing challenges raise a wide variety of human fears and uncertainties that must be understood and addressed by both the buyer and the seller. For affected employees and others in the transactional ecosystem, it is a time of uncertainty, chaos, and even trauma. Leaders of companies need to have a game plan to ensure that all affected parties continue to thrive amidst the turmoil. The fear of the unknown experienced by the seller's employees must be addressed and put to rest; otherwise, the employees' stress and distraction will affect the seller's performance and the viability of the transaction. Since roughly 30 percent of the employees in a typical transaction will be redundant, many will focus not on their day-to-day tasks, but instead on wondering who will stay, who will go, and who will be reclassified, relocated, or reassigned. The need to integrate the two corporate cultures quickly also raises personal and psychological issues that must be addressed. Once word of a deal leaks out to employees, the uncertainty associated with the change is likely to lead to widespread insecurity and fear of job loss at all levels of the organization. Everyone affected by the transaction, either directly or indirectly, will inevitably ask four key questions:

1. What's going to happen to me?
2. What's expected of me?
3. What's in it for me?
4. How will my roles and responsibilities be affected?

Be sure that post-closing planning and communication address these three fundamental human concerns. Take control of the rumor mill before it takes control of you and your transaction. Most rumor mills begin as a result of an information gap. It is the responsibility of senior management to fill this void with clear and consistent information at all levels, even if some of the data shared involves bad news. Leaving the door open to watercooler-driven information channels will often lead to the best and the brightest people heading for the exits, when it is often those exact folks who need to be directly motivated, given incentives, and retained. These issues are particularly challenging in cross-border transactions, where cultural, language, and legal differences may complicate these matters further.

Many of the fears experienced by the employees of *both* the buyer and the seller result from expectations of downsizing to cut costs, avoid duplication, and achieve the economies of scale potential provided by the transaction.

Another common problem is the psychological consequences of "seller's remorse," particularly when the seller remains on-site in a consulting capacity or even as a minority owner. The seller can be so accustomed to managing the business that he may not be open to the changes in strategies or policies implemented by the buyer. The seller undermines the buyer's efforts or contradicts its authority. These sellers often want the *benefits* of the bargain but seem unwilling to accept the *burden* of the bargain and relinquish control of the company. These problems are particularly common in mergers, where the management and flow of the deal may be one of shared objectives and values, as opposed to an acquisition, which more clearly has a designated quarterback.

In attempting to realize the true value of a merger or acquisition, the buyer must coordinate a smooth and efficient post-closing process. Important issues that need to be managed fall into three areas: people, places, and things. Some issues are addressed in the closing documents. Most require forethought in order to anticipate potential pitfalls. Some of the strategic issues that must be addressed are listed in Figure 13-2, and some of the more common problems are addressed in Figure 13-3. The bottom line is that if the buyer doesn't plan to address the following issues, the chances for failure or for not fully realizing success are greatly increased.

Figure 13-2. Strategic Post-closing Issues

Who should lead the transition team?

Which changes should be made, and how quickly?

How will the changes be presented and sold?

How can the seller's transition from owner to employee status be managed?

How can "turf wars" be avoided?

Figure 13-3. Common Post-closing Problems

Lack of communication

Weak leadership

Mistakes made in due diligence process

Realization of efficiencies and synergies took too long (or were obsolete or stale by the time they were achieved)

Unexpected rapid shift in post-closing market or economic conditions

Unexpected post-closing third-party claims on liabilities

Cultural differences greater than predicted

Market share or valuation failed to be accretive

Indecisiveness as to timing and details of integration

Inexperience among executives or advisors

Post-closing synergies overestimated or unrealistic

Stakeholder resistance underestimated

Customer and channel partner loyalty overestimated

Technology integration or infrastructure costs well above budget

STAFFING LEVELS AND RELATED HUMAN RESOURCES CHALLENGES

One of the primary areas that an acquiring company looks to in order to realize the projected return on its investment is the new company's level of staffing, along with certain qualitative challenges for the workforce in the new entity. After a merger or an acquisition, the numbers must, indeed, work, but success depends on the people. If a certain number of employees can be eliminated, it is more likely that earnings projections will be met or exceeded. The hard part is deciding who stays, and in what positions, and who goes. Much of this depends on the nature of the acquisition. On the one hand, if the terms dictate that the acquired firm is to maintain its independence, it is much more difficult to reduce staffing levels. On the other hand, if the acquired firm is absorbed into the acquirer, staff cutbacks are probably appropriate and healthy. This is the greatest source of employee fear and is the fuel that powers the rumor mill. But some of these fears are valid. An April 2005 report published by Challenger, Gray & Christmas indicated that job cuts following M&A deals in the first quarter of 2005 soared to nearly 77,000, more than six times the rate of the last quarter of 2004 and three times the rate of the first quarter of 2004. The biggest cuts during that period came in the telecommunications and high-tech industries. Some of the biggest cuts were in the manufacturing (impact of automation and robotics and plant closing) and retail (impact of e-commerce and web2.0) sectors.

The first step in determining staffing levels is to divide the workforce into management and staff/labor. These two groups must be distinguished because their terms of employment are often quite different. Management employees often have employment contracts and may receive deferred compensation or stock options, or present other issues. Staff members can be protected by union contracts as well as by federal or state and even local employment laws and regulations.

Management

In many ways, management staffing is a much easier problem to resolve. Most employment agreements or management benefits can be quantified to determine the cost of such decisions. This should have been examined during the due diligence process and worked into the pricing for the transaction.

The primary task in resolving the level of management staffing is to determine where there are redundancies and who the most qualified candidates are. Such a process is normally driven by the acquiring company, but it is not a bad idea to involve the acquired company as well. Only in this way can a true evaluation be made. Failure to consider all candidates fairly may result in a lower return on the investment.

All candidates must be evaluated objectively. It is often difficult to do so because emotions often cloud the judgment of the evaluators. For the acquiring company, choosing the incumbent management team is an easy decision. However, a formal evaluation of all candidates can lead to a stronger, more diverse team. While change can be difficult, it is necessary to embrace the change inherent in acquisitions to enhance your chances of success.

Labor and Staffing Issues

Labor is often protected by union contracts and labor laws. This limits the options available when deciding who should stay and who should go. However, it should not prevent the buyer from evaluating all employees. By evaluating first and then worrying about possible protections, the buyer gains a much better sense of the quality of the workforce that ultimately does remain.

The same rules apply to evaluating labor as to evaluating management. Be objective. Be balanced. Be honest. The buyer shortchanges itself by not doing so. Develop a selection methodology by targeting certain employees for layoff or retention based on performance and experience. Make sure that the applied criteria are documented and objective and are supported by a performance evaluation and that any review of personnel files and performance evaluations is confidential. This may require the formation of a review committee made up of representatives from each organization to ensure that the terminations occur according to agreed-upon procedures.

Once the selections are made, they must be examined from a legal point of view. The following is a checklist of legal considerations to be examined:

- ► Employment agreements that may contain conditions that are unacceptable to the buyer or conditions that may be triggered in the event of a merger or acquisition.
- ► Employees who are on family leave, pregnancy leave, workers' compensation, or disability who have certain rights to comparable positions upon their return to work, which may or may not be consistent with staffing plans after the acquisition.
- ► Whistle-blowers who could bring claims of wrongful discharge.
- ► WARN (Workers Adjustment and Retraining Notification) notices, which the seller must send to its employees sixty days in advance if it is planning to close facilities.
- ► Union contracts that could fall under the National Labor Relations Act (NLRA), which protects the rights of both union and nonunion employees on matters of wages, hours, and working conditions.
- ► Race, religion, or sex discrimination for which the buyer may be held accountable under civil rights legislation, even

if claims are filed based on events that occurred before the acquisition.

▶ Age discrimination under the Age Discrimination in Employment Act (ADEA) and/or the Older Workers Benefit Protection Act (OWBPA), which protect workers against changes in the workforce or changes in benefit plans that would discriminate against workers over forty or make age-based distinctions.

▶ Compliance with the Americans with Disabilities Act (ADA), which, among other things, requires a review of job descriptions to ensure that there is a distinction between essential and nonessential duties and a review of property leases to determine who is responsible (the lessee or the lessor) for renovations required under the ADA.

▶ Violations of the Fair Labor Standards Act (FLSA) or the Equal Pay Act, especially concerning the determination of exempt versus nonexempt positions; a violation in this area could lead to substantial payments to current and former employees for overtime that was worked but not paid.

▶ Problems that could develop under the Occupational Health and Safety Act (OSHA) if current compliance is not verified and the cost of future compliance is not factored into operating results.

▶ Whether the employees being acquired are legally able to work in the United States; the burden of compliance is on the employer under the Immigration Reform and Control Act (IRCA).

▶ Whether there is compliance with the Drug-Free Work Place Act and various government contract laws, since lack of compliance can lead to suspended payments or terminated contracts for a seller that is a federal government contractor.

▶ Whether state law counterparts to federal employment laws have precedence.

The bottom line is that the buyer needs to conduct a thorough labor and employment review. This entails examination of all manner of documents related to such issues. Each transaction is unique in that these issues will apply to differing degrees.

CUSTOMERS

When a buyer acquires a business, one of the most valuable assets is its customer base. One of the post-closing challenges is to determine the profitability of the customers. Often the acquired company has legacy customers that it has been unwilling or unable to terminate even though they are unprofitable or difficult to manage. The acquirer should review all customers for profitability and sustainability. It makes little sense to keep a customer if it is not possible to make a profit on the relationship, unless the customer enables the merged company to penetrate a new market or helps the merged company achieve economies of scale, thereby enabling other customers to be profitable. However, even in these cases, there is a limit to the amount of losses that make financial sense. In addition, the customer may be a direct competitor of the buyer or of one of the buyer's customers. As a result, it is important to evaluate the seller's customer base. It may be necessary to discount the value of the acquisition to account for a customer base that is unprofitable or duplicative and that provides little additional strategic value.

Perhaps more important, however, is for the seller to transfer the goodwill of its customers to the buyer. A disgruntled employee can very quickly destroy this goodwill and perhaps jeopardize a significant income stream on which the value of the acquisition was based. The key steps to transferring this goodwill are:

- ▶ Personal introductions to customer contacts
- ▶ Social events to acquaint customers with the new owners
- ▶ Letters from both the seller and the buyer that thank customers for their business and announce the new management and plans for the merged entity

VENDORS

Suppliers are overlooked much more often than customers. Buyers assume that, after all, any vendor can easily be replaced. Since this is often true, it is necessary for the buyer to conduct a thorough review of the existing suppliers to ensure that the seller is getting the best prices and terms. However, there are certain suppliers whose replacement would cause significant disruption. This can occur in situations where there is only one supplier of a given product or service, or when the supplier is an integral part of a just-in-time inventory system. Essential vendors are a key component of a company's continued success and uninterrupted operation.

Of special importance are suppliers that provide professional services—in particular, bankers, accountants, and lawyers. The standard assumption is that the combined company will use the buyer's professional suppliers, but this may not always be desirable or feasible. If a buyer is purchasing a business in a different industry, its bankers may not have the appropriate expertise. The seller's legal counsel may be better suited to deal with certain local matters or be more cost-effective. The seller's accountants may be providing outsourcing of certain tasks that it may not be practical to change immediately. These factors should be considered carefully before any key relationships are terminated. Ultimately, it may be best to continue to use both firms for certain purposes, subject to any potential conflicts of interest being resolved.

PHYSICAL FACILITIES

Rent and lease payments are a natural place for a buyer to focus when evaluating the efficiencies to be gained by a merger, as these are often one of the larger expenses on the income statement. This would seem to be an easy issue to resolve: In acquiring this company, we can reduce the staff by x percent, which means that we need x percent less square footage in which to work. In addition, the seller has x percent more square footage per employee than our company. As a result, total square footage can be reduced by x percent, thereby saving x. But very few decisions in a merger or acquisition can be resolved with a simple mathematical equation. There usually are people involved, and with people come emotions and unpredictability. These have to be accounted for when looking at space, just as much as when examining staffing levels.

When examining the space requirements of the combined entity, it is certainly helpful to consider the square footage. The space should be evaluated to determine if the rent is higher or lower than that for other company space and if the amount of space is more than is needed. This will go a long way toward helping to cut expenses in order to reach the target return.

However, there must also be human considerations. How long have the employees been in this space? How does the commute compare to that for the places where they might be relocated? How much interaction is required between the staff members being relocated and staff members in a different location? How much reconfiguration of the office and facilities of each company will be required to accommodate additional staff members or functions? How much productivity can be expected from these people during the course of the move?

Failure to explore these and other related questions can open up a can of worms. Location is a factor that can affect the overall integration of the buyer and the seller and can lead to significant turnover. It is taken very personally by many employees. Our suggestion is to take steps to maximize the efficiency of your use of space and property, but to consider the human elements of the changes in doing so.

PROBLEMS INVOLVING ATTITUDES AND CORPORATE CULTURE

The mating dance was fun. The due diligence was outright friendly. The negotiations were cordial. All has gone well. Now, let's get on with the business. And by the way, I think we'll do things our way. After all, we are the buyer.

This is a perfect example of how to ruin months of goodwill with the seller and its employees. It is a perfect example of how to cause problems at the level of corporate culture. Many of the problems associated with mergers and acquisitions are rooted in a lack of sensitivity to the cultures of the combining entities.

There are four keys steps in making sure that such issues don't cloud the success of an otherwise wonderful marriage. First, allow cultural differences to play a part when determining the value of the deal. Second, realize that the cultures of both companies are important. Third, admit that it is not in either company's interest to maintain both cultures (unless the organizations are going to remain autonomous, in which case the cultural differences may be immaterial to continued performance). And fourth, figure out how to combine the two cultures in a way that will prevent the deal from exploding.

If cultural differences are not uncovered during the due diligence process and incorporated into the terms of the deal, the return on the investment will usually be disappointing. The primary reason that this issue can affect the value of the deal is that cultural differences often lead to decreased productivity, which leads to lower revenues and income, and hence the combined entity may be worth less than expected. As a result, it is often wise to place a conservative value on at least the first year's earnings and cash flow. After that, the value should depend on the experience the buyer has obtained as a result of prior acquisitions. If this is the buyer's first acquisition and there are no staff members with experience in such matters, the buyer would be well advised to be conservative in future years as well!

Because of the longevity of the companies that are now seeking to create a single operating entity, the culture of each is usually deeply ingrained. If this were not the case, the companies probably would not be successful and hence would not be attractive merger candidates. In many cases, company employees are unaware of the strength of the culture and how it affects their daily activities.

Recognizing that it is not feasible to keep both cultures seems obvious. Doing so would translate into having two different ways to perform each function. This is a clear recipe for chaos and lack of unity, factors that are normally noticed by outsiders even though efforts are made to hide them. The bottom line is that if the two companies don't act as one, the chances of success are greatly minimized. There will be both internal problems (low morale, disparate goals, redundancy) and external ones (poor customer service, disenchanted investors, and negative press).

The most difficult part of merging two corporate cultures is to identify the common ground. Believe it or not, this usually exists. Look not at the operational level, but at the philosophical level. Once a common primary goal can be agreed upon, and referred back to on many occasions, the true process of merging the cultures can begin. This primary goal must be agreed upon at the top and communicated to all levels. Only then can functional-level details be worked out.

Corporate culture is such a nebulous, personal concept that it can often be difficult to get your arms around it. This makes planning for it and incorporating it into any merger planning difficult. But if it is ignored, it is an issue that can linger for years and ultimately contribute to disappointment on many levels, including return on investment!

Another major cultural challenge is the degree of engagement by the workforces of *both* buyer and seller. According to the December 2016 (updated) Gallup Study on the State of the American Workforce, nearly 20 percent are highly disengaged, 51 percent are disengaged, 25 percent are engaged, and only 4 percent are highly engaged.

There is no guaranty that a merger or acquisition will *improve* these levels of disengagement and, in many cases, it is a distraction that only fuels further dysfunctionality.

BENEFIT AND COMPENSATION PLANS

With the advent of the Employee Retirement Income Security Act (ERISA) and other legislation concerned with compensation and benefits, managing the merging of benefit and compensation plans has taken on added importance. All of the issues concerned with benefit and compensation plans should be worked out in the course of negotiations. Failure to do so, especially with regard to pension plans, can result in costly surprises that cannot be readily addressed afterwards.

As a result of the elaborate structure of such plans, the primary concern should be the ERISA-covered plans—in particular, defined-benefit pension plans. The options available for ERISA-covered pension plans (both defined-benefit and defined-contribution) include terminating the existing plan, freezing the benefits accrued up to the time of the acquisition, merging the two companies' plans, maintaining two plans, or converting to an entirely different plan. Each of these options has benefits and pitfalls, but the primary issue is the potential costs. These costs include required contributions, the amount of unfunded liabilities (in the case of defined-benefit plans), and cash flow requirements. Only after evaluating the magnitude of these costs can an educated decision be made as to the course to take.

Another issue to consider is the integration of other compensation and benefit components, such as medical, life, and disability insurance; severance policies; and reimbursement of medical and childcare expenses. The options available are similar to those for ERISA-covered plans: Maintain separate systems, choose one system over the other, or choose a combination of the two systems. The method of integration chosen is often driven by the costs involved, but it should also take into account the overall compensation and benefits philosophy.

Believe it or not, making these choices is the easy part. The hard part comes with the closing of the transaction and the need to integrate the plans of the two companies. The first step is to set the objectives of the integration. The objectives should cover such factors as the cost, funding, adequacy, and competitive position of the plan.

Once the objectives have been set, the premerger plans of both organizations should be reviewed relative to the objectives outlined for the choice made. In addition, the option chosen should be compared to the general marketplace. Finally, the plan should be evaluated by a representative group of employees. Assuming that the plan has passed all of these tests, it is now time to implement it. As with most post-closing issues, implementation determines the success or failure of the plan. The key function in a successful implementation of benefit and compensation plans is communication. Without good communication of the plan's objectives and details, implementation will be moderately successful, at best. The importance of benefit and compensation plans at every level of the workplace means that, without successful implementation of such plans, no matter how well other aspects of the consolidation may be handled, the situation can spell disaster for employee morale and the ability of the combined entity to work as one.

CORPORATE IDENTITY

Now that the two companies have become one, it stands to reason that the merged entity is different from what existed before. Yet this is a point that can often be forgotten when it comes to corporate identity. Since there is essentially a *new* company, it may be important to consider a new corporate identity in the form of the company name and/or logo.

This may seem obvious, but the real issue goes much deeper. A corporate identity defines what makes a corporation unique. The company name and logo are merely manifestations of that identity. Before such issues can be decided, it must be determined what the corporation stands for, where it is going, and how it is different from other corporations. Only then does it make sense to put a name on it and identify an image with it.

There are several aspects of a corporation that go into its identity. These include market share, industry group identification, customer base, employees, and direction. Most, if not all, of these aspects are altered in some way as the result of a merger or acquisition. The key is to identify what changes have occurred and to respond to them by shaping the image or identity that is communicated to the public.

LEGAL ISSUES

Following the closing of the transaction, there are many legal and administrative tasks that the acquisition team must accomplish in order to complete the transaction. The nature and extent of these tasks will vary, depending on the size of the acquisition and the type of financing method selected by the purchaser. The parties to any acquisition must be careful to ensure that the jubilation of closing does not cause any post-closing matters to be overlooked.

In an *asset acquisition,* these post-closing tasks typically include the following:

- ▶ Final verification that all the assets acquired are free of liens and encumbrances
- ▶ Recording of financing statements and transfer tax returns
- ▶ Recording of any assignments of intellectual property with the Library of Congress or the Patent and Trademark Office
- ▶ Notification of the sale to employees, customers, distributors, and suppliers
- ▶ Adjustments to bank accounts and insurance policies

In addition to these tasks, a stock acquisition may also include the following:

- ▶ Filing articles of amendment to the corporate charter or articles of merger
- ▶ Completion of the transfer of all stock certificates
- ▶ Amendments to the corporate bylaws
- ▶ Preparation of all appropriate post-closing minutes and resolutions

Such actions require legal counsel familiar with the issues of corporate governance and intellectual property. While the buyer's legal counsel attends to these matters, management can more readily focus on the other aspects of the business combination for which it is better qualified and more effective.

MINIMIZING BARRIERS TO THE TRANSITION

No matter how hard you try and how well you anticipate the issues that need to be addressed, the natural response of most people is to avoid change. As a result, it is important that you be aware of the various aspects of change management and address them as well. The primary emotion that will be encountered in dealings with various groups will be *fear*. There will be fear on the part of employees, related to such things as job security, workplace location, and reporting structure. But you may also have to deal with fear on the part of customers (the buyer may discontinue a product line) and suppliers (the buyer may already have a company that supplies that good).

Communication Is Hypercritical

The primary tool for dealing with fear, and with many of the other emotions that surface during the course of an acquisition transition, is communication. If a merger is thought of as the beginning of a marriage, think of the amount of communication that is necessary in the first few weeks and months of such a relationship. As with any relationship, a lack of communication typically means a lack of success.

In a merger, the two keys to effective communication are to determine (1) the importance of the information and (2) who should communicate it. Information should be communicated in the order of its importance. This means that you first want to communicate that information that affects people directly, including changes in:

▶ The organization, especially who is staying and who is leaving
▶ Reporting structures
▶ Job descriptions and responsibilities
▶ Titles, compensation, and benefits
▶ Job location and operating procedures

Because of the importance of this information, the person who is communicating it is also important. Using a trusted person from the seller's side along with an important person from the buyer's side works best. This will assist in the transition and will add credibility to the process.

The next most important information is the introduction of the new management team and the transition to new managers and employees. It is a bit disconcerting to walk the halls in an organization and not know people. Think of how it feels on the first day of a new job. Well, that's how it feels for all the employees of an acquired company. If the buyer makes an effort to introduce the key players, people are more comfortable. The key is to involve employees in the post-closing integration process in order to create a positive momentum. This can help alleviate some fears of insecurity and uncertainty that are a natural consequence of a merger or an acquisition. Employees can match a name with a face and know who is being referred to in discussions. This can help overall efficiency because employees will be focusing on doing their jobs rather than on wondering who someone is and how that person might affect their careers. It also helps in the process of socialization among the employees, which in turn contributes to efficiency. This, of course, becomes more difficult as organizations grow larger. You can, however, introduce those people who are most likely to run into each other.

Effective communication helps in achieving an effective cultural alignment after integration, an issue that often has not been given the attention it requires. When initiating a deal, one must anticipate complexity, have fruitful discussions and, if required, constant communication with stakeholders, and have a continual focus on cultural integration. The extent of the sustainable value creation will ultimately depend on how productive the cultural alignment is. The importance of this is further increased when a post-merger manager is dealing with a cross-border deal. For example, an American buyer must ensure the retention and effective blending of certain core cultural aspects of the European target within the context of the larger picture. The wheels of American capitalism may not (and, indeed, will not) run smoothly on the relatively protectionist European tracks. This blending requires proper use of communication skills by post-merger managers in order to achieve continued success.

Finally, communicate the new reporting structure and have individual managers introduce the two sides when there will be day-to-day interaction. If possible, have the prior manager make some kind of handover to the new leadership. Some kind of group meeting or social gathering among the employees of various departments, especially those that interact regularly, can go a long way toward making everyone more comfortable with the new faces, functions, and procedures.

Post-merger Task Force

One of the tools through which communication can be made more effective is a *post-merger task force*. Such an entity should be composed of a representative group from both sides of the transaction and should be formed after the due diligence process. The role of such a group, which needs to be defined and communicated early, is to uncover, evaluate, and resolve post-merger problems.

The importance of communicating the role of the task force effectively cannot be emphasized enough. Failure to do so will limit its effectiveness and call the resolve of the new organization into question. In a very real sense, this is the first operating decision to be seen by the seller's employees, and thus it will greatly influence the new employees' perception of the acquiring organization.

The composition of the task force has a bearing on its effectiveness and on the integrity of the buyer, as viewed by the seller's employees. As a result, the CEO should probably avoid making herself a member. An honest assessment of those being considered for the task force will go a long way toward establishing its credibility. If one of the members from the seller's side is an employee who is not respected by the majority of the workforce, people will not take the task force seriously.

The role of the task force is best kept simple. It can serve as a conduit from labor to management to resolve problems that arise during the course of the merger. In this way, a dialogue can be opened, and people will get the impression that actions are being taken to address their concerns. The task force can also be used to organize the information that needs to be communicated to the new employees. The amount of information to be communicated can be overwhelming, and the way in which it is communicated can also cause problems. The task force can serve to communicate the issues in order of importance and to address them accurately. This helps prevent the grapevine from disseminating erroneous information. Creating the dialogue and organizing the information helps to reduce or eliminate the fear discussed earlier.

Once its work is completed, the task force must be dissolved. This is easier said than done, as it is much easier to say when the merger activity begins than to define when it is over. The first sign that the end of the task force's life is near is when all the information related to the merger that was deemed to be important has been disseminated. An additional indication is that the amount of information flowing back from the employees to the task force has significantly waned. Nonetheless, it is often helpful to give the task force a set life at its beginning—sixty or ninety days—and to evaluate the situation after that period. The final call will come from the CEO, when it is determined that the value of the task force has been expended and it is now time to get to work to realize the true value of the combination.

POST-MERGER INTEGRATION KEY LESSONS AND BEST PRACTICES

Here are some key lessons learned for developing an effective post-closing integration plan:

- *Pick your poison.* Many deals fail because a strategy for integrating (or not integrating) the two cultures was never clearly defined. Will the seller's culture become dominant? Will the buyer's culture be absorbed by the seller's team and employees? Or, if this is feasible, will the cultures be allowed to "peacefully coexist"? Or will the resulting culture be a hybrid driven by compromise and merit (i.e., they do *that* better but we do *this* better, so let's find ways to truly combine the best of the best in each area). Buyers should not lose sight of the value of the culture that they are buying just because their ego or their ignorance assumes that *their* culture must be dominant on a post-closing basis.

- *Align cultural decisions with the overall M&A goals and growth strategy.* Employees want to see a *fit* between the post-closing integration decisions that are made and the overall strategy that is driving the transaction. If the CEO of BuyerCo talks about the need to cut costs, but nobody is fired, then employees are relieved (for now) but confused. If the BuyerCo CEO talks about the need for geographic expansion, but then closes offices and plants, these decisions do not appear to be aligned with the strategy that has been articulated.

- *Compatibility does not always mean an exact match.* Post-closing, executives and consultants will often force-feed a quest for "sameness" that is unnecessary. Cultures can be compatible and functional even if they are not an exact mirror image of each other. For example, both could be focused on merit-driven performance and rewards, even if the rewards are not exactly the same. Both could be driven by customer service excellence, even if that excellence manifests itself in very different ways, especially if the two companies are in different types of businesses.

■ *Communicate early and communicate often.* The more that can be done to reduce or eliminate the stress and fear of the typical employee, the better. If the leadership is perceived as playing its cards too close to the vest or being fearful of making the hard decisions, both cultures will erode quickly, resulting in a significant adverse effect on the value of the entity on a post-closing basis.

■ *Reach for the stars, but be realistic about post-closing objectives.* The excitement and optimism expressed during the transaction are wonderful and provide energy that should be contagious, but post-merger goals should be realistic and attainable. Goals that are neither believable nor achievable will only disappoint the investors, employees, vendors, and customers and reflect poorly on the management team of the recently integrated company. I am sure that every CEO of BuyerCo believes in his "heart of hearts" that getting this deal done will increase the value of the company by tenfold or even twentyfold down the road . . . but is that realistic in the near term? And if not, is it realistic to have employees believe that a tenfold increase in value in the near term is the actual goal, only to be disappointed when the results are nowhere even close?

■ *Meaningful systems need to be in place to set, measure, and adjust the goals of the transaction.* A clear set of twelve-, twenty-four-, and thirty-six-month "goals and objectives" to be achieved as a result of *this* transaction should be articulated as part of the post-merger integration plans. Yes, some portion of the results will be intangible and difficult to measure (e.g., our customers just "feel better" about us now), but even goodwill should manifest itself in higher customer loyalty and increases in sales that can be easily measured. Repeat sales, upsales, renewals of commitments, and lower turnover rates *can* all be measured and closely monitored.

■ *Treat both sets of customers as gold.* At the end of the day, you can write up all the press releases in the world, but if customers are not convinced that this M&A deal is good for *them*, then the objectives of the deal will *not* be met. Take the time to explain the post-closing value proposition to both sets of customers. If the deal will result in lower costs or better pricing, then tell them so and show them how and why. If the deal will result in higher prices but better service and support, then be ready to justify and explain the value of the trade-off. If the deal will result in broader and better product lines or service offerings, then have your cross-selling strategies and tools ready to go. Remember that your competitors will try to attack the deal and market to your customers if they see the opportunity; you need to be ready to push back.

■ *Don't hide the poop under the rug.* In an attempt to paint a rosy post-closing picture, buyers and sellers may choose to defer problems and challenges that were identified before the closing to some undefined time period after the closing. This "we'll get to it later" approach is a time bomb just waiting to explode, and the cleanup will not be pretty. The failure to unearth lurking problems, or worse, the intentional decision to ignore them, is a recipe for disaster. Problems in such areas as human resources, environmental liabilities, lack of clear ownership of intellectual property, poorly drafted earn-outs, unpaid taxes, unclear major customer commitments, or under-funded pension plans are not going to go away with the waving of a post-closing magic wand. The parties may feel pressure from the marketplace or from their advisors or from their sources of capital to "just go ahead and get this deal closed, and we'll figure out how to deal with these problems later," but this is bad advice and a bad strategy. The delays in closing that solving these problems would create are viewed as the evil, instead of the problems themselves. Yes, momentum is important, and there may be minor problems that are not worth derailing a transaction over, but material issues and challenges *must* be resolved prior to closing.

■ *Do your due diligence the right way the first time.* Improper or hasty due diligence often results in post-merger integration plans going awry. Key issues that should have been discovered and dealt with before closing wind up being a source of tension and dispute after closing because due diligence was piecemeal or improperly staffed. Due diligence staffing means having the right number of people with the right skill sets who are prepared to invest the time and effort needed to ask the right questions and challenge the answers that don't make sense. Subject matter experts should be brought in when necessary, especially for high-tech or biotech/life science transactions. For example, if you are buying a government contractor and one of the key assets is a long-term supply contract with the Department of Defense for providing advanced technology and support, then those contracts had *better* be reviewed by someone more senior and more knowledgeable than a second-year general corporate practice associate at your local law firm.

COMMON AREAS OF POST-CLOSING DISPUTES AND LITIGATION

When a post-closing integration plan goes awry or if there are significant post-closing breaches of covenants in the definitive purchase documents, the parties may need to turn to the courts to resolve disputes, or at the very least to post-closing negotiation, mediation, or arbitration. Post-closing disputes come in a variety of forms, from basic breaches of the representation and warranties, to violations of post-closing covenants (such as non-competes or nondisclosures), to accounting, tax, and financial claims (often relating to disputes in liability calculation, holdbacks, or allocation of risk to loss of key customers, vendors, or employees, which the financial premise of the transaction relied upon to stay in place). These disputes can cut deeply into the value proposition of the transaction and delay or derail the financial upside to both the buyer and the seller.

Disputes may arise either directly between the parties, or be initiated by an affected third party, such as a lender or investor, or be brought as a derivative action, when a stockholder steps into the shoes of the harmed corporate buyer or seller and sues on the company's behalf for damages to the company. The key determinants are *who* suffered the alleged harm and *who* would receive the benefit of any remedy. Most claims revolve around some fundamental flaw in the M&A process, whether overvaluation (underpayment *or* overpayment), waste and inefficiency, mismanagement, dilution, or some fundamental breach of the fiduciary duty that the officers and directors of both parties owe to their respective stakeholders. Some cases have even named the financial or professional advisors as parties to the fraud or breach of duty.

In 2007, about 44 percent of M&A deals worth over $100 million were the subject of some form of a post-closing dispute. By 2014, that percentage had peaked by rising to over 90 percent, representing nearly every large transaction across a wide spectrum of industries. In 2016, the percentage had "stabilized" to under 80 percent, as courts began to push back on this proliferation of M&A-related litigation, especially when many cases generated more in legal fees than the actual damages that wound up in the hands of the affected shareholders.

At the heart of many of these disputes are whether the officers and directors of each entity satisfied their duty of care and their duty of loyalty. The *duty of care* requires fiduciaries to inform themselves about the transaction in a deliberate manner of all reasonable available material *before* giving their respective approvals. Failure to be diligent and thorough in the review of the information available could be an actionable breach of this duty. The *duty of loyalty*–related disputes usually revolve around conflicts of interest, improper payments or personable benefits, acts taken in bad faith or in knowing violation of the law, or international misconduct. Specific claims could include improper dividends, excessive salary or benefits, special treatment in stock purchases or redemption or other acts of bad faith, unfairness, or self-dealing by leaders or majority shareholders at the expense of the minority stakeholders. Financial advisors and investment bankers need to be aware of potential liability for "aiding and abetting claims" even if they are third parties with no fiduciary relationship to the buyer or seller or its shareholders.

CONCLUSION

The importance of a well-planned and smooth post-closing transition cannot be emphasized enough. Without the proper attention to these matters, the value of the transaction may never be realized. This will require assembling a team with proven implementation skills and a desire to see the transaction work. The sheer number of issues that need to be addressed can seem overwhelming. But the importance of these issues in the success of a business combination cannot be overemphasized. By planning properly, paying attention to the details, and picking the right people for the job, a buyer will gain confidence in its ability to successfully integrate the seller into its operations. The key is to understand that this planning process for post-merger integration begins well before the process is initiated. There must be clear rules for assessing the best fit, and if preliminary investigations reveal a likelihood of potential issues arising, the buyer must be prepared to stop the process and clarify those issues prior to closing. This requires a deeper due diligence, something that, when avoided, results in post-integration shocks. Engaging in it will serve to encourage further growth through mergers and acquisitions.

14.

Special Challenges (and Opportunities) in Cross-Border Transactions

As our marketplaces become increasingly global in nature, the rise in cross-border deals continues to grow, both in frequency and complexity. Leaders of companies from all over the globe are looking at acquisitions abroad in order to drive globalization objectives, fight market saturation or slowdown in core markets, enhance diversification, address regulatory uncertainty in home markets, access new perspectives in innovation and business models, and counter the high repatriation costs of overseas earnings by investing excess earnings in local markets. In 2016, companies in China, the United States, and Canada were the top three investors or buyers, and the top three markets for investment targets were the United States, Switzerland, and the United Kingdom (pre-Brexit).

Activity in the United Kingdom may slow down a bit in 2017–2018 as other parts of Europe become more robust. In Switzerland, the deal activity swelled to such an impressive level that, by summer 2017, cash reserves in the Bank of Switzerland had reached in excess of $750 billion.

Company leaders interviewed in late 2016 by Deloitte cited the following strategic reasons for the uptick in cross-border deals, with a focus on the strategic objectives shown in Figure 14-1.

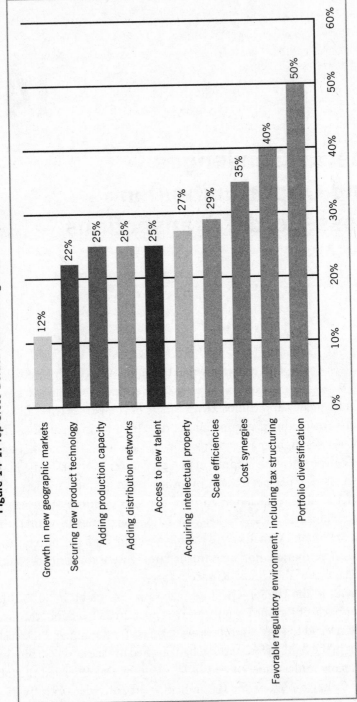

Figure 14-1. Top Cross-Border M&A Strategic Deal Objectives

1. Source—Deloitte, Fall 2016
2. Value might not add up to 100 percent because respondents could select more than one answer.

China struck $25 billion in deals in 2016 to acquire companies around the globe, a record-breaking figure that may not be matched any time soon. By 2017, Chinese government and business leaders had already pulled back a bit on overseas M&A, concerned that too much capital was leaving its borders. Several Chinese leaders in early 2017 observed that "too many deals were done too quietly" in 2016 and that some deals reflected a "blind and irrational M&A investment strategy." But as China slowed down, companies from Japan and other countries kept their appetites healthy for U.S. and European targets. See Figure 14-2.

Figure 14-2. Global M&A Data Set: M&A Drivers and Trends Across the Globe	
NORTH AMERICA **$1.5 Trillion** *2016 vs. 2015* -23 percent	2016 was a strong year for U.S. M&A, despite the significant decline from 2015 record levels. TMT and Energy were the strongest sectors after a slow start to the year. Foreign investment (particularly Chinese) continued, leading to a 2 percent rise in inbound M&A. U.S. bidders targeted Europe, doing some of the largest U.S. outbound deals on record (Qulacomm/NPX, Praxair/Linde, Twenty-First Century Fox/Sky). Strategic buyers are dominating U.S. M&A activity with cash, strong stock prices, and cheap debt being used to finance deals. Private equity sponsors remain cautious. Fewer mega-deals were tabled and broken deals hit record levels—principally due to antitrust concerns (e.g., Honeywell/UTC) and the clampdown on tax inversions (e.g., Pfizer/Allergan).
LATIN AMERICA **$90 Billion** *2016 vs. 2015* 0 percent ═	LatAm M&A was flat year on year, as strong investment from Asia Pacific, particularly China (e.g., State Grid Corporation/CPFL Energia), countered an otherwise slowing M&A market. Hotspots were Mexico, Peru, Argentina, and Chile. It remains to be seen what effect the Trump administration will have on M&A activity in the region (particularly Mexico). Growth in M&A is being held back by economic slowdowns and political uncertainty, particularly in Brazil, where deep recession and political scandals are impediments to M&A. Distressed M&A is prevalent as Brazilian companies struggle to access capital; large companies (e.g., Petrobras and Vale) are undertaking asset sales to cut leverage. Deals are increasingly delayed and difficult to complete because of extensive due diligence and tax, regulatory, or compliance issues, with rising concerns over bribery and corruption.

(continued on next page)

Figure 14-2. Global M&A Data Set: M&A Drivers and Trends Across the Globe (cont.)

EUROPE **$781 Billion** *2016 vs. 2015* -11 percent	European M&A activity is down 11 percent year on year, as European businesses reacted with caution to political and economic events. Overseas investment continued unabated through 2016, with inbound M&A up to 36 percent (principally from China and Japan) focused on European industrials and advanced tech (e.g., Midea/Kika, SoftBank/ARM Holdings), as well as energy (e.g., CTG/WindMW). Germany is the European M&A hot spot, where M&A activity rose 27 percent year on year, fueled partly by a surge in Chinese investment. Italy recorded its second best year for M&A since 2007. Spanish M&A also strengthened after the formation of a new government in October 2016. In CEE, FIG deals in Poland and real estate in the Czech Republic were active. Largely driven by Brexit uncertainty, UK M&A had a bumpy year, with value levels down 55 percent.
AFRICA/MIDDLE EAST **$90 Billion** *2016 vs. 2015* +52 percent	M&A levels held up despite the sustained period of low oil prices hurting the economies of oil producers such as Nigeria, Angola, and Algeria. We see a noticeable shift from West to East Africa, with Kenya and other East African counties becoming favored investment destinations. Stable countries are being targeted to act as regional hubs from which investors can access growth in nearby economies. The consumer sector saw Africa's largest deals in 2016, as multinational corporates purchased market share and South African retail majors reorganized capital structures to facilitate outbound acquisitions. Mining, power, and telecoms are active as Africa's infrastructure deficit drives M&A activity. Despite continued weak oil prices, 2016 was a strong year for Middle East M&A, with deal values more than doubling year on year. Increased liquidity, government-sponsored mergers (particularly in Banking) and energized regional private equity firms drove activity. Banking will continue to see activity in 2017 as central bank policy drives further consolidation. Standout sectors include tech (particularly online retailers and payment solutions services) and health care (partly driven by deregulation, e.g. Saudi).
ASIA PACIFIC **$738 Billion** *2016 vs. 2015* -22 percent	M&A values in Asia Pacific fell year on year, as the Japanese and Chinese prioritized outward investment over intra-regional activity (Japan intra-regional M&A -75 percent; Chinese intra-regional M&A -53 percent). Hot spots are consumer/TMT assets in Southeast Asia (boosted by investment in China's One Belt One Road initiative) and power and infrastructure assets in Indonesia (e.g. Nebras/Paiton).

Cross-border deals present a wide variety of legal, financial, cultural, regulatory, and compliance challenges in both due diligence, financing, deal structuring, and post-closing integration. Due diligence considerations often focus on political stability, cultural differences, compliance with the Foreign Corrupt Practices Act (FCPA), and parallel anti-bribery and anti–money laundering regulations in the United States and Europe.

Key risk factors include tax considerations, regulatory compliance, shifts in consumer demand and buying patterns, cultural and work habit issues, political stability and predictability, and access to human capital talent/staffing.

Best practices for cross-border M&A include:

▶ Ensure that the deal thesis and deal objective drives all phases of the M&A life cycle.

▶ Adapt the deal methodology and playbook to specific deal circumstances to preempt global M&A challenges.

▶ Integrate pre-deal due diligence with pre-close planning activities to prevent handoff misses.

▶ Structure the deal so it has the best chance of meeting its objectives.

▶ Define the overall integration scope, approach, and plan for achieving both day-one and end-state goals.

▶ Organize a global integration program that has representation from both acquirer and target around key work streams and regions/countries.

▶ Focus efforts on effectively planning pre- and post-close integration in detail, with dependencies and critical path clearly outlined.

Figure 14-3. Key Due Diligence and Structural Challenges in Cross-Border M&A

➡ *Political Considerations.* Identifying and evaluating the actual or potential political implications should be accomplished in advance of initiating any M&A or strategic investment transaction. It is imperative that the likely concerns of federal, state, and local government agencies, employees and unions, customers, suppliers, communities, and other interested parties be thoroughly considered ▼

and, if possible, addressed strategically prior to any acquisition or investment proposal becoming knowing to the public. Many parties—other than the executive branch of the federal government in the applicable jurisdictions—have potential leverage (economic, regulatory, public relations, etc.) that can bear on a cross-border transaction.

➡ *U.S. Law Compliance.* Complying with applicable U.S. law can be troublesome for non-U.S. entities during both the deal-making process and post-closing integration phase in private transactions as well as public deals. In private transactions, U.S. laws such as the Foreign Corrupt Practices Act can pose pre-closing due diligence disclosure issues or post-closing compliance obstacles for non-U.S. entities in many regions—particularly outside of the EU. Another example is a foreign target's historical business activities that do not comply with U.S. export and sanctions laws. In cross-border public deals, disclosure/governance compliance regulations, SEC rules, the Sarbanes-Oxley Act, and stock exchange requirements can present certain challenges for non-U.S. companies. The actual and potential impact of these compliance issues should be evaluated to ensure compatibility with home country rules and to be certain that the non-U.S. target will be able to comply. For inbound public transactions, rules relating to director independence, internal controls reports, and loans to officers and directors, among others, can frequently raise issues for non-U.S. companies that become subject to U.S. listing requirements.

➡ *Cultural and Communication Obstacles.* Cross-border transactions —inbound or outbound—present a unique set of issues that are compounded by the scale and geographic scope of the deal. Parties to the deal often come from divergent cultural backgrounds, have multiple language requirements, have different business practices, and are in distant locales. Overlooking these issues often results in a failed deal or in unsuccessful business integration. Most cultural and communication obstacles to a deal are best addressed with early and consistent recognition in the deal process of the breadth of these obstacles.

➡ *U.S. Attorney-Client Privilege.* The attorney-client privilege is one of the oldest tenets of the U.S. legal system and perhaps the most important evidentiary privilege in the United States It aims to protect confidential attorney-client communications that relate to legal advice from disclosure to third parties—including disclosure to the government. The purpose of the attorney-client privilege is to promote full and frank communications between attorneys and their clients. This privilege is generally extended by U.S. courts to in-house counsel. However, in many countries, the rules related to privilege are quite different. Failing to recognize the risks posed for cross-border transactions and developing appropriate strategies to protect sensitive information can be catastrophic. In cross-border transactions this privilege can be inadvertently waived—or even found not to exist in many circumstances (this is especially so for in-house counsel who may work on a transaction but not be licensed in various foreign jurisdictions).

➡ *Employment and Labor.* Labor and employment issues in cross-border transactions can be quite complex because of the differences in local jurisdiction requirements or customs and practices. The depth of challenges in this area can become compounded by the scale and geographic scope of the transaction. Many countries severely restrict the ability to terminate employees, and local labor laws may also impact or regulate employee work hours and benefits including overtime, vacation, and severance. For example, France does not recognize "at will" employment and, as such, the employer must provide each employee with a written contract and may only terminate the employee for cause. In Japan, long-held traditional local customs and practices based on expectations of "lifetime employment" for employees were recently codified into statute. Chinese law stipulates the amount of severance to be paid to an employee terminated without cause. Labor unions play a large role in M&A negotiations in countries such as France and Germany, where union collective bargaining agreements typically define employee wage levels, work conditions, and termination conditions.

➡ *Tax and Accounting Considerations.* Tax issues are typically critical to structuring the transaction. Non-U.S. acquirers contemplating a dividend stream flowing from the U.S. target need to structure the transaction to deal with withholding tax requirements and should consider the possibility of utilizing a subsidiary located in a country that has a favorable tax treaty network or other tax attributes that will minimize the taxes imposed on the dividends as they cross borders. The proportion of debt and equity will be important from a tax perspective, as will obtaining U.S. interest deductions on indebtedness. For cross-border stock-for-stock mergers or acquisitions that are intended to be tax-free, special rules applicable to these types of transactions may be relevant. Also, different countries have different accounting rules.

➡ *Post-closing Integration.* One of the reasons deals often fail to meet their pre-closing objectives on financial goals is poor post-acquisition integration, particularly in cross-border deals where multiple cultures, languages, and historic business methods may create friction and post-closing challenges. If possible, the executives and consultants who will be responsible for integration should be involved in the early stages of the deal so that they can help formulate and "own" the plans that they will be expected to execute. Too often, a separation between the deal team and the integration/execution teams invites slippage in execution of a plan that in hindsight is labeled by the new team as unrealistic or overly ambitious. However, integration planning needs to be carefully phased in, as implementation cannot occur prior to the time most regulatory approvals are obtained.

➡ *Antitrust and Anticompetition Issues.* To the extent that a non-U.S. acquirer directly or indirectly competes or holds an interest in a company that competes in the same industry as the target company, antitrust concerns may arise either at the federal agency or state attorney general level. Although less typical, concerns can also occur if the foreign acquirer competes either in an upstream or downstream market of the target. Pre-closing planning integration efforts should also be sensitive to antitrust considerations.

➡ *Transaction Structure.* A variety of potential transaction structures should be considered when developing the deal structure, especially in sensitive transactions. Choosing the right deal structure is often critical to successfully closing the transaction and optimizing post-closing integration and operations. Structures used successfully on past deals have their place, but today other structures can be helpful in many circumstances. Examples of these deal structures include no-governance and low-governance investments, minority ownership stakes or joint ventures (with the potential for future increase in ownership or governance over time), and making an acquisition of a U.S. business utilizing a controlled or partly controlled U.S. acquisition vehicle.

➡ *Due Diligence.* Wholesale application of the acquirer's domestic due diligence standards to the target's jurisdiction can cause delay, waste time and resources, or result in missing key issues. Due diligence methods must take into account the target jurisdiction's legal regime and, particularly important in a competitive auction situation, take into account the local customs and practices. Making due diligence requests that appear to the target as particularly unusual or unreasonable (not uncommon in cross-border deals) can easily cause a party to lose credibility. Similarly, missing significant local issues for lack of target country knowledge can be highly problematic. These issues can be typically addressed by engaging and soliciting input from experienced local counsel.

15.

Alternatives to Mergers and Acquisitions

You will recall that in Chapter 1 we established that mergers and acquisitions, at least from the buyer's perspective, were an inorganic growth strategy. The buyer's acquisition plan identifies one or more transactions that will enhance its market share, create economies of scale, penetrate new geographic and categorical markets, and provide a basis for raising additional capital. Hopefully, at this point, you feel comfortable with the logistics, challenges, and mechanics of this strategy as well as the legal, financial, and strategic aspects of mergers and acquisitions.

However, there is a wide variety of alternative strategies that focus on the building of *external* relationships that achieve many of these same objectives. The primary difference among these strategies is the *degree of control* that results between the parties after the consummation of the relationship. If you take a look at Figure 15-1, you will see that mergers and acquisitions appears at the far left as being the growth strategy that results in the strongest level of control, since it doesn't get much stronger than 100 percent ownership! As you move toward the right, you will see strategies such as joint ventures, franchising, licensing, strategic alliances, and distributorships. These are alternatives to mergers and acquisitions in that all of these strategies and relationships envision a dynamic and synergistic working relationship but fall short of a metamorphosis.

Figure 15-1. Growth Strategies Horizon

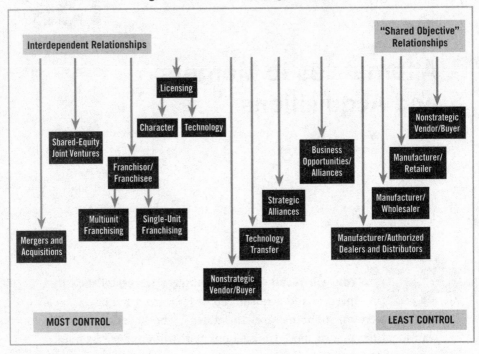

In 2017 and beyond, these strategic alternatives to M&A became more important than ever before, given the muted appetite for risk and concern for overpayment with tightly controlled access to the capital markets. In lieu of establishing direct company-owned units, either in the United States or abroad, at a very high cost of capital, many companies turned to franchising and licensing as a way to pursue new opportunities and penetrate new markets. In order to reduce the risk of a hasty transaction that would inevitably lead to post-closing problems, many companies took a more gradual approach through a multistage relationship, such as joint ventures and strategic alliances. Instead of complex rollups, many like-minded companies with common needs or potential shared efficiencies turned to cooperatives, federations, and networks as a way of working together, thereby taking a page out of the playbook of well-established structures such as Sunkist, Ace Hardware, FTD, and Best Western.

In some cases, these strategies and relationships are designed to be long-term and truly independent, and in other cases the relationships are more noncommittal and merely have "shared objectives." Let's take a look at a few of these alternatives.

GROWTH STRATEGY ALTERNATIVE 1:
JOINT VENTURES

One strategic alternative to an acquisition that is available to today's small and growing companies is a legal structure known as a *joint venture*. A joint venture is typically structured as a partnership or as a newly formed co-owned corporation where two or more parties are brought together to achieve a series of strategic and financial objectives on a short-term or a long-term basis. Emerging growth and middle-market companies that want to explore this strategy should give careful thought to the type of partner they are looking for and what resources they will be contributing to the newly formed entity. As in the raising of a child, each parent will be making its respective contribution of skills, abilities, and resources.

Joint ventures, strategic partnering, cross-licensing, and technology transfer agreements are all strategies designed to obtain one or more of the following: (1) a direct capital infusion in exchange for equity and/ or intellectual property or distribution rights, (2) a "capital substitute" where the resources that would otherwise be obtained with the capital are obtained through joint venturing, or (3) a shift of the burden and cost of development (through licensing) in exchange for a potentially more limited upside.

Embarking on a search for a joint venture partner is a bit like searching for a spouse. Care should be taken to truly conduct a thorough review of prospective candidates, and extensive due diligence should be done on the final few that are being considered. Develop a list of key objectives and goals to be achieved by the joint venture or licensing relationship, and compare this list with the objectives and goals of your final candidates. Take the time to understand the corporate culture and decision-making process within each company. Consider some of the following issues: (1) How does this fit with your own processes? (2) What about each prospective partner's previous experiences and track record with other joint venture relationships? (3) Why did these previous relationships succeed or fail?

Wahaha Joint Venture Company was a joint venture, formed in 1996, between the Hangzhou Wahaha Group, China's largest beverage producer, and Danone, one of the largest food conglomerates in the world. At the time it was formed, this joint venture was referred to as a showcase joint venture by a popular business magazine, but it has since resulted in much bitterness, including several lawsuits between the two companies in 2009. While there were several issues at play, the massive cultural clashes between the Chinese and French companies that formed the joint venture were a key issue, a lesson for all of us considering cross-border joint ventures. Other recent joint ventures that have gone awry and resulted in litigation included KapuGems/Diamond Imports (billing and accounting issues), Verizon/Redbox (unclear timetable and consumer adoption), Crossfit/Northstar (fraud claims), and Iridium (too many chefs in a nineteen-company JV kitchen).

In mid-2009, Delta and Virgin Blue announced plans to form a joint venture to better compete in the market for flights between the United States and Australia. The joint venture allowed the companies to collaborate on product offerings as well as expand their value to customers by expanding the reach of their frequent-flyer program benefits and granting access to airport lounges through reciprocity agreements, and has to date been very successful.

In 2016 and 2017, in the face of falling oil barrel prices, many energy companies turned to joint ventures (often in lieu of M&A) to drive new innovation, new markets, and operational efficiencies. These included joint ventures between BP and Shanghai's SECCO Petrochemical (a division of Sinopec), Exelon and JATC (Japan Atomic Power Company), and Hanwha (based in South Korea) and TOTAL to expand both of their refinery and petrochemical platforms. In April 2017, a joint venture was announced between BP and DuPont's subsidiary BUTAMAX to add to their ethanol production capabilities. 2017 also saw joint venture activity in the health-care, defense, cybersecurity, and automotive industries, namely Eaton/Cummins (to produce automated transmissions) and Zenvity (the joint venture between Autoliv and Volvo to produce autonomous vehicles). We also saw strange pairings between old media and new media companies, such as Alibaba partnering with Marriott to attract more Chinese travel customers, Airbnb/ Hearst teaming up to create a new travel magazine, and Dish Network partnering with Amazon to be more competitive in the wireless business. We have also seen online and brick and mortar M&A such as Amazon/Whole Foods and online retailers turning to traditional format stores, such as Warby-Parker and Bonobos (acquired in 2017 by WalMart).

In many cases, smaller companies that are looking for joint venture partners wind up selecting a much larger Goliath with a wide range of financial and nonfinancial resources that will allow the smaller company to achieve its growth plans. The motivating factor for the larger company under these circumstances is to get access and distribution rights to new technologies, products, and services. In turn, the larger company offers access to pools of capital, research and development, personnel, distribution channels, and general contacts that the small company desperately needs.

But proceed carefully. Be sensitive to the politics, red tape, and different management practices that may be in place at a larger company that will be foreign to many smaller firms. Try to distinguish between what is being promised and what will actually be delivered. If the primary motivating force for the small firm is really only capital, then consider whether alternative (and perhaps less costly) sources of money have been thoroughly explored. Ideally, the larger joint venture partner will offer a lot more than money. If the primary motivating force is access to technical personnel, then consider whether purchasing these resources separately might be a better decision than entering into a partnership in which you give up a certain measure of control. Also, consider whether strategic relationships or extended payment terms with vendors and consultants can be arranged in lieu of the joint venture.

Why Consider a Joint Venture or Strategic Alliance?

▶ Develop a new market (domestic or international).
▶ Develop a new product.
▶ Develop or share technology.
▶ Combine complementary technologies.
▶ Pool resources to develop a production or distribution facility.

- ▶ Acquire capital.
- ▶ Execute a government contract.
- ▶ Access a distribution network or sales or marketing capability.

For example, suppose that an emerging company named Product-Corp has the patents to protect the technology necessary to produce a wide range of new consumer products. It can commence a search for a capital-rich partner that will invest money in the construction of a manufacturing facility, to be owned and operated by the newly established entity. As an alternative, ProductCorp could enter into a joint venture with a larger competitor that already has the manufacturing capability to produce the products.

Each strategy has advantages and disadvantages, and it is important to understand the key differences as demonstrated in Figure 15-2. The capital-rich joint venture partner brings the necessary financial resources to achieve company objectives, but it cannot contribute experience in the industry. On the other hand, the larger competitor may offer certain operational and distribution synergies and economies of scale, but it may seek greater control over ProductCorp's management decisions.

	JOINT VENTURES	STRATEGIC ALLIANCES
Figure 15-2. Understanding the Difference Between Joint Ventures and Strategic Alliances		
Term	Usually Medium-to Long-Term	Short-Term
Strategic Objective	Often serves as the Precursor to a Merger	More Flexible and Noncommittal
Legal Agreements and Structure	Actual legal entity formed	Contractual-Driven
Extent of Commitment	Shared Equity	Shared Objectives
Capital and Resources	Each party makes a capital contribution of cash or intangible assets	No specific capital contributions (may be shared budgeting or even cross-investment)
Tax Ramifications	Be on the lookout for double taxation unless pass-through entities are utilized	No direct tax ramifications

Unlike franchising, distributorships, and licensing, which are almost always vertical in nature, joint ventures can be structured at *either* horizontal or vertical levels of distribution. At the horizontal level, the joint venture is almost an alternative to a merger, with two companies operating at the same level in the distribution channel joining together (either by means of a partnership-type agreement or by joint ownership of a specially created corporation) to achieve certain synergies or operating efficiencies.

Consider the following key strategic issues before and during joint venture or strategic alliance negotiations:

- ▶ Exactly what types of tangible and intangible assets will be contributed to the joint venture by each party? Who will have ownership rights in the property contributed during the term of the joint venture and thereafter? Who will own property developed as a result of joint development efforts?
- ▶ What covenants of nondisclosure or noncompetition will be expected of each joint venturer during the term of the agreement and thereafter?
- ▶ What timetables or performance quotas for completion of the projects contemplated by the joint venture will be included in the agreement? What are the rights and remedies of each party if these performance standards are not met?
- ▶ How will issues of management and control be addressed in the agreement? What will be the respective voting rights of each party? What are the procedures in the event of a major disagreement or deadlock? What is the fallback plan?

Once the two parties have discussed all of the preliminary issues, a formal joint venture agreement or corporate shareholders' agreement should be prepared with the assistance of counsel. The precise terms of the agreement between the two joint venturers will naturally depend on the specific objectives of the parties. At a minimum, however, the following topics should be addressed in as much detail as possible:

- ■ *Nature, purpose, and trade name for the joint venture.* The legal nature of the parties' relationship should be stated, along with a clean statement of purpose to prevent future disputes. If a new trade name is established for the venture, provisions should be made concerning the use of the name and any other trade or service marks should the project be terminated.

- **Status of the respective joint venturers.** Clearly indicate whether each party is a partner, shareholder, agent, independent contractor, or some combination thereof.

- **Representations and warranties of each joint venturer.** Standard representations and warranties will include obligations of due care and due diligence, along with mutual covenants governing confidentiality and anticompetition restrictions.

- **Capital and property contributions of each joint venturer.** A clear schedule of all contributions should be established, whether those contributions are in the form of cash, shares, real estate, or intellectual property. Detailed descriptions will be particularly important if the distribution of profits and losses is to be based on each party's overall contribution. The specifics of the allocation and distribution of profits and losses among the venturers should also be clearly defined.

- **Management, control, and voting rights of each joint venturer.** If the proposed venture envisions joint management, it will be necessary to specifically address the keeping of books, records, and bank accounts; the nature and frequency of inspections and audits; insurance and cross-indemnification obligations; and the responsibility for administrative and overhead expenses.

- **Rights in joint venture property.** Each party must be mindful of intellectual property rights, and the issues of ownership use and licensing entitlements should clearly be addressed, not only for the venturers' presently existing property rights, but also for the future use of rights (or products or services) developed in the name of the venture itself.

- **Default, dissolution, and termination of the joint venture.** The obligations of the venturers and the distribution of assets should be clearly defined, along with procedures in the event of bankruptcy and grounds for default.

GROWTH STRATEGY ALTERNATIVE 2:
FRANCHISING

Over the last two decades, franchising has emerged as a popular expansion strategy for a variety of product and service companies, especially for smaller businesses that cannot afford to finance internal growth. Recent International Franchise Association (IFA) statistics demonstrate that retail sales from franchised outlets make up nearly 60 percent of all retail sales in the United States, estimated at over $2.3 trillion, and the outlets employed more than 20 million people in 2016. Notwithstanding these impressive figures, franchising as a method of marketing and distributing products and services is really appropriate only for certain kinds of companies. Despite the favorable media attention that franchising has received over the past few years, this strategy is not for everyone. This is because there are a host of legal and business prerequisites that must be satisfied before any company can seriously consider franchising as a method for rapid expansion.

Many companies prematurely select franchising as a growth alternative and then haphazardly assemble and launch the franchising program. Other companies are urged to franchise by unqualified consultants or advisors who may be more interested in professional fees than in the long-term success of the franchising program. This has caused financial distress and failure at both the growing company and the franchisee level, usually resulting in litigation. Current and future members of the franchising community must be urged to take a responsible view toward the creation and development of their franchising programs.

Reasons for Franchising

There are a wide variety of reasons cited by successful growing companies as to why they have selected franchising as a method of growth and distribution. These reasons include:

- ► Obtain operating efficiencies and economies of scale.
- ► Achieve more rapid market penetration at a lower capital cost.
- ► Reach the targeted consumer more effectively through cooperative advertising and promotion.

▶ Sell products and services to a dedicated distributor network.

▶ Replace the need for internal personnel with motivated owner/operators.

▶ Shift the primary responsibility for site selection, employee training and personnel management, local advertising, and other administrative concerns to the franchisee, licensee, or joint venture partner with the guidance or assistance of the growing company.

In the typical franchising relationship, the franchisee shares the risk of expanding the market share of the growing company by committing its capital and resources to the development of satellite locations modeled after the proprietary business format of the growing company. The growing company's risk of business failure is further reduced by the improvement in competitive position, reduced vulnerability to cyclical fluctuations, the existence of a captive market for the growing company's proprietary products and services (because of the network of franchisees), and reduced administrative and overhead costs.

The Foundation for Franchising

Responsible franchising is the *only* way in which growing companies and franchisees will be able to coexist harmoniously in the twenty-first century. Responsible franchising means that there must be a secure foundation from which the franchising program is launched. Any company that is considering franchising as a method of growth and distribution or any individual considering franchising as a method of getting into business must understand the components of this foundation (see Figure 15-3). The key components of this foundation are as follows:

- *A proven prototype* location (or chain of stores) that will serve as a basis for the franchising program. The store or stores must have been tested, refined, and operated successfully and be consistently profitable. The success of the prototype should not be too dependent on the physical presence or specific expertise of the founders of the system.

- *A strong management team* made up of internal officers and directors (as well as qualified consultants) who understand both the particular industry in which the company operates and the legal and business aspects of franchising as a method of expansion.

■ *Sufficient capitalization* to launch and sustain the franchising program and to ensure that enough capital is available to allow the growing company to provide both initial and ongoing support and assistance to franchisees. (A lack of a well-prepared business plan and adequate capital structure is often the principal cause of demise of many early-stage franchisors.)

Figure 15-3. Foundation for Successful Franchising Systems

➡ *A distinctive and protected trade identity* that includes federal and state registered trademarks as well as a uniform trade appearance, signage, slogans, trade dress, and overall image.

➡ Proprietary and proven *methods of operation and management* that can be reduced to writing in a comprehensive operations manual, that are not be too easily duplicated by competitors, that are able to maintain their value to the franchisees over an extended period of time, and that can be enforced through clearly drafted and objective quality control standards.

➡ A comprehensive training program for franchisees, both at the company's headquarters and on-site at the franchisee's proposed location, at the outset of the relationship and on an ongoing basis.

➡ Field support staff members who are skilled trainers and communicators and who are available to visit, inspect, and periodically assist franchisees, and also to monitor quality control standards.

➡ A set of comprehensive *legal documents* that reflect the company's business strategies and operating policies. Offering documents must be prepared in accordance with applicable federal and state disclosure laws, and franchise agreements should strike a delicate balance between the rights and obligations of the growing company and the franchisee.

➡ A demonstrated *market demand* for the products and services developed by the growing company that will be distributed through the franchisees. The growing company's products and services should meet certain minimum quality standards, not be subject to rapid shifts in consumer preferences (e.g., fads), and be proprietary in nature. Market research and analysis should be ▼

sensitive to trends in the economy and the specific industry, the plans of direct and indirect competitors, and shifts in consumer preferences.

➡ A set of carefully developed, uniform *site selection criteria and architectural standards* that can be readily and affordably secured in today's competitive real estate market.

➡ A genuine understanding of the competition (both direct and indirect) that the growing company will face in marketing and selling franchises to prospective franchisees and that franchisees will face when marketing the company's products and services.

➡ Relationships with suppliers, lenders, real estate developers, and other key resources as part of the operations manual and system.

➡ *A franchisee profile and screening system* developed by the growing company in order to identify the minimum financial qualifications, business acumen, and understanding of the industry that will be required to be a successful franchisee.

➡ An effective system of *reporting and recordkeeping* to maintain the performance of the franchisees and ensure that royalties are reported accurately and paid promptly.

➡ Research and development capabilities for the introduction of new products and services to consumers through the franchised network on an ongoing basis.

➡ A *communication system* that facilitates a continuing and open dialogue with the franchisees, and as a result reduces the chances for conflict and litigation with the franchise network.

➡ National, regional, and local *advertising, marketing, and public relations programs* designed to recruit prospective franchisees and to attract consumers to the sites operated by the franchisees.

Regulatory Issues

The offer and sale of a franchise is regulated at both the federal and the state level. At the federal level, the Federal Trade Commission (FTC) in 1979 adopted its trade regulation rule 436 (the FTC Rule), which specifies the minimum amount of disclosure that must be made to a prospective franchisee in any of the fifty states. In addition to the FTC rule, more than a dozen states have adopted their own rules and regulations for the offer and sale of franchises within their borders. Known as the *registration states*, these states generally follow a more detailed disclosure format known as the Franchise Disclosure Document (FDD).

Each of the registration states has slightly different procedures and requirements for the approval of a growing company before offers and sales are authorized. In all cases, however, the package of disclosure documents is assembled, consisting of an FDD, a franchise agreement, supplemental agreements, financial statements, a franchise roster, an acknowledgment of receipt form, and the special disclosures that are required by each state, such as corporation verification statements, salesperson disclosure forms, and consent to service of process documents. The specific requirements of each state should be checked carefully by the growing company and its counsel.

Structuring and Preparing Franchise Agreements. The franchise agreement is the principal document that sets forth the binding rights and obligations of each party to the franchise relationship. The franchise agreement contains the various provisions that will be binding on the parties for the life of their relationship and therefore must maintain a delicate balance of power. It must give the franchisor enough control to enforce uniformity and consistency throughout the system, yet at the same time be flexible enough to respond to changes in the marketplace that require modifications to the franchise system and to meet the special considerations or demands caused by a franchisee's local market conditions.

The franchise agreement can and should reflect the business philosophy of the franchisor and set the tenor of the relationship. If well drafted, it will be the culmination of literally thousands of business decisions and hundreds of hours of market research and testing. The length, term, and complexity of the agreement will (and should) vary from franchisor to franchisor and from industry to industry. Many start-up franchisors make the critical mistake of "borrowing" the terms of a competitor's franchise agreement. Such a practice can be detrimental to both the franchisor and the franchisee, since the agreement will not accurately reflect the actual dynamics of the relationship. Early-stage franchisors should resist the temptation to copy from a competitor or to accept the "standard form and boilerplate" from an inexperienced attorney or consultant. The relationship between the franchisor and the franchisee is far too complex to accept such compromises in the preparation of such a critical document.

Regardless of the franchisor's size or stage of growth, industry dynamics, or specific trends in the marketplace, all basic franchise agreements should address the following key topics:

- *Recitals.* The recitals, or "introduction to the purpose of the agreement," essentially set the stage for the discussion of the contractual relationship. This section provides the background information regarding the development and ownership of the proprietary rights of the franchisor that are being licensed to the franchisee. The recitals should always contain at least one provision specifying the obligation of the franchisee to operate the business format in strict conformity with the operations manual and quality control standards provided by the franchisor.

- *Grant, term, and renewal.* The typical initial section of the franchise agreement is the grant of a franchise for a specified term. The length of the term is influenced by a number of factors, including market conditions; the franchisor's need to change certain material terms of the agreement periodically; the cost of the franchise and the franchisee's expectations in relation to start-up costs; the length of related agreements necessary to the franchisee's operations, such as leases and bank loans; and anticipated consumer demand for the franchised goods and services. The renewal rights granted to a franchisee, if they are included at all, will usually be conditioned upon the franchisee's being in good standing under the agreement (e.g., there have been no material defaults by the franchisee). Other issues that must be addressed in any provision regarding renewal include renewal fees, obligations to execute the "then-current" form of the franchise agreement, and any obligations of the franchisee to upgrade its facilities to the "latest" standards and design. The franchisor's right to relocate the franchisee, adjust the size of any exclusive territory granted, or change the fee structure should also be addressed.

- *Territory.* The size of the geographic area granted to the franchisee by the franchisor must be specifically discussed in conjunction with what exclusive rights, if any, will be granted to the franchisee with respect to this territory. These provisions address whether the size of the territory is a specific radius, city, or county and whether the franchisor will have a right to either operate company-owned locations and/or grant additional franchises within the territory. After conducting market research, some franchisors will designate a specific territory in which a specific number of franchises could be successful without market oversaturation, and then will sell that exact number of franchises, without regard to the specific locations selected within the geographic area. Any rights of first refusal for additional locations, advertising restrictions, performance quotas relating to territory, and policies of the franchisor with regard to territory are addressed in this part of the agreement.

■ *Site selection.* The responsibility for finding the specific site for the operation of the franchised business can rest with either the franchisor or the franchisee. If the franchisee is free to choose its own site, then the franchise agreement will usually provide that the decision is subject to the approval of the franchisor. Some franchisors provide significant amounts of assistance in site selection in the form of marketing and demographic studies, lease negotiations, and securing local permits and licenses, especially if a "turnkey" franchise is offered. Site selection, however, can be the most difficult aspect of being a successful franchisee, and as a result, most franchisors are reluctant to take on full responsibility for this task contractually. For additional protection and control, some franchisors will insist on becoming the franchisee's landlord through a mandatory sublease arrangement once an acceptable site has been selected. A somewhat less burdensome method of securing similar protection is to provide for an automatic assignment of the lease to the franchisor upon termination of the franchise.

■ *Services to be provided by the franchisor.* The franchise agreement should clearly delineate which products and services will be provided to the franchisee by the franchisor or its affiliates, in terms of both the initial establishment of the franchised business (pre-opening obligations) and any continuing assistance or support services provided throughout the term of the relationship (post-opening services). The pre-opening obligations will generally include a trade secrets and copyrights license for the use of the confidential operations manual; recruitment and training of personnel; standard accounting and bookkeeping systems; inventory and equipment specifications and volume discounts; standard construction, building, and interior design plans; and grand opening promotion and advertising assistance. The quality and extent of the training program is clearly the most crucial pre-opening service provided by the franchisor; it should include both classroom and on-site instruction. Post-opening services provided to the franchisee on a continuing basis generally include field support and troubleshooting, research and development for new products and services, development of national advertising and promotional campaigns, and the arrangement of group purchasing programs and volume discounts.

- *Franchise, royalty, and related fees payable to the franchisor, and reporting.* The franchise agreement should clearly set forth the nature and amount of the fees that will be payable to the franchisor by the franchisee, both initially and on a continuing basis. The initial franchise fee is usually a nonrefundable lump-sum payment that is due upon execution of the franchise agreement. Essentially, this fee is compensation for the grant of the franchise, the trademark and trade secret license, pre-opening training and assistance, and the initial opening supply of materials, if any, to be provided by the franchisor to the franchisee. A second category of fees is the continuing fee, usually in the form of a specific royalty on gross sales. This percentage can either be fixed or be based on a sliding scale for different ranges of sales achieved at a given location. Often minimum royalty payments will be required, regardless of the franchisee's actual performance. These fees should be payable either weekly or monthly and should be submitted to the franchisor together with some standardized reporting form for internal control and monitoring purposes. A weekly or monthly payment schedule will generally allow the franchisee to budget for this payment from a cash flow perspective, and also provide the franchisor with an early warning system if there is a problem, enabling the franchisor to react before the past due royalties accrue to a virtually uncollectible sum. The third category of recurring fees is usually in the form of a national or regional cooperative advertising and promotion fund. This promotion fund may be managed by the franchisor, by an independent advertising agency, or even by a franchisee association. Whoever manages it, the franchisor must build a certain amount of control over the fund into the franchise agreement in order to protect the company's trademarks and ensure consistency in marketing efforts. Other categories of fees payable to the franchisor may include the sale of proprietary goods and services to the franchisee, consulting fees, audit and inspection fees, lease management fees (where the franchisor is to serve as sub-lessor), and renewal or transfer fees. The obligations of the franchisee to provide the franchisor with periodic weekly, monthly, quarterly, and annual financial and sales reports should also be addressed in the franchise agreement.

- *Quality control.* A well-drafted franchise agreement will always include a variety of provisions designed to ensure quality control and consistency throughout the franchise system. Such provisions often take the form of restrictions on the franchisee's sources of products, ingredients, supplies, and materials, as well as strict guidelines and specifications for operating procedures. These operating procedures will usually specify standards of service, trade dress and uniform requirements, the condition and appearance of the facility, hours of business, minimum insurance requirements, guidelines for trademark usage, advertising and promotional materials, accounting systems, and credit practices. Any restrictions on the ability of the franchisee to buy goods and services or requirements that it purchase from a specific source should be carefully drafted within the perimeter of applicable antitrust laws. If the franchisor is to serve as the sole supplier or manufacturer of one or more products to be used by the franchisee in the day-to-day operation of the business, then such exclusivity must be justified by a product that is truly proprietary or unique, such as the blend of eleven special herbs and spices that has been protected for many decades by KFC.

- *Insurance, recordkeeping, and other related obligations of the franchisee.* The minimum amounts and types of insurance that the franchisee must carry in connection with its operation of the franchised businesses should also be included. Typically, the franchisor is named as an additional insured under these policies. Other related obligations of the franchisee that must be set forth in the franchise agreement include keeping proper financial records (which must be made available for inspection by the franchisor upon request); the obligation to maintain and enforce quality control standards with its employees and vendors; the obligation to comply with all applicable employment laws, health and safety standards, and related local ordinances; the duty to upgrade and maintain the franchisee's facilities and equipment; the obligation to continue to promote the products and services of the franchisor; the obligation to reasonably process requests by patrons for franchising information; the obligation to refrain from producing goods and services that do not meet the franchisor's quality control specifications or that may be unapproved for offer at the franchisee's premises (such as video games at a fast-food restaurant or X-rated material at a bookstore); the obligation not to solicit customers outside its designated territory; the obligation of the franchisee to personally participate in the day-to-day operation of the franchised business (required by many but not all franchisors); and the general obligation of the franchisee to refrain from any activity that may reflect adversely on the reputation of the franchise system.

■ *Protection of intellectual property and covenants against competition.* The franchise agreement should always contain a separate section on the obligations of the franchisee and its employees to protect the trademarks and trade secrets being licensed against misuse or disclosure. The franchisor should provide for a clause that clearly sets forth that the trademarks and trade names being licensed are the exclusive property of the franchisor and that any goodwill established is to inure to the sole benefit of the franchisor. It should also be made clear that the confidential operations manual is "on loan" to the franchisee under a limited-use license, and that the franchisee or its agents are prohibited from the unauthorized use of the trade secrets, both during and after the term of the agreement. To the extent that such provisions are enforceable in local jurisdictions, the franchise agreement should contain covenants against competition by a franchisee, both during the term of the agreement and following its termination or cancellation.

■ *Termination of the franchise agreement.* One of the most important sections is the section discussing how a franchisee may lose its rights to operate the franchised business. The various "events of default" should be carefully defined and tailored to meet the needs of the specific type of business being franchised. Grounds for termination can range from the bankruptcy of a franchisee to failure to meet specified performance quotas or to strictly abide by quality control standards. Certain types of defaults will be grounds for immediate termination, while other types of default will provide the franchisee with an opportunity to fix its mistakes within a certain time period prior to termination. This section should address the procedures under which the franchisor will provide notice to the franchisee of the default(s) and clearly explain how much time the franchisee will have to rectify the problem(s), as well as the alternative actions that the franchisor may pursue to enforce its right to terminate the franchise agreement. Such clauses must be drafted in light of certain state regulations that limit franchise terminations to "good cause" and have certain minimum procedural requirements that must be followed. The obligations of the franchisee upon default and notice of termination must also be clearly spelled out, such as the duty to return all copies of the operations manuals, pay all past-due royalty fees, and immediately cease the use of the franchisor's trademarks.

- *Miscellaneous provisions.* Like any well-prepared business agreement, the franchise agreement should include a notice provision, a governing law clause, severability provisions, an integration clause, and a provision discussing the relationship of the parties. Some franchisors may want to add an arbitration clause, a "hold harmless" and indemnification provision, a reservation of the right to injunctions and other forms of equitable relief, specific representations and warranties of the franchisee, attorney's fees for the prevailing party in the event of dispute, and even a contractual provision acknowledging that the franchisee has reviewed the agreement with counsel and has conducted an independent investigation of the franchise, and is not relying on any representations other than those expressly set forth in the agreement.

GROWTH STRATEGY ALTERNATIVE 3:
TECHNOLOGY AND MERCHANDISE LICENSING

Licensing is a contractual method of developing and exploiting intellectual property by transferring the rights of use to third parties *without* the transfer of ownership. Virtually any proprietary product or service may be the subject of a license agreement, ranging from the licensing of the Mickey Mouse character by Walt Disney Studios in the 1930s to modern-day licensing of computer software and high technology. From a legal perspective, licensing involves complex issues of contract, tax, antitrust, international, tort, and intellectual property law. From a business perspective, licensing involves a weighing of the economic and strategic advantages of licensing against other methods of bringing the product or service to the marketplace, such as direct sales, distributorships, or franchises.

Many of the benefits of licensing to be enjoyed by a growing company closely parallel the advantages of franchising, namely:

- ▶ To spread the risk and cost of development and distribution
- ▶ To achieve more rapid market penetration
- ▶ To earn initial license fees and ongoing royalty income
- ▶ To enhance consumer loyalty and goodwill
- ▶ To preserve the capital that would otherwise be required for internal growth and expansion
- ▶ To test new applications for existing and proven technology
- ▶ To avoid or settle litigation regarding a dispute over ownership of the technology

The disadvantages of licensing are also similar in nature to the risks inherent in franchising, such as:

- ▶ A somewhat diminished ability to enforce quality control standards and specifications
- ▶ A greater risk of another party infringing upon the licensor's intellectual property
- ▶ Dependence on the skills, abilities, and resources of the licensee as a source of revenue
- ▶ Difficulty in recruiting, motivating, and retaining qualified and competent licensees
- ▶ The risk that the licensor's entire reputation and goodwill may be damaged or destroyed by the act or omission of a single licensee
- ▶ The administrative burden of monitoring and supporting the operations of the network of licensees

Failure to consider all of the costs and benefits of licensing could easily result in a regretful strategic decision or being stuck with the terms of an unprofitable license agreement because of either an underestimation of the licensee's need for technical assistance and support or an overestimation of the market demand for the licensor's products and services. In order to avoid such problems, the licensor should conduct a certain amount of due diligence prior to engaging in any serious negotiations with a prospective licensee. This preliminary investigation will generally include market research, legal steps to fully protect intellectual property, and an internal financial analysis of the technology with respect to pricing, profit margins, and costs of production and distribution. It will also include a more specific analysis of the prospective licensee with respect to its financial strength, research and manufacturing capabilities, and reputation in the industry. Once the decision to enter into more formal negotiations has been made, the terms and conditions of the license agreement should be discussed. Naturally, these provisions will vary, depending on whether the license is for merchandising an entertainment property, exploiting a given technology, or distributing a particular product to an original equipment manufacturer or value-added reseller.

There are two principal types of licensing: (1) technology licensing, where the strategy is to find a licensee for the exploitation of industrial and technological developments, and (2) merchandise and character licensing, where the strategy is to license a recognized trademark or copyright to a manufacturer of consumer goods in markets that are not currently served by the licensor.

Technology Licensing

The principal purpose behind technology transfer and licensing agreements is to make a marriage between the technology proprietor, as licensor, and an organization that has the resources to properly develop and market the technology, as licensee. This marriage is made between companies and inventors of all shapes and sizes, but it often involves an entrepreneur who has the technology but lacks the resources to adequately penetrate the marketplace, as licensor, and a larger company that has sufficient research and development, production, human resources, and marketing capability to make the best use of the technology. The industrial and technological revolution has a history of very successful entrepreneurs who have relied on the resources of larger organizations to bring their products to market, such as Chester Carlson (xerography), Edwin Land (Polaroid cameras), Robert Goddard (rockets), and Willis Carrier (air-conditioning). As the base for technological development becomes broader, large companies look not only to entrepreneurs and small businesses for new ideas and technologies, but also to each other, foreign countries, universities, and federal and state governments to serve as licensors of technology.

In the typical licensing arrangement, the proprietor of intellectual property rights (patents, trade secrets, trademarks, and know-how) permits a third party to make use of these rights pursuant to a set of specified conditions and circumstances that are set forth in a license agreement. Licensing agreements can be limited to a very narrow component of the proprietor's intellectual property rights, such as one specific application of a single patent, or be much broader in context, such as in a classic "technology transfer" agreement, where an entire bundle of intellectual property rights is transferred to the licensee in exchange for initial fees and royalties. The classic technology transfer arrangement is actually closer to a sale of the intellectual property rights, with the licensor having the right to get the intellectual property back if the licensee fails to meet its obligations under the agreement. An example of this type of transaction might be bundling a proprietary environmental cleanup system together with technical support and training services to a master overseas licensee, with reversionary rights in the event of a breach of the agreement or the failure to meet a set of performance standards.

Merchandise and Character Licensing Agreements

The use of commonly recognized trademarks, brand names, sports teams, athletes, universities, television and film characters, musicians, and designers to foster the sales of specific products and services is at the heart of today's merchandise and character licensing environment. Manufacturers and distributors of a wide range of products and services license these words, images, and symbols for use with a range of products from clothing to housewares to toys and posters. Certain brand names and characters have withstood the test of time, while others have fallen prey to fads, consumer shifts, and stiff competition.

The trademark and copyright owners of these properties and character images are motivated to license them for a variety of reasons. Aside from the obvious desire to earn royalty fees and profits, many manufacturers view this licensing strategy as a form of merchandising to promote the underlying product or service. The licensing of a trademark for use on a line of clothing helps to establish and reinforce brand awareness at the consumer level. For example, when R.J. Reynolds Tobacco Company licenses a leisure apparel manufacturer to produce a line of Camel wear, it is hoping to sell more cigarettes, appeal to the lifestyle of its targeted consumers, maintain consumer awareness, *and* enjoy the royalty income from the sale of the clothing line. Similar strategies have been adopted by manufacturers in order to revive a mature brand or failing product. In certain instances, the spin-off product that has been licensed has been almost as financially successful as the underlying product that it was intended to promote.

Brand-name owners, celebrities, and academic institutions must be very careful not to grant too many licenses too quickly. The financial rewards of a flow of royalty income from hundreds of different manufacturers can be quite seductive, but it must be weighed against the possible loss of quality control and dilution of the name, logo, or character. The loyalty of the licensee network is also threatened when too many licenses for closely competing products are granted. Retailers will also become cautious when purchasing licensed goods from a licensee if they fear that quality control has suffered or that the popularity of the licensed character, celebrity, or image will be short-lived. This may result in smaller orders and an overall unwillingness to carry inventory. This is especially true in the toy industry, where purchasing decisions are being made based on (or at least influenced by) the whims of a five-year-old child, who may strongly identify with a character image one week and then turn her attention to a totally different character image the next week. It is incumbent on the manufacturers and licensees to develop advertising and media campaigns that will hold the consumer's attention for an extended period of time. Only then will the retailer be convinced of the potential longevity of the product line. This will require a balancing of the risks and rewards between the licensor and the licensee in the character licensing agreement in the areas of compensation to the licensor, advertising expenditures by the licensee, scope of the exclusivity, and quality control standards and specifications.

In the merchandise licensing community, the name, logo, symbol, or character is typically referred to as the *property*, and the specific product or product line (e.g., the T-shirts, mugs, posters, and so on) is referred to as the *licensed product*. This area of licensing offers opportunities and benefits to both the owners of the properties and the manufacturers of the licensed products. For the owner of the property, brand recognition, goodwill, and royalty income are strengthened and expanded. For the manufacturer of the licensed products, there is an opportunity to leverage the goodwill of the property to improve sales of the licensed products. The manufacturer has an opportunity to "hit the ground running" in the sale of merchandise by gaining access to and using an already established brand name or character image.

Naturally, each party should conduct due diligence on the other. From the perspective of the owner of the property, the manufacturer of the licensed product should demonstrate an ability to meet and maintain quality control standards, should possess financial stability, and should offer an aggressive and well-planned marketing and promotional strategy. From the perspective of the manufacturer of the licensed property, the owner of the property should display a certain level of integrity and commitment to quality, should disclose its future plans for the promotion of the property, and should be willing to participate and assist in the overall marketing of the licensed products. For example, if a star basketball player were to be unwilling to appear for promotional events designed to sell his own specially licensed line of basketball shoes, this would present a major problem and would be likely to lead to a premature termination of the licensing relationship.

The Licensing Agreement

As a general rule, any well-drafted licensing agreement should address the following topics:

- *Scope of the grant.* The exact scope and subject matter of the license must be initially addressed and carefully defined in the license agreement. Any restrictions on the geographic scope, rights of use, or permissible channels of trade; restrictions on sublicensing; limitations on assignability; or exclusion of improvements to the technology covered by the agreement should be clearly set forth in this section.

- *Term and renewal.* The commencement date, duration, renewals and extensions, conditions for renewal, procedures for providing notice of intent to renew, grounds for termination, obligations upon termination, and licensor's reversionary rights in the technology should all be included in this section.

- *Performance standards and quotas.* To the extent that the licensor's consideration will be dependent on royalty income that will be calculated from the licensee's gross or net revenues, the licensor may want to impose certain minimum levels of performance in terms of sales, advertising and promotional expenditures, and human resources to be devoted to the exploitation of the licensed property or technology. Naturally, the licensee will argue for a "best efforts" provision that is free from performance standards and quotas. In such cases, the licensor may want to insist on a minimum royalty level that will be paid regardless of the licensee's actual performance.

- *Payments to the licensor.* Virtually every type of license agreement will include some form of initial payment and ongoing royalty to the licensor. Royalty formulas vary widely, however, and may be based upon gross sales, net sales, net profits, a fixed sum per product sold, a minimum payment to be made to the licensor over a given period of time, or even a sliding scale in order to provide the licensee with some incentive as a reward for performance.

- *Quality control assurance and protection.* Quality control standards and specifications for the production, marketing, and distribution of the products and services covered by the license must be set forth by the licensor. In addition, procedures should be included in the agreement that give the licensor an opportunity to *enforce* these standards and specifications, such as a right to inspect the licensee's premises; a right to review, approve, or reject samples produced by the licensee; and a right to review and approve any packaging, labeling, or advertising materials to be used in connection with the exploitation of the products and services that are within the scope of the license.

- *Insurance and indemnification.* The licensor should take all necessary and reasonable steps to ensure that the licensee has an obligation to protect and indemnify the licensor against any claims or liabilities resulting from the licensee's exploitation of the products and services covered by the license.

- *Accounting, reports, and audits.* The licensor must impose certain reporting and recordkeeping procedures on the licensee in order to ensure an accurate accounting for periodic royalty payments. Furthermore, the licensor should reserve the right to audit the records of the licensee in the event of a dispute or discrepancy, along with provisions as to who will be responsible for the cost of the audit in the event of an understatement.

■ *Duties to preserve and protect intellectual property.* The obligations of the licensee and its agents and employees to preserve and protect the confidential nature and acknowledge the ownership of the intellectual property being disclosed in connection with the license agreement must be carefully defined. Any required notices or legends that must be included on products or materials distributed in connection with the license agreement (such as the status of the relationship or the actual owner of the intellectual property) are also described in this section.

■ *Technical assistance, training, and support.* Any obligation of the licensor to assist the licensee in the development or exploitation of the subject matter being licensed is included in this section of the agreement. The assistance may take the form of personal services or documents and records. Either way, any fees due to the licensor for such support services that are over and above the initial license and ongoing royalty fee must also be addressed.

■ *Warranties of the licensor.* A prospective licensee may demand that the licensor provide certain representations and warranties in the license agreement. These may include warranties regarding the ownership of the technology, such as absence of any known infringements of the technology or restrictions on the ability to license the technology, or that the technology has the features, capabilities, and characteristics previously represented in the negotiations.

■ *Infringements.* The license agreement should contain procedures under which the licensee must notify the licensor of any known or suspected direct or indirect infringements of the subject matter being licensed. The responsibilities for the cost of protecting and defending licensed technology should also be specified in this section.

GROWTH STRATEGY ALTERNATIVE 4:
DISTRIBUTORSHIPS AND DEALERSHIPS

Many growing product-oriented companies choose to bring their wares to the marketplace through independent third-party distributors and dealerships. This type of arrangement is commonly used by manufacturers of electronics and stereo equipment, computer hardware and software, sporting goods, medical equipment, and automobile parts and accessories. These dealers are generally more difficult to control than a licensee or franchisee and, as a result, the agreement between the manufacturer and the distributor will be much more informal than a franchise or license agreement.

In developing distributor and dealership agreements, growing companies must be careful to avoid being included within the broad definition of a "franchise" under the Federal Trade Commission rule 436, which would require the preparation of a disclosure document. To avoid such a classification, the agreement must impose minimal control over the dealer, the sale of products must be at bona fide wholesale prices without any form of initiation fee, and the company must provide minimal assistance in the marketing or management of the dealer's business. A well-drafted distributorship agreement should, however, address the following key issues:

1. What is the scope of the appointment? Which products is the dealer authorized to distribute, and under what conditions? What is the scope, if any, of the exclusive territory to be granted to the distributor? To what extent will product, vendor, customer, or geographic restrictions be applicable?

2. What activities will the distributor be expected to perform in terms of manufacturing, sales, marketing, display, billing, market research, maintenance of books and records, storage, training, installation, support, and servicing?

3. What obligations will the distributor have to preserve and protect the intellectual property of the manufacturer?

4. What right, if any, will the distributor have to modify or enhance the manufacturer's warranties, terms of sale, credit policies, or refund procedures?

5. What advertising literature, technical and marketing support, training seminars, or special promotions will be provided by the manufacturer to enhance the performance of the distributor?

6. What sales or performance quotas will be imposed on the dealer as a condition of its right to continue to distribute the manufacturer's

products or services? What are the manufacturer's rights and remedies if the dealer fails to meet these performance standards?

7. What is the term of the agreement, and under what conditions can it be terminated? How will post-termination transactions be handled?

Differences Between Distributors and Sales Representatives

Distributors are often confused with sales representatives. There are many critical differences that must be understood. Typically, a distributor buys the product from the manufacturer, at wholesale prices, with the intent to resell it to a retailer or directly to the customer. The distributor usually pays no actual fee for the grant of the distributorship, and the distributor will typically be permitted to carry competitive products. The distributor is expected to maintain some retail location or showroom where the manufacturer's products are displayed. It must also maintain its own inventory storage and warehousing capabilities. The distributor looks to the manufacturer for technical support; advertising contributions; supportive repair, maintenance, and service policies; new product training; volume discounts; favorable payment and return policies; and brand-name recognition. The manufacturer looks to the distributor for in-store and local promotion, adequate inventory controls, financial stability, preferred display and stocking, prompt payment, and qualified sales personnel. Although a distributorship network offers a viable alternative to franchising, it is not a panacea. The management and control of distributors may be even more difficult than that involved in franchising (especially without the benefit of a comprehensive franchise agreement), and the termination of these relationships is regulated by many state and anti-termination statutes.

The sales representative or sales agent is an independent marketing resource for the manufacturer. The sales representative, unlike the distributor, typically does not actually purchase the merchandise for resale, nor is she typically required to maintain inventories or retail locations or to engage in any special price promotions unless instigated by the manufacturer.

Index